The Texas Legation Papers
1836–1845

The Texas Legation Papers

1836–1845

Kenneth R. Stevens, EDITOR

Gregg Cantrell and Nancy R. Stevens,
ASSOCIATE EDITORS

TCU PRESS

Library of Congress Cataloging-in-Publication Data
The Texas Legation papers, 1836–1845 / Kenneth R. Stevens, editor.
p. cm.
"A joint project of The Center for Texas Studies at TCU and TCU Press."
Summary: The papers of the Republic of Texas between independence and statehood.
Includes bibliographical references and index. ISBN 978-0-87565-393-8
(hardcover: alk. paper)
1. Texas. Legation (U.S.)--Sources. 2. Diplomatic and consular service--
Texas--History--Sources. 3. Statesmen--Texas--Correspondence. 4. Texas--
History--Republic, 1836–1846--Sources. 5. Texas--Foreign relations--United
States--Sources. 6. United States--Foreign relations--Texas--Sources. I.
Stevens, Kenneth R.,– II. Texas Christian University. Center for Texas Studies.
III. TCU Press.
F390.T3852012
976.4'04--dc23
2012014458

TCU Press
P. O. Box 298300
Fort Worth, Texas 76129
817.257.7822
www.prs.tcu.edu

To order books: 1.800.826.8911

Designed by Barbara Mathews Whitehead

Contents

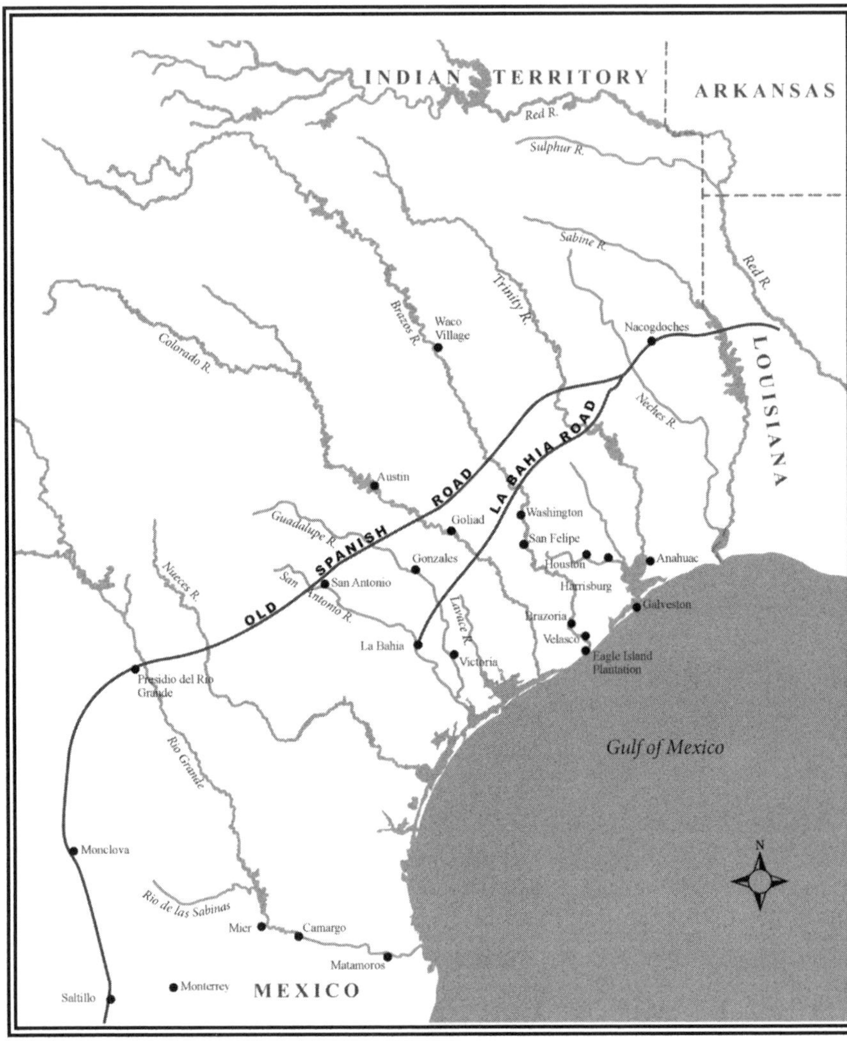

Map of Texas, ca. 1836
By Tracy Ellen Smith, 2012

Foreword

THE REPUBLIC OF TEXAS maintained a diplomatic legation to the United States from 1836 until achieving statehood in 1845. When the legation office closed in 1845, its papers were moved to the Office of the US Adjutant General in Washington, DC. In 1846 the newly elected US senator from Texas, Sam Houston, was directed to take control of all of the documents and convey them to the Texas secretary of state in Austin. For some reason, Senator Houston instead took them to his home. Most were ultimately turned over to the state, but a single box containing over 250 documents was not and over the ensuing 161 years passed through the family of Sam Houston's son, Andrew Jackson Houston, and eventually to other people.

The documents were exposed to humidity and heat, and in 1961 they were almost casualties of Hurricane Carla when the house in which they were held was wrecked by the hurricane and then damaged by fire. Following the hurricane, the documents remained in a private home, for a period in the trunk of a car and then in a bank vault. Most of the documents were damaged by water or fire. Nonetheless, the documents survived and in 2006, as part of an auction benefiting the Texas State Historical Association, came into the custody of the Center for Texas Studies at TCU and TCU's Special Collections in the Mary Couts Burnett Library. The documents were held by TCU for a period of five years for exhibition and scholarship.

As part of the scholarly effort, all of the documents, many of which are copies of known documents along with others that had never previously been seen, were transcribed. The initial phase of the transcription and annotation process was undertaken by students in a graduate history seminar led by Dr. Gregg Cantrell, who holds the Erma and Ralph Lowe Chair of Texas History at TCU. Professor Kenneth R. Stevens completed the final transcriptions and annotations, and the headnotes preceding the documents. The results are presented in this volume, one intended to preserve an important portion of the correspondence that passed through the Texas legation during the time of the Texas Republic and make it available to scholars and others who treasure the legacy of the State of Texas.

Many others contributed to making this project possible. The papers would not have come into TCU's hands had not Mary Ralph Lowe, J. P. Bryan, and TCU Chancellor Victor Boschini recognized their importance and contributed the necessary funds to secure the possession and exhibition rights for TCU at the Texas State Historical Association auction in 2006. Moreover, the Jane and John Justin Foundation subsequently underwrote Professor Stevens's scholarship and the publication of this book. The Justin Foundation also funded the creation of a website through the Center for Texas Studies at TCU where all of the original documents will be available for viewing. The Center for Texas Studies at TCU and the TCU Press are indebted to each of these proud Texans, including honorary Texan Victor Boschini, for making this project possible.

Mary L. Volcansek, PhD
Executive Director
Center for Texas Studies at TCU

Acknowledgments

THE EDITORS WOULD like to thank the many persons who have contributed to this volume. In addition to Mary Ralph Lowe, J. P. Bryan, Chancellor Victor Boschini, and the Jane and John Justin Foundation, thanks are also due to Mary Volcansek, the executive director of the Center for Texas Studies, and Gene Allen Smith, the director, who have been consistently encouraging and helpful. So, too, have our colleagues in the Department of History and Geography at TCU. Department Chair Peter W. Worthing and Dean Andrew Schoolmaster have been ever supportive.

The staff of the TCU library has provided invaluable support. We owe special thanks to the good folks in Interlibrary Loan—Kay Edmondson, Clare Taylor, and Jill Kendle—who always manage to track down obscure things; James Lutz, the director of Administrative Services, who found working space for the project in the library; Roger Rainwater, the head of Special Collections, for taking care of the Legation Papers while attending to our requests; and especially to Dean of the Library June Koelker, who makes the library a wonderful place to get things done.

We appreciate the hard work, talent, and patience of the staff at TCU Press, especially Editor Kathy Walton, Production Manager Melinda Esco, Director Dan Williams, and Press Intern Ben Wright.

We thank Tracy Ellen Smith for her fine work in producing the map used in this book.

Finally, thanks again, to Nancy, for everything.

Editorial Method

LETTERS AND DOCUMENTS in this volume are printed in chronological order, except that enclosures immediately follow the document they accompanied. The point of origin and the dates of the letters have been placed at the upper right side of each letter using the language of the original author. If information has been included by the editors, it appears in square brackets [ ]. Complimentary closings, which often took up multiple lines in the custom of the day, have been run continuously as the last line of the text.

These letters and documents are reproduced as true to the original as possible. Misspellings have been retained without the use of *sic*, and punctuation is left as the authors employed it, though periods have been added when necessary to indicate the ends of sentences.

Many of these documents have been damaged, and in some cases there are substantial gaps in the text. We have elected to publish them even in their damaged or incomplete condition because the available portion may include information of value to a reader. When text is missing, the missing material is indicated by the use of <...>, with the number of ellipses to approximate the missing space. In instances where the editors have not been able to decipher the writer's words, this has been indicated by <illegible>. When text missing in the document due to paper damage has been found and provided from another source, it is indicated within angle brackets < >. Words or parts of words that have been added because they can be reasonably inferred around damaged paper or from mostly illegible text are indicated in square brackets [ ].

Most identifications and annotations are brief. Persons are identified only the first time they appear, and generally only in the context of Texas history. The page on which a person is identified for the first time is indicated by boldface type in the index. The Texas State Historical Association *Handbook of Texas Online* has been an invaluable source for identifications of Texas persons, places, and events. Another excellent source for Texas information is the Portal to Texas History website, which is maintained by the University of North Texas Digital Projects Unit.

Abbreviations and Short Titles

ALS	Autographed letter signed
Austin Papers	Eugene C. Barker, ed., *The Austin Papers,* 3 vols. in 4. (Washington, DC: American Historical Association, and Austin: University of Texas, 1919-1928).
Cong. Globe	*Congressional Globe*
DS	Document signed
Gammel	H. P. N. Gammel, comp., *The Laws of Texas, 1822–1897,* 10 vols. (Austin: Austin Book Company, 1898).
DCRT	George P. Garrison, ed., *Diplomatic Correspondence of the Republic of Texas,* Annual Report of the American Historical Association, 1907–1908, 3 vols. (Washington, DC: Government Printing Office, 1908–1911).
IAA	William Ray Manning, comp., *Diplomatic Correspondence of the United States: InterAmerican Affairs, 1831–1860,* 12 vols. (Washington, DC: Carnegie Endowment for International Peace, 1932–1939).

LS	Letter signed
Niles'	*Niles' Weekly Register*
Intelligencer	Washington, DC, *Daily National Intelligencer*
Messages and Papers	James D. Richardson, ed., A *Compilation of the Messages and Papers of the Presidents, 1789–1897,* 10 vols. (Washington, DC, 1896–1899).
Secret Journals	*Secret Journals of the Senate, Republic of Texas, 1836–1845* (Austin: Texas Library and Historical Commission, 1911).
TLP	Texas Legation Papers
Treaties	Hunter Miller, ed., *Treaties and Other International Acts of the United States of America,* 8 vols. (Washington, DC: Government Printing Office, 1931–1948).
Tx	Texas State Library and Archives Commission, Austin
TTR	*Telegraph and Texas Register*

Introduction

On March 1, 1836, representatives from across the Mexican province of Texas held a convention at Washington-on-the-Brazos. The weather was cold, and the unfinished building in which they met had neither doors nor glass windows, but the delegates remained intent on completing their business. The next day, March 2, they declared independence from Mexico and soon thereafter named Sam Houston commander of Texan military forces. By the middle of the month, they had written a constitution and selected interim officials for the government.

The first Anglo-Americans came to Texas in the 1820s when Mexico established the empresario system, which allowed selected individuals to distribute land to colonists from the United States. Stephen F. Austin's first settlers—the Old Three Hundred—were among these. By 1836 there were a number of other grants under the empresario system. But relations between the government of Mexico and Anglo-Texans were often turbulent. Though they were generally evaded, Mexican laws restricted slavery and required colonists to adopt Roman Catholicism; Mexican and Anglo legal norms differed; and land titles were often confused. Disturbances at several places between 1825 and 1832—including Fredonia, Anahuac, Nacogdoches, and Velasco—illustrated the problems. Anglo-Texans held a Convention at San Felipe in 1833 and passed resolutions expressing their concerns. Austin was chosen to present them to the government, but in Mexico City he was arrested and held prisoner until July 1835.

More trouble occurred in October 1835, when Texans fought and bested Mexican soldiers who had been ordered to recover a small cannon at Gonzales. While Mexican forces retreated toward San Antonio, Texans held a General Consultation at San Felipe. The Consultation established a provisional government with a council made up of representatives from the municipalities, and selected

Henry Smith as interim governor. The delegates established a regular army under the command of Sam Houston. And they appointed Branch T. Archer, William H. Wharton, and Stephen F. Austin as commissioners to the United States for the purpose of raising funds and generating public support. The diplomacy of the Republic of Texas had begun even before independence was declared.

The Texas Legation Papers
1836–1845

Stephen F. Austin

Portrait by Louis Eyth (1838-1889). Texas Senate Chamber, Austin, Texas. Courtesy of the State Preservation Board, Austin, TX; Accession ID: CHA 1989.101. Photography by Perry Huston, January 5, 1995, post conservation.

The financial difficulties the new republic had to overcome were formidable. On November 12, 1835, the provisional government established by the Consultation appointed Branch T. Archer, Stephen F. Austin, and William H. Wharton as commissioners to the United States, authorized, among other duties, to contract loans to the republic that would be secured by Texas land (Gammel, 1: 534; Commission of Austin, Archer, and Wharton, December 7, 1835, DCRT, *1: 51–55). On January 10, 1836, they reported that they had succeeded in negotiating a $250,000 loan (Archer, Austin, and Wharton to Henry Smith,* DCRT, *1: 55–57). Even so, the republic's money troubles were far from over.*

Loan Contract, April 2, 1836

WHEREAS, Branch T. Archer,[1] William H. Wharton and Stephen F. Austin, Commissioners on behalf of the Provisional Government of Texas, obtained money from certain individuals in the United States, upon two Loans, one for *two hundred thousand Dollars,* the other for *fifty thousand Dollars,* upon conditions, a part of which, the Government of Texas are desirous of being relieved from, by giving an equivalent therefor:

Now, in consideration of the said Lenders agreeing to have the Loan redeemed in Land, at fifty cents per acre, with the privilege of locating the same on any vacant Land held at any time by the Government, or which may accrue to the Government, except by purchase or donation, and holding the said Land on the same conditions that they are held by the Citizens of Texas, the Lenders or their Assignees, residing where they please, and the relinquishment by the said Lenders of all the other conditions of said contracts, except the mode of transferring scrip and titles: The Government of Texas agrees to give a premium of *thirty-two leagues of Land,* to be divided between the two Loans aforesaid, in proportion to their amounts; the takers of the first, or two hundred thousand Dollars Loan, relinquishing their priority of location over the takers of the second, or fifty thousand Dollars Loan, and every one else; and furthermore, relinquishing their right to take more of it than to the amount paid up: by way of being more explicit, the takers of the two hundred thousand Dollars Loan get four shares of the premium, and the takers of the fifty thousand Dollars Loan, one share. The said premium to be divided into shares of six hundred and forty acres, as the balance is now held, and all to be held upon the same terms, with the privilege of locating wherever vacant or Government Land, as aforesaid, can be obtained. The understanding is furthermore, that if said Scrip shall at any time be laid on Land to which the Government has not the prior right, the same may be removed to other Land; and the said Lenders may also buy of individuals Land to the amount of one hundred thousand Dollars, and hold the same upon the same terms as the former named Land, except as to settlement, as hereinafter set forth: provided, however, that no such purchase shall be made within twelve months from this date. It is understood, that the sections aforesaid, are to be surveyed as near as may be with the cardinal points and in squares, having regard to the necessary variation to be produced by bounding on rivers and other adjoining surveys. Furthermore, so much as may be purchase of individual Citizens of Texas, shall be settled as follows: within ten years from this time, there shall be at least one settler upon the same for every twelve hundred and eighty acres. It is understood, that the Scrip before the Land is surveyed, and the grants or titles for the same afterwards issued, shall be considered on the footing of personal property, and transferable as Scrip or Bank Stock may be transferred by the Laws of the Republic, or as set forth in the contract for the Loan aforesaid. It is the intention of the Executive, to give the Executors, Administrators or Assigns of Aliens, such powers to dispose of the Land aforesaid, as shall prevent its being beyond the reach of purchasers at any time; wherefore, it is understood, that the same shall be subject to sale in the same manner as goods and chattels generally are; and when sold by the original proprietor, his executor or administrator, the purchaser shall have all the right under the assignment or transfer which the original proprietor had.

William H. Wharton
Artist unknown, ca. 1850. Courtesy Friends of the Governor's Mansion, Austin, Texas.

The Deeds for Land bought of individuals, as herein before set forth, shall be recorded in any designated Office, hereafter to be named by Congress: and in the meantime, when the said transfers are recorded in other offices, a report shall be made to the Office of the Secretary of State, and his acknowledgment of such report shall be necessary to make said record valid: and in case the amount of the said one hundred thousand Dollars shall be exceeded, in purchase of individuals, to the amount of the overplus thereof, the same shall be void,

David G. Burnet

Portrait by William H. Huddle (1847-1892). Courtesy of the State Preservation Board, Austin, TX; Accession ID: CHA 1989.105. Photography by Eric Beggs, August 13, 1983, post conservation. © State Preservation Board (2012), all rights reserved.

null, and of no effect.

The Scrip aforesaid shall be issued to the said contractors, when prepared and presented to them for signature, in a neat and proper form, and after their signatures are affixed to this agreement or it shall be issued to those who shall at any time have signed it in the ratio of thei<r interest in said> contracts, provided they agree to the terms <hereof within sixty days after the publications of notice of> this agreement in the City of New-Orleans; and when the holder of any of the aforesaid Scrip, shall be under the terms of this agreement file the same, together with the boundaries of the Lands intended to be covered by said Scrip, in the Office of the Secretary of State, Titles shall issue for the same in the usual form.

In Testimony whereof, the Members of the Executive Government of Texas, of the one part, and the Contractors aforesaid, have hereunto set their hands, and affixed their private seals, this first day of April, eighteen hundred and thirty-six, in the Town of Harrisburg, and Republic of Texas.

The Lenders and Contractors aforesaid, of both Loans, in proportion to their original subscription, shall have the privilege of paying up the remainder of the Loan, to wit: one hundred and eighty thousand Dollars, or any part thereof, on the terms specified in the original contract, and of this compromise after sixty days' notice of this modification; and, shall have the option to take Lands on the same terms provided for the payment of the Loans already received by this contract (but without the premium,) or the principal and interest on the same, as stipulated in the original contract. The Lands, if taken, to be at fifty cents per acre, and held on the timers compromised for, in this contract, except the right to buy of individuals.

Done at Harrisburg, this second of April, eighteen hundred and thirty-six, by and with the advise and consent of my Cabinet.

David G. Burnet,[4]
President of the Republic of Texas

Lorenzo De Zavala,[5]
Vice-President of Texas.
Samuel Carson,[6]
Secretary of State.
Thomas J. Rusk,[7]
Secretary of War.
Bailey Hardeman,[8]

Secretary of Treasury.
David Thomas,[9]
Attorney General.
Robert Triplett,[10]
W. F. Gray[11]

✦✦✦

Print. Damaged, with missing text. Tx, TLP. Published in John H. Jenkins, ed., *The Papers of the Texas Revolution, 1835–1836,* 10 vols. (Austin: Presidial Press, 1973), 5: 271–273 (# 2510). Missing text added from Jenkins.

1. Branch Tanner Archer (1790–1856), of Virginia, attended William and Mary College and earned a medical degree at the University of Pennsylvania in 1808. Archer came to Texas in 1831. An early advocate of Texas independence, he was a member of the Convention of 1833 and was elected chair of the Consultation. He later served in the First Congress of Texas and as President Mirabeau B. Lamar's secretary of war, 1838–1841.

2. William Harris Wharton (1802–1839), from Nashville, Tennessee, graduated from the University of Nashville and was admitted to the state bar in 1826. He came to Texas in 1827, where he married Sarah Ann Groce (1810–1878), the daughter of wealthy planter Jared E. Groce, one of Stephen F. Austin's original settlers. Jared Groce gave the couple Eagle Island Plantation in Brazoria County as a wedding gift. Wharton was an early advocate of Texas independence. He was a delegate to the Convention of 1832, was president of the Convention of 1833, and was a delegate at the Consultation of 1835. Wharton was elected to the Senate of the First Texas Congress, but resigned when President Houston appointed him the first Texan minister to the United States. Wharton was killed after returning to Texas, when his pistol accidently discharged.

3. Stephen Fuller Austin (1793–1836) was born in Virginia and raised in Missouri. His father, Moses Austin (1761–1821), obtained a grant to introduce settlers to Texas, but died before he could do so. Stephen Austin carried through his father's legacy by introducing three hundred families to Texas by 1825 and even more thereafter. Austin was imprisoned by Mexican officials from 1833 to 1835 and upon release supported independence for Texas. Upon his return to Texas following his stint as commissioner, Sam Houston defeated him in the Texas presidential contest. Houston appointed Austin secretary of state, but worn down by the hardships he had suffered, the "Father of Texas" died December 27, 1836.

4. David Gouverneur Burnet (1788–1870) studied law in Ohio and first came to Texas in the 1820s, settling permanently on Galveston Bay in 1831. He entered into several unsuccessful economic ventures and political efforts. He was ad interim president of Texas from March 17 to October 22, 1836, and was elected vice president in Mirabeau B. Lamar's administration in 1838.

5. Manuel Lorenzo Justiniano de Zavala Sáenz (1788–1836) was a newspaper

editor and a key figure in the Federalist movement in Mexico. He held several important posts in government until Santa Anna assumed dictatorial power in 1834. Zavala came to Texas in 1835 and supported the independence movement. He was a member of the Consultation and the Convention of 1836. Elected ad interim vice president in 1836, he resigned due to poor health in October 1836 and died of pneumonia in November.

6. Samuel Price Carson (1798–1838), from North Carolina, served four terms in the US House of Representatives, in the Nineteenth through Twenty-Second Congresses, from 1825 to 1832. In Texas he was a member of the Convention of 1836 and signed the Declaration of Independence. He was elected ad interim secretary of state in 1836, a position he quit before the year was out.

7. Thomas Jefferson Rusk (1803–1857), secretary of war, ad interim. Rusk had been a lawyer and investor in Georgia gold mines before coming to Texas in 1834. He took an active part in the independence movement and signed the Declaration of Independence as a representative of Nacogdoches at the Convention of 1836. The Convention appointed him ad interim secretary of war, a position he held for a time into the Houston administration. Rusk represented Nacogdoches in the Texas Congress from September 1837 to May 1838. Congress selected Rusk as major general of the militia, and in 1838 he put down the Cordova Rebellion and pursued Caddoes into Louisiana in November of that year. He took part in the Cherokee War and was at the Battle of the Neches. In December 1838 Rusk became chief justice of Texas, a position he held until 1840 when he resigned to resume his own very successful law practice and legal partnership with J. Pinckney Henderson. Following annexation, Rusk was elected to the US Senate; he served in the Twenty-Ninth through Thirty-Fifth Congresses, 1845–1857.

8. Bailey Hardeman (1795–1836) was a fur trapper in New Mexico and a store owner and tavern keeper in Tennessee before moving with his extended family to Texas in 1835. He participated in the revolution and took part in the convention that drafted the Texas Declaration of Independence and the constitution. In addition to his service as secretary of the treasury, Hardeman was also acting secretary of state in the absence of Samuel Carson and negotiated the two Velasco treaties.

9. David Thomas (1801–1836) came to Texas from Tennessee in 1835. He represented Refugio at the Convention of 1836 and signed the Declaration of Independence. The Convention elected him ad interim attorney general, and when Rusk left the cabinet he became acting secretary of war. Thomas was killed by the accidental discharge of a firearm while traveling on a steamboat.

10. Robert Triplett (d. 1853), from Kentucky, was a land speculator and agent for Texas based in New Orleans.

11. William Fairfax Gray (1787–1841), of Virginia, an attorney and land agent, provided financial support to Texas. He authored a perceptive travel diary, *From Virginia to Texas, 1835–1837*, edited by Paul D. Lack (Dallas: DeGolyer Library and William P. Clements Center for Southwest Studies, Southern Methodist University, 1997).

Mexico was not willing to lose Texas without a fight. In January 1836 President General Antonio López de Santa Anna led an army into Texas. On February 23 he reached San Antonio, where the Texans had taken up a position in the Alamo, a former mission. On March 6, after a thirteen-day siege, the Alamo fell, and all the defenders were killed. As Santa Anna's forces continued their advance, Sam Houston and his army retreated. At Goliad more than three hundred Texan troops under the command of Colonel James W. Fannin, who had surrendered with the understanding that they would be treated as prisoners of war, were instead massacred on the direct order of Santa Anna.

Despite such discouragements, Houston held his army together and finally at San Jacinto prepared to battle. On the afternoon of April 21, 1836, with shouts of "Remember the Alamo!" and "Remember Goliad!" Texans attacked Santa Anna's army, taking them by surprise. The battle lasted only eighteen minutes, but the killing went on longer. Mexican losses were 630 dead and 730 taken prisoner. Texan losses came to nine killed and about thirty wounded. Among the wounded was Houston himself, who received a severe bullet wound in the ankle. Santa Anna escaped the battleground, but was taken prisoner the next day wearing the uniform of a common soldier. Though his captors did not recognize him, his identity was given away when other Mexican prisoners saluted the general and addressed him as "El Presidente."

On May 14, 1836, Santa Anna signed the public and secret Treaties of Velasco (see below). In the public treaty Santa Anna agreed to withdraw Mexican forces beyond the Rio del Norte (the Rio Grande) and not to take up arms against the Texans again. Prisoners on both sides would be released. Santa Anna would be freed and returned to Mexico. In the secret treaty Santa Anna promised to "so prepare matters" that Mexico would acknowledge the independence of Texas.

Santa Anna and his entourage boarded the Texas war schooner Invincible *on June 1 for his return to Mexico, but new volunteers from New Orleans blocked the departure. Santa Anna was removed from the vessel and jailed. On July 4, 1836, Santa Anna wrote Andrew Jackson advising him that because he had not been able to use his good offices while a prisoner, Mexican forces were now positioned at the Nueces ready to renew hostilities. War was "inevitable, unless a powerful hand interpose." Jackson could "render so great a service to humanity" by using his influence to see that the Velasco agreements were fulfilled (Santa Anna to Jackson, July 4, 1836,* DCRT, *1: 106–107).*

Jackson's response, on September 4, 1836, was a model of caution. Nonetheless, in November, Santa Anna and his aide Juan Nepomuceno Almonte, accompanied by Colonel George W. Hockley, Barnard E. Bee Sr., and Major William H. Patton, began a journey to Washington, DC, to visit President Jackson.

Andrew Jackson to Antonio López de Santa Anna

Hermitage, September 4. 1836.

Sir:

I have the honor to acknowledge the receipt of your letter of the 4th of July last,[1] which has been forwarded to me by General Samuel Houston,[2] under cover of me from him, transmitted by an express from General Gaines, who is in command of the United States forces on the Texan frontier.[3] The great object of these communications appears to be to put an end to the disaster which necessarily attend the civil war now raging in Texas and asking the interposition of the United States in furthering so humane and desirable a purpose. That any well-intended effort of yours in aid of this object <should> have <been> defeated <is calculated to excite the regret of all who justly appreciate the blessings of peace, and who take> an interest in the causes which contribute to the prosperity of Mexico in her domestic as well as her foreign relations.

General D. Antonio López de Santa Anna, president of the Republic of Mexico
Print by A. Hoffy, Philadelphia, published July 1847. Courtesy Library of Congress Prints and Photographs Division, Washington, DC 20540. LC-USZ62-21276

The Government of the United States is ever anxious to cultivate peace and friendship with all nations, but it proceeds on the principle that all nations have the right to alter, amend, or change their own Government as the sovereign power (the people) may direct. In this respect, it never interferes with the policy of other powers, nor can it permit any on the part of others with its internal policy. Consistently with this principle, whatever we can do to restore peace between contending nations, or remove the causes of misunderstanding, is cheerfully at the service of those who are willing to rely upon our good offices as a friend or mediator.

In reference, however, to the agreement, <which> you as the representative <of Mexico, have made> with <Texas, and which invites the interposition of the United States, you will at once> see

Sam Houston

Daguerreotype by Matthew Brady's studio, ca. 1848-1850. Library of Congress Prints and Photographs Division, Washington, DC 20540. LC-USZ62-110029

that we are forbidden by the character of the communications made to us through the Mexican Minister,[4] from considering it. That Government has notified us that, as long as you are a prisoner, no act of yours will be regarded as binding by the Mexican authorities.[5] Under these circumstances, it will be manifest to you that good faith to Mexico, as well as the general principle to which I have adverted as forming the basis of our intercourse with all foreign powers, make it impossible for me to take any step like that you have anticipated. If, however, Mexico should signify her willingness to avail herself of our good offices in bringing about the desirable result you have described, nothing could give me more pleasure than to devote my best services to it. To be instrumental in terminating the evils of civil <war, and in substituting in their stead the blessings of peace, is a divine privilege.>

Every government and the people of all countries should feel it their highest happiness to enjoy an opportunity of thus manifesting their love of each other, and their interest in the general principles which apply to them all as members of the common family of man.

Your letter, and that of General Houston, commander-in-chief of the Texan army, will be made the basis of an early interview with the Mexican minister at Washington. They will hasten my return to Washington, to which place I will set out in a few days, expecting to reach it by the 1st of October. In the meantime, I hope Mexico and Texas, feeling that war is the greatest of calamities, will pause before another campaign is undertaken, and can add to the number of those scenes of bloodshed which have already marked <the progress of their contest,> and have <given so much pain to their Christian friends throughout the world.> This is sent under cover to General Houston, who will give it a safe conveyance to you.

I am very respectfully, Your obedient servant,
(signed) Andrew Jackson.

✦✦✦

Copy. Tx, TLP. Damaged. Published in *Cong. Globe,* 24th Cong., 2d Sess., January 18, 1837, p. 109. Missing text copied from *Cong. Globe.* Antonio López de Santa Anna (1794–1876), Mexican military leader and president. Andrew Jackson (1767–1845), president of the United States, March 4, 1829–March 3, 1837.

1. Santa Anna to Jackson, July 4, 1836, *DCRT,* 1: 106–107; also in *Cong. Globe,* 24th Cong., 2d Sess., January 18, 1837, pp. 108–109.

2. Samuel Houston (1793–1863) was born in Virginia and moved with his family to Tennessee after the death of his father. As a teenager he ran away from home and lived with the Cherokees, who called him "The Raven." Houston joined the army at the outbreak of the War of 1812 and served with Andrew Jackson in his victory over the Creeks at the Battle of Horseshoe Bend. After the War of 1812, Houston began a law practice and was elected attorney general for Nashville. He was elected to the US House of Representatives for the Eighteenth through Nineteenth Congresses, 1823–1826. In 1827 Houston was elected governor of Tennessee, but in 1829, after the collapse of his brief marriage to Eliza Allen, Houston abruptly resigned from office and made his way to Indian Territory, where he rejoined the Cherokees who had taken him in before. He remained with the Cherokees for three years. Houston came to Texas in 1832 and soon immersed himself in political affairs. He was a delegate from Nacogdoches to the Convention of 1833 and to the Consultation of 1835 and was a delegate from Refugio at the Convention of 1836 at Washington-on-the-Brazos. At

the Consultation he was appointed major general of the army. In command of the Texas army, Houston defeated General Santa Anna at the Battle of San Jacinto on April 21, 1836, and captured Santa Anna the following day. Houston was president of Texas from October 22, 1836, to December 10, 1838. He was a member of the Texas Congress in the House of Representatives from 1838 to 1841. Houston served a second term as president from December 12, 1841, to December 9, 1844. When Texas joined the Union in 1845, Houston was selected one of its two US senators. He served in the US Senate from February 21, 1846, to March 4, 1859, in the Twenty-Ninth through Thirty-Fifth Congresses. In 1859 Houston was elected governor of Texas. Houston opposed Texas secession after the election of Abraham Lincoln and refused to take a loyalty oath to the Confederate States of America. The legislature removed him from office on March 16, 1861. Houston retired to Huntsville, where he died in 1863.

3. General Edmund Pendleton Gaines (1777–1849) was a career soldier. In 1836, he commanded the US Army's Southwest Military Division.

4. Manuel Eduardo de Gorostiza (1789–1851), a playwright, was minister to the United States in 1836. He subsequently served as Mexico's finance minister, interior minister, foreign minister, and as envoy extraordinary to the United States in 1844.

5. See Manuel Eduardo de Gorostiza to John Forsyth, July 9, 1836, *IAA*, 8: 331–333.

On December 30, 1835, the Mexican Congress, at Santa Anna's urging, enacted a decree that all foreigners taken in arms against Mexican authority would be executed as pirates. Such was the fate of the defenders of the Alamo. Near the village of Goliad on March 27, 1836, Mexican soldiers massacred 342 Texan soldiers. The men, under the command of Col. James W. Fannin Jr. plus a contingent of Georgia volunteers taken prisoner at the Battle of Refugio, had surrendered to General José Urrea on the condition that they would be treated as prisoners of war. The surrender, however, was "subject to the disposition of the supreme government." Urrea recommended parole for the prisoners, but Santa Anna ordered them killed. The deed dramatically increased support for Texas in the United States and increased the determination of Texans to resist the Mexican army.

Peyton Sterling Wyatt to William H. Wharton

[November 8, 1836]
Charlotte C. H. Virginia

Dear Sir,

A few weeks since while in Huntsville Alabama, I received a communication from Mr. [William H.] Christy,[1] the distinguished friend of Texas in New Orleans, in reply to a proposition of mine, advising me not to make an exertion to send on more volunteers as "It was a well settled belief, that the War in that Country was at an end." Recent reports from Mexico however, seem to warrant a different conclusion, and are of a more warlike character, indicating a reinvasion of Texas. In that event, I desire you to acquaint me forthwith of the first demonstrations made by the enemy so that I may be enabled to join you in time to participate in the operations of the Army, and if possible, avenge the death of that portion of my brave Company who fell at Goliad and the Mission del Refugio.

My friend Mr. Jno. D. Phelan[2] having as I learn, made known to you my character, I have the taken the freedom to address this letter to you, as a gentleman, who correctly estimates me. I beg, therefore, to be allowed to look upon you as my friend.

I have several Letters to you and your Brother The Hon. John A. Wharton,[3] still in my possession, which I was unable to deliver in Texas. I sincerely regret that I was prevented from seeing either you or him, during my stay in that Country.

Be pleased, Sir, to address your reply to me at "Huntsville, Alabama" care of J. D. Phelan Esqr.

Since leaving Texas in June last, I have been engaged in the Creek War, acting as Aid-de-Camp to Maj. Gen. Patterson;[4] and very recently only have been discharged from the Service of the U. S.

Acknowledging myself, however, still subject to the orders of the Texian Government, I am With great consideration and regards Your Obt. Sevt.

P. S. Wyatt

✦✦✦

ALS. Tx, TLP. Peyton Sterling Wyatt (1804–1847), of Huntsville, Alabama, recruited and led a company of volunteers to Texas at the beginning of the revolution. While he was on a recruiting trip to the United States, most of the men who had originally come to Texas with him were massacred at Goliad.

1. William H. Christy (1791–1865), a New Orleans attorney, was an ardent supporter of the cause of Texas. He helped Archer, Austin, and Wharton secure two loans totaling $250,000. In 1836 the US government charged him with violating neutrality law, but he was acquitted.

2. John Dennis Phelan (1810–1879), a Huntsville attorney.

3. John Austin Wharton (1806–1838) followed his brother, William, to Texas. He was a delegate to the Consultation of 1835 and served as Houston's adjutant during the revolution. He was Texas secretary of war in 1836 and a member of the Texas Congress in 1836 to 1838.

4. Wyatt means to refer to Maj. Gen. Benjamin Patteson (1789–1862). He was a US Marshal in Huntsville, Alabama. Creek resistance to white encroachments on their land led to the Alabama Creek War of 1836. Their defeat led to additional forced removals to Indian Territory.

In the Transcontinental Treaty of 1819, US Secretary of State John Quincy Adams and Spanish Minister Luis de Onís set the eastern boundary of Texas from the mouth of the Sabine River along its western bank to the 32nd parallel, then due north to the Red River. In his letter of November 17, 1836, Richard Ellis suggested changes to the agreement.

Richard Ellis to William H. Wharton

Columbia 17th Novr 1836

Esteemed friend

At your request I with great pleasure make the following Breef Sugestions.

1 The reason for fixing the boundiary line in the middle of the Sabine River is by the constitution of Louisiana adopted 1812. That is

the extreme limit of that state, and therefore would leave the western half of that stream subject to no Jurisdiction whatever.[1] I need only to sugest to you what a fine field for Smuggling & Piricy lay on Sour Island west [of] the middle of that stream, and too for Robers & Banditi.

2 From where the 32 degree of North Latitude intersects the Sabine is not more than 56 miles. It can be run by a Skillful Engineer in 12 or 15 days after the point of departure shall have been accurately ascertained; have the kindness to urge the necessity of running that line with the least possible delay for the following reasons—1st in a National point of view that we may know where the lands lye belonging to our citizens, that they may be subject to Taxation, so indispensable at this time to our infant Republic struggling for its existence, 2nd it affords an almost safe hiding place for rogues and Bandits of all discriptions, destructive alike to the peace and Security of the good people of Louisana & this Republic.

I feel confident if those weighty reasons, and, others that your own beter judgment and reflection will sugest, need only to be stated to the Chief Magistrate of the U.S. (the Honest & virtous Patriot alike distinguished in Peace and in War whom from my first acquaintance with him I have most delited to honour) and he will act at once with his accustomed promptness & energy, for he will See it is of the highest importance to run the line even if we are annexed to the U S—for it would be to me a source of the highist gratification, if we could add another Laurel to his brow by yealding up this mighty Region of country, with all its vast resources, than he Should for a moment think of the litle strip of country between the Neches and Sabine Rivers is its self of but lit[t]le value.

3rd. The reason I described the boundary line on Red River in my Report as Chairman of the committe on Foreign Relations, at the lowest water mark is, because by the Chartered limits of Arkansaw as amended by Congress the South line of that state is to run down the South bank of Red River and with the Mexican line to that of Louisiana.

If we canot describe the line at lowest water mark, we may have the same <illegible> in future as New York or N Jersey cannot establish lines—& I cannot write this letter legible. I fear you know the cause & can excuse.

Your friend & Obet Servant
Richard Ellis

✦✦✦

ALS. Tx, TLP. Richard Ellis (1781–1846), an Alabama plantation owner and state judge, moved to Pecan Point, disputed territory along the Red River between Texas and Arkansas, in 1834. He was elected to the Texas Constitutional Convention, at which he presided as president. He served as senator from Red River County in the First through Fourth Texas Congresses, 1836–1840.

1. Constitution of Louisiana, 1812, in Benjamin Perley Poore, comp., *The Federal and State Constitutions, Colonial Charters, and other Organic Laws of the United States*, Part I, 2nd ed. (Washington, DC: Government Printing Office, 1878), 700–709. The preamble of the Louisiana Constitution of 1812 includes the following: "Beginning at the mouth of the river Sabine; thence by a line to be drawn along the middle of said river, including all islands, to the thirty-second degree of north latitude."

President Houston nominated William H. Wharton as the republic's first Minister Plenipotentiary to the United States on November 16, 1836. The Texas Senate confirmed his appointment the same day.

Stephen F. Austin to William H. Wharton

Republic of Texas
Department of State
Columbia Novr. 18th 1836

General instructions to the Hon. W. H. Wharton, Minister Plenepotentiary to the United States of America

Sir,

You will herewith receive your Commission and Credentials as Minister Plenepotentiary of Texas, to the United States of America, and also copies of the declaration of Independence, of the Constitution, and other acts and proceedings in relation to the organization of the Government of Texas, to be used as you may deem expedient in presenting the objects of your Mission.[1] The most importent of these objects are,

First, The recognition of the Independence of Texas.

Second, The annexation of this Country to the United States.

You will proceed to the City of Washington with the least possible delay, and your own judgment and sound discretion are relied upon fully in selecting the best and most expeditious mode of bringing these subjects before the Government, or Congress of the United States. Should difficulties arise as to receiving you formally as Minister until after the question of recognition is settled, you will urge that subject as the Agent of this Government, for which purpose seperate credentials are furnished you to be used in case it should be necessary.

Possessing as you do, the full confidence of the Government and being acquainted from long residence, with the situation and wants of this country, and the sentiments of the people, you will consider yourself vested with very ample powers in effecting the before mentioned objects of your Mission, and that the following instructions are given in explanation of the views of the Government, more as a general guide, than as a positive mandate. It is not intended to embarrass the negotiations with the United States by any onerous conditions or restrictions on our part. A just reciprocity is our basis, in the full confidence that a similar one will influence the counsels of the United States; you will therefore observe the utmost frankness and candor in all your intercourse with the government.

Texas claims the right of being recognized as an independent Nation, on the broad basis that she is so de jure, and de facto, that she has organized her political and civil government, which has been and is in undisturbed operation—and that she is fully competent to sustain her independence and fulfill the duties and obligations of an independent power.

It can not properly be made a question by a foreign nation whether Texas is independent de jure and had a constitutional right to seperate from Mexico, and form a government for herself; but it may notwithstanding add much to the moral force of our claims, to shew, that we were in fact made independent by the federal constitution of Mexico, in consequence of the revolution that destroyed the federal compact, which alone bound Texas in common with the other States to the Mexican confederation.[2] The destruction of that compact and constitution by revolutionary, violent and unconstitutional means, and the consequent change in the system and form of government, evidently severed all the bonds which united this country to Mexico, and absolved the people of Texas from all allegiance to the federal union, which ceased to exist, and left them free to take care of themselves. It is equally evident that the mere establishment of a new government by force of arms and usurpation, cannot and does not impose upon Texas nor upon any other of the former States, any obligations either moral or political, to resign the rights and sovereignty with which she was invested by the adoption of the federal union, or to acknowledge any allegiance or subjection whatever to such new and usurped government, other than by the free and voluntary consent of the people. It is therefore evident that the charge made by the present government of Mexico, that Texas has rebelled against the constitutional authority, or in any manner violated the allegiance that united it with that nation, is unfounded and recoils with all its force upon those who make it. But besides this fact, the right of the people of Texas to provide for their own security and welfare, and do what they consider necessary for self-preservation, cannot be questioned, for it is a natural right that every people possess; more especially when the nation to which they had been previously united is distracted by revolutions, and affords no protection whatever, political or civil, as was the case with Mexico in relation to Texas, at the time of the seperation of the latter, and for years previous. Your knowledge of this branch of the subject will however enable you to handle it in a proper manner, should you deem it necessary to touch upon it at all.

The most important point, and the only one about which the United States Government will probably require definite or special information, is whether Texas is independent de facto, and has established a regular government and is competent to sustain herself, and fulfil the duties of an independent nation. On this point, the declaration of Independence, the Constitution, the organization of the several branches of Government, the acts of Congress &c. are conclusive evidence that a political and civil government is established, and is republican and liberal. The fundamental laws are all adopted, and are in full force and operation. The constitutional executive and Congress have been duly elected and installed, and the latter has progressed with the details of legislation, with great rapidity and wisdom considering all the circumstances. The several subordinate departments of the Government are all organized and in full operation, many of the most important laws for the civil and military government of the Republic have been passed, or are in a great state of forwardness, such as the Judiciary law, that regulating the revenue, imposts, taxes &c, that organizing the army, and many others. These facts it is hoped, will be satisfactory and conclusive, that a government is established that is fully competent to fulfil the duties and obligations contemplated by the law of nations and required by the situation of Texas, and consequently it is believed that no material objection will be made to our independence on this point after it is fully explained by you.

In regard to the physical capacity of Texas to sustain herself, the signal and total defeat by General Houston of the army that invaded Texas, last spring commanded by the President Genl. Santa Anna in person, at the memorable battle of San Jacinto on the 21st. of April—the flight and dispersion of the remnant of that army, and the total abandonment of all the territory of Texas, by the forces of Mexico, and its peaceable possession by those of this Republic, afford evidence which certainly ought to be conclusive of the physical power of this republic to sustain its independence. This fact cannot admit of a single doubt, when it is considered that the invasion of General Santa Anna was made under the most favorable auspices for Mexico, and the most discouraging for Texas. The former was then united under a popular leader whose influence gave him almost dictatorial powers. He brought a well appointed and disciplined regular army to Texas, of about 8000 men, attached to their leader and confident of victory. On the other hand, Texas was totally unprepared for the contest, without organization, civil government, an army, or resources. At the present time however, this state of things is reversed. Mexico is in revolution and disorganized, its army dispersed and dispirited. Texas is looked upon as a dangerous and formidable enemy. The Mexican president

Genl. Santa Anna, the leader of her army, is a prisoner, and acknowledges that this country is able to sustain its independence and is lost to Mexico, the same is admitted in substance by General Filosola in his published defence of his conduct as the second in command under Santa Anna.[3] Most or all of the officers of the defeated army, state the same thing, and declare they will never return to this country. Texas at this time, has an organized government, in full and undisturbed operation, an army, a navy, and the people are all united and confident in their strength, the population has augmented and is rapidly increasing &c.

When all these circumstances are considered it cannot reasonably be supposed that any doubts can exist, as to the physical capacity of Texas to sustain her independence.

Your own judgment will suggest to you such other reasons and arguments as you may deem necessary to bring into view, according to circumstances and the nature of the objections that may be raised to an acknowledgment, should there be any.

Amongst others it may be important to argue that this measure is fully justified by precedent, in the case of South America, and is called for by the great principles of liberty, phylanthropy, and impartial justice, which form the basis for the institutions of the United States and of their exterior policy. On this basis, the republics of South American and Mexico were ushered by the United States into the family of nations. The political situation of Texas is certainly much better than most of those States were, particularly Mexico, when President Monroe recommended their recognition, by his Message of 8th March 1822.[4] Mexico at that time had not adopted any permanent fundamental law or Constitution, and did not adopt any until the 4th. of October 1824.[5] Spain still held possession of the Castle of San Juan de Ulloa,[6] and the people all over the nation were divided into factions, and in constant political ferment and revolution. A comparison between such a state of things, and that which exists in Texas, is so decidedly in favor of the latter, that it must be obvious, and have its due weight in an impartial Scale. In addition to these considerations it is evident that the elements and materials of Texas for forming an independent Republic on the broad basis of self government, will bear a very favorable comparison with those of any of said States, whose people had been for ages kept in ignorance and abject subjection by the despotic government of Spain.

Texas has those claims upon the good will and confidence of the United States, which common origen, language, habits, religion, political principles, kindred and education naturally create. We are in fact one people, seperated only by a line similar to that which divides the possessions of a son from those of his father.

Sound policy seems to urge the friendly interposition of the United States for the purpose of terminating the contest between Texas and Mexico, which if continued by the active renewal of hostilities, must inevitably be carried beyond the Rio Bravo into the thickly populated parts of Mexico, and become in the highest degree injurious to that country, and thus inflame the prejudices against Citizens of the United States there, and perhaps produce some outrage upon their rights by land or sea that would disturb the friendly relations and commercial intercourse that now exists between those nations. The effect this war will have upon the tranquility of the Southwest frontier of the United States is at least quite problematical. The Indians of that frontier are numerous and warlike, and may be disposed to take part on one side or the other, and thus the war whoop and savage barbarities will swell the tide of human sufferings, and in all probability force the United States into a war with those Indians, or lay her liable to the charge of cold indifference to the calamities of a suffering and innocent people should she fail to restrain the Indians from taking part against Texas, or of having evaded or violated the Treaty with Mexico, should she not restrain them from making predatory incursions against the Mexicans.

As to the second great object of your Mission, which is the annexation of Texas to the United States, you will make every exertion to effect it with the least possible delay, using your discretion as to the proper mode of bringing it before the Executive or Congress. It is probable that no action can be had on this point, until <u>after</u> the recognition of our Independence, unless the act of recognition and annexation should be simultaneous. The views of this Government are, that the annexation should be made on the broad basis of equitable reciprocity.

It must be effected by a formal treaty, which must be ratified by the Senate of Texas, in conformity with the constitution. In negotiating and forming this treaty, while you bear in mind that it is a favorite measure with the people of Texas and much desired by them, as is proven by their almost unanimous vote in favor of it at the September election;[7] you must not lose sight of the fact, that it is to decide the political fate and interests of the people of Texas, who have acquired many rights, under the laws of the former and present governments, and also by their toils and sufferings in redeeming this country from the wilderness, and achieving its independence, which must be duly respected and secured beyond the possibility of doubt, cavil or constructions at any future period. This Government has the most unbounded confidence in the magnanimity, justice, and liberality of the United States, and has no fears that any attempt will be made by them to invade any of the vested or equitable rights of the people of Texas.

It is believed that the sovereignty of this Country as an integral part of the American Union, on an equal footing with the other States is all that the United States will desire, but in the transfer of this Sovereignty it is very important that the rights of the people of Texas, should be clearly defined, understood, and guaranteed in order to avoid those kind of doubts and constructions which are always a fruitful source of disputes and litigations.

In forming said Treaty of annexation, the right ought therefore to be secured to Texas, of becoming a State of the American Union, on an equal footing with the other States, and as such to adopt her constitution and present it to the next Congress of the United States for approval and to organize her state Government without delay, so soon as the Treaty of annexation shall be duly ratified by both parties. The authorities of the Republic that may be in office at the ratification of said Treaty, should continue administering the government under the Constitution and laws of this Republic, which are not contrary to those of the United States, until the State government is organized, so as to avoid an interregnum. Possession should be taken by the United States immediately after the ratification of the Treaty, and Military posts established competent to protect it from indian or other enemies, especially on the Southwest and Northwest frontiers.

As regards the boundaries of Texas, perhaps this question cannot be definitely settled at present, it may however be important for you to explain the views of this government, on this point. You will therefore use the following as you may deem necessary. We claim and consider that we have possession to the Rio Bravo del Norte, taking this as the basis, the boundary of Texas would be as follows. Beginning at the mouth of said river on the Gulf of Mexico, thence up the middle thereof following its main channel, including the Islands to its most northerly Source, thence in a direct line to the United States boundary under the treaty of De Onis[8] at the head of Arkansas River, thence down said river and following the United States line as fixed by said De Onis treaty to the Gulf of Mexico at the mouth of Sabine, thence Southwardly along the shore of said Gulf, to the place of beginning, including the adjacent Islands, soundings &c. The said treaty of De Onis calls for the West bank of Sabine, and the South bank of Red and Arkansas rivers as the Line. It is believed that the chartered limits of Louisiana calls for the middle of Sabine, if so there will probably be no difficulty in making our line correspond with that of Louisiana—so as to give to us the right of landing, ferries &c without molestation on the West Side.

The same alteration should be made if practical as to the Red and Arkansas River lines, by fixing them in the middle of those Rivers, but should this be objected to, it is presumed the right of landing, and the free use and control of the banks on our side to low water mark will be secured to us. Should it appear that very serious embarrassments or delays will be produced by insisting on the above described line, the following alterations might be made on the Western boundary—Instead of the Rio Bravo, beginning on the west of the Gulf of Mexico, half way between the mouth of the Bravo and the inlet of Corpus Christi, which is the main outlet of the Nueces River and bay into the Gulf, thence in a Northwestwardly direction following the dividing Ridge of high land that divides the waters of the Nueces River and bay, from those of the River Bravo, to the hills or mountains in which the main branch of the said Nueces River has its Source, and thence following said ridge or chain of mountains westerly so as to strike the River Puerco or Pecos five leagues above its mouth (This river Puerco or Pecos enters the Bravo about fifty or sixty miles above the old

Presidio of Rio Grande now called Guerero situated on the main road from Bexar to Monclova) from the place where the line will strike the Puerco, it is to follow the ridge or mountain that divides its waters from those of Rio Bravo and to continue along said mountains above the head of said Puerco or Pecos, to the United States line, at the head of the Arkansas River. The Bravo as a line would cut off many settlements and some villages of Native Mexicans and divide the populous valley of New Mexico. It therefore may be seriously objected to. The other line along the dividing ridge includes no Mexican population except Bexar and Goliad, whose inhabitants have joined the cause of Texas and are represented in Congress—it will include in Texas all the vallies of the Nueces and Puerco and all the waters of the Red River and those of the south Side of Arkansas, west of De Onis' line, all of which naturally belongs to Texas and we have peaceable possession of it. The Salt lakes or ponds between the Nueces and Rio Bravo are of incalculable value and would supply a great amount of this article in the chrystalized form—the last mentioned line would divide them, the first would include them all. They are distributed over an extensive tract of sandy country which is of but little value for farming or pasture.

In relation to the future subdivision of Texas into several States, the broad basis of equity upon which it is contemplated to unite this country with the United States, seems to require that all future subdivisions should be left entirely to the option and decision of the people of Texas, when the increase and extension of population should render it necessary to the public convenience or interest. The treaty stipulations agreeably to this principle should only extend to limiting the number or territorial extent of said New States hereafter to be formed, and guaranteeing their admission into the Union on an equal footing with the other States, when petitioned for by the Legislature of Texas in conformity with the Constitution and laws of the United States.

The future location of Indians within the limits of Texas, south of Red River should be carefully guarded against, and the removal on just such terms of indemnity of those who are now residing there with acknowledged rights, should be provided for. The reasons for this measure are evident, when it is considered that they are now partially, and soon will be closely surrounded and intermingled with the

White population. This stipulation however need not prevent the location of Indians by the United States, between Red and Arkansas Rivers west of the De Onis line, should any important advantages be gained by such a concession, or should the United states earnestly desire it.

Should it be stipulated that Texas is to pay her own debts, she will of course retain the absolute disposal of all the Public Lands, and should the United States assume our debts, the public lands may be relinquished to them, but in the latter case, liberal allowances for Schools, Colleges, internal improvements &c ought to be made, and the Salt lakes or Ponds and Springs retained.

All laws civil or penal, acts and obligations either legal or equitable of the present Government of Texas, or of the provisional, and <u>ad interim</u> governments which preceded it, must be respected and held valid.

The legislation of the present Congress will no doubt settle most or all questions relative to land claims, by legislative provisions, but should any thing prevent or retard its completion until the annexation to the United States, all <u>bona fide</u> settlers in Texas must be protected in their rights to so much land as they can rightfully claim in virtue of the laws under which they emigrated, and their titles must not be adjudged defective nor questioned for want of mere matters of form, or for any failure to comply with formal and unessential requisitions, such as being a Roman Catholic, cultivation in toto or in any limited time or specific manner, alienation in a limited time, classification of the land, erecting stone or mud corners, paying dues to the Government by a fixed day, and the like. On the subject of land claims, the same broad and fundamental principles of equity should be observed, which are to form the basis of our connection with the United States. In order therefore to present this part of the subject in its true and proper light, it must be borne in mind that the people of Texas have undergone great privations, embarrassments and impediments owing to the wilderness situation of the country in times past, Indian hostilities, and especially to the revolutionary state of Mexico, and the consequent want of adequate protection, or even of local authorities; which impediments have in many instances rendered it impracticable for them comply strictly with all the minute conditions of the Colonization laws, altho' they have complied with the spirit and evident intention of said laws, by populating the country and contributing by their presence, and personal services to its improvement and defence. Great care should therefore be taken not to leave the just titles of any such, subject to doubts or to be questioned. Their claims are founded upon actual settlement, the sufferings of families, the redemption of this country from the wilderness, and opening the way for easy emigration, in short, they have laid a foundation by their labors and past sufferings, for independence and all the results that will follow.

There must be no special restrictions or limitations as to Slavery in Texas, different from what are imposed by the Constitution of the United States, upon other Slave holding States of that nation, and all persons of African derivation now in Texas, and held as Slaves shall be respected as the property of their Respective owners.

A reasonable time should be allowed to persons who may owe debts to citizens of foreign countries, contracted previous to coming here, before they can be molested by suits or the payment demanded.[9]

In conclusion the President directs that you express in the strongest terms the friendly disposition and warm attachment of the Citizens of this Republic towards the Government and citizens of the United States, and the high respect and consideration of this government and people for the venerable Chief Magistrate of that Great and prosperous Republic.

RespectfullyYour most ob't
S.F. Austin
Secy. of State

✦✦✦

LS. Tx, TLP. Published in *DCRT,* 1: 127–135.

1. Wharton's commission is in *DCRT,* 1: 140–141. For the "acts and proceedings" up to the date of this instruction, see Gammel, 1: 505–1093 (for the Declaration of Independence see pp. 1063–1067, and for the constitution see pp. 1069–1085).

2. At the Consultation of 1835, Texans declared that Santa Anna and other military chieftains had violated the Mexican Constitution of 1824 "by force of arms, overthrown the federal institutions of Mexico, and dissolved the social compact which existed between Texas and the other members of the Mexican confederacy" (Gammel, 1: 522). The Texas Declaration of Independence of March 2, 1836, reiterated those assertions (Gammel, 1: 1063-1067).

3. Following the defeat at San Jacinto on April 21, 1836, Santa Anna, then a prisoner of the Texans, ordered his second-in-command, General Vicente Filisola

[vice Filosola] (1789–1850), to withdraw the Mexican army from Texas. When he was accused of cowardice for carrying out those orders, Filisola published a defense of his actions, which was translated into English by George L. Hammeken and published in Texas as *Evacuation of Texas: Translation of the Representation Addressed to the Supreme Government by Gen. Vicente Filisola, in Defence of his Honor, and Explanation of his Operation as Commander-in-Chief of the Army Against Texas* (Columbia, TX: G. & H. T. Borden, 1837).

4. *Messages and Papers,* 2: 116–118.

5. Gammel, 1: 59–93.

6. Spain occupied the fortress of San Juan de Ulúa at Vera Cruz until November 1825.

7. The Texas Congress noted that "only ninety-three of the whole population" voted against annexation to the United States (Gammel, 1: 1089).

8. The 1819 treaty with Spain signed by John Quincy Adams and Luis de Onís, in *Treaties,* 3: 3–64.

9. This paragraph is omitted in *DCRT.*

Stephen F. Austin to William H. Wharton

Private and Special instructions to the Hon. W. H. Wharton Minister Plenepotentiary to the United States of America

Republic of Texas
Department of State
Columbia Novr 18th 1836.

Sir,

In addition to your general instructions of this date, you will be governed by the following, as your private and special instructions.

You will use every possible exertion to bring the question of recognition and annexation, to an issue during the present session of the United States Congress.

In forming the treaty of annexation it is highly important that no principles or rights should be surrendered that will probably be disapproved of by the people of Texas, or cause discontent, and be rejected by our Senate; and thus defeat the annexation. Be very particular to urge the importance and necessity of this point, in your conferences with the President, Secretary of State &c.

Notwithstanding the vote of the people at the September election in favor of annexation, you are aware that very many persons of influence who voted for that measure, merely yielded to the peculiar circumstances of the times, and incline strongly to the opinion, that Texas ought to remain a seperate and independent Republic.

Should our affairs assume a more favorable aspect by a termination of the war, and a treaty with Mexico, and by the manifestation of a friendly disposition towards us by England and France, it will have a powerful influence on public opinion, and in all probability decide it in favor of remaining independent. England, France and Mexico therefore have it in their power to influence very materially in fixing the political position of Texas. Suppose the two former and especially England should pursue the course which sound policy evidently dictates, and interpose their influence with Mexico to procure an acknowledgment of our Independence, and it was known in Texas that favorable Treaties could be made with those nations. And suppose at the same time that indifference is manifested by the United States as to receiving us, or that unjust and hard terms should be insisted on, or they should cavil about minute particulars &c.—What would be the consequence?—The answer is evident—Texas would at once say "we first applied to the land of our Nativity and have been coldly received or treated like strangers, we therefore abandon all idea of annexation and will proceed to perfect our institutions and extend our foreign relations where our interest can be best promoted." It should be borne in mind, that Texas makes a great sacrifice by agreeing to the annexation at all, even were the prospect of a continuance of the war greater than it now is, a Sacrifice that would be incalculable should the aspect of our affairs change as before indicated, as there is probability they will, within a short time. It should also be remembered that many are of the opinion that the vote of Septbr. was more the result of attachment to the native government of the great mass of the people, of the ties of kindred, the reminiscences of the past, and confidence in the liberal munificence of that government, than of mature reflection, on the future glory, interest and prosperity of Texas. This view of the subject affords to us a powerful argument which may be advantageously used by you so as to have its proper weight with the government of the United States, and with the Ministers of England, France and other foreign nations. It is a correct exhibition of facts, and of what will certainly take place, should the course and policy of the United States be adverse or illiberal, or should she refuse to allow not only liberal, but even munificent terms to Texas. In the event therefore of discovering any such disposition in the Government or Congress of the United States you will have full and free conversations with the British, French and other foreign Ministers, on the Texas question, explaining to them the great commercial advantages that will result to their nations from our Cotton &c. and finding a market here for their merchandise, and an outlet for their surplus population, on the basis of a system of low duties and liberal encouragement which it would be our interest to establish. And you will endeavor to enlist their governments through them, in favor of Texas, to acknowledge our Independence and interpose their friendly influence with Mexico, to procure a similar acknowledgment, with the boundary line first mentioned in your General instructions, which is the Rio Bravo on the west &c. Should both the recognition, and annexation be effected, all farther relations of a belligerent or peaceful character, will of course cease between Texas and Mexico and all other foreign powers. If however, these happy events should not take place, other and very important duties will devolve upon you.

Should the United States acknowledge independence but decline annexation on such terms as Texas can admit, it will then be your duty to propose and form a Treaty of Amity, limits, and commerce with that government, on the basis of a just reciprocity, and if possible, also a Treaty of alliance, keeping this Government regularly and minutely informed by your correspondence with the State department of what occurs, that the necessary instructions may be given.

You will ascertain as soon as possible whether a treaty of alliance can be made with the United States, and aid in money, troops or vessels of War can be procured under it, or otherwise, against Mexico, and if to be had, procure it without delay. You will also extend, so far as possible, your friendly intercourse with the foreign ministers of Washington, and sound them as to the dispositions of their governments.

You will not lose sight of the Indian question, and make such arrangements as will prevent the United States Indians from taking part with Mexico against Texas.

Should neither recognition, or annexation be effected you will then endeavor to procure the mediation of the United States for the purpose of terminating the war with Mexico, on the basis of a recognition of our independence, and you will also secure all the support and good will you can from the foreign ministers at Washington.

As a proof of our perfect reliance on the magnanimity of the United Sates, you will, as soon as may be proper, after your first interview with the Secretary of State, exhibit to him your general instructions in extenso, as a plain view of the subject, which may serve in affording information that may be useful to both parties in settling the question on the basis of equity and just reciprocity.

President Burnet wrote officially to Genl. Gaines, that it would be agreeable to the Government of Texas, should he establish his headquarters at, or occupy the post of Nacogdoches for the purpose of restraining the Indians.[1]

You will endeavor to ascertain the real views of the United States government in occupying that post, and whether it is seriously contemplated to insist on the River Neches as the constructive line under De Onis's treaty, instead of the Sabine as laid down in Millish's Map of 1818, which is positively and definitely fixed by said treaty as the boundary line.[2] This government cannot admit of any construction that will fix the line at the Neches, or make any variations of this kind from the said Treaty of De Onis, and should there be any attempt on the part of the United States government to move the line to the Neches and thus claim the country between that river and Sabine, you will solemnly protest against it as an infraction of said Treaty of De Onis, and an invasion of the rights and territory of Texas.

The confidence of this government in the justice and liberality of the United States is unbounded, and consequently it is not believed that any conditions or restrictions will be insisted on that are likely to be seriously disapproved by the people of Texas, or rejected by our Senate and thus defeat the annexation in toto. It is however highly important that the following stipulations should be kept in view pending the negotiations, as being particularly interesting to this country.

That allowing Texas to enter the American union as a State without passing through the intermediate stage of a territorial government, and that the authorities in office, and the laws in force, ~~not repugnant to the constitution of the United States,~~[3] at the ratification of the treaty of annexation, should continue until the state constitution and Government is formed and organized by the installation of the State authorities, and the enactment of State laws.

That no future subdivision of the territory of Texas, south of Red River, into a plurality of States or territories shall ever be made except on the petition of the Legislature of Texas founded upon that of the people of the particular section of country which is to be erected into such new state or territory. The country between Red and Arkansas Rivers may be excepted from this stipulation, and relinquished to the United States in full, on terms that will be equitable to both parties.

That relative to Slavery. On this point you must <u>insist</u> that no kind of restriction whatever, shall be imposed, different from the constitution of the United States, with respect to the other slave holding States of that Republic.

That confirming land titles of actual and <u>bona fide</u> settlers so as to secure them from the heartless grasp or persecution of speculators.

That recognizing as valid the legislation and acts of the present and past governments of Texas.

That allowing liberal donations to Texas of lands &c for Schools, Colleges, internal improvements &c. in case the United States assume our debts and take the vacant lands.

That prohibiting the location of Indians, south of the Red River, and all other stipulations of a similar character which involve interests of vital importance, or principles that may materially affect the future liberties or prosperity of Texas.

Should objections be made to the admission of Texas as a state without dividing or cutting off any of the territory South of Red River and between it and the Coast, and between the Sabine and the western boundary of Texas, on account of the size thereof, (an objection which it is not contemplated will be made) it will be your particular duty to show, as you can do, that many exaggerated and erroneous impressions have influenced public opinion in the United States, in relation to the extent or size of Texas. The map of this country compiled by S. F. Austin and published by Tanner,[4] was formed at an early day, when the interior of Texas was but imperfectly known, and makes this country much larger than it really is—for example, the general course of Red River as correctly ascertained is on or near the parallel of 33° North latitude but on said map it is extended near to latitude 34°. The distance on the map from Sabine to the Nueces and Rio Grande, is greater than it is in fact. The coast of the gulf is put down on the map many miles east and South east of what it really is—The river Puerco and the great bend of the Rio Bravo is put down on the map, much too far West. An accurate delineation therefore of the true size of Texas would show a territory much less than the said Map represents, and would not be any thing like so extensive as is generally supposed. It probably will not greatly exceed One hundred thousand square miles, supposing the western boundary to be on the dividing ridge between the Rivers Nueces and Puerco, and the River Bravo, which it is probable will be the line finally established.

It must also be remembered that a large tract on the Western and North western frontiers is of but little value and can never be densely populated. The country on the Puerco South of the latitude of the heads of Red River is represented as very mountainous and barren in general.

In conclusion the President relying fully on your prudence and judgment, confides the important objects of this mission to you in the confidence, that you will devote to it all the attention and activity which it requires, and that you will keep this government fully and minutely informed of every thing of public interest.

Respectfully Your most obed't
S F Austin
Sec. of State

N. B.[5] You will bear in mind, that all that part of your instructions relative to cultivating a <u>close</u> and intimate friendly intercourse with the foreign ministers at Washington, is based <u>solely</u> upon the <u>contingency</u> that the policy of the United States towards Texas should be indifferent or adverse, a contingency which it is not expected will take place; but if unfortunately it should, the duty of this government evidently requires of them to seek and procure all the aid they can from other Quarters. You will therefore be very careful not to commit yourself in any manner whatever with any of said foreign ministers untill you have had full time and a fair opportunity of investigating the subject, and understanding fully, so far as may be practicable, what are the views of the U.S. Govt. and of the said foreign ministers as to Texas, and then act in this particular, as in your judgement the interests of Texas may require.

S. F. Austin
Sec. of State

✦✦✦

Copy. Tx, TLP. It appears that Austin's signature was cut from the manuscript. Published in *DCRT,* 1: 135–140.

1. Burnet wrote Gaines that if he thought it "expedient and likely to secure peace among those Tribes to establish his head quarters at Nacogdoches, such a measure would be perfectly satisfactory to this government" (Burnet to Collinsworth and Grayson, July 8, 1836, *DCRT,* 1: 104–105).

2. Secretary of State John Quincy Adams and Spanish minister Luis de Onís used John Melish's [vice Mellish] (1771–1822) 1818 "Map of the United States with the Contiguous British and Spanish Possessions" in the 1819 treaty. That map depicted the Texas-Louisiana border at the Sabine River.

3. This phrase, which is struck out in the manuscript, is not struck out in *DCRT.*

4. Austin began working on a map of Texas in 1822, which he completed in 1829 and arranged to have published by Philadelphia cartographer Henry S. Tanner. A color plate of the map is in James C. Martin and Robert Sidney Martin, *Maps of Texas and the Southwest, 1513–1900* (Austin: Texas State Historical Association, 1999).

5. This *nota bene* addition to the instruction is in Austin's hand. It differs in many particulars from the text published in *DCRT.*

Stephen F. Austin to William H. Wharton

Republic of Texas
Department of State
Colombia Novr. 19th, 1836

The President has directed me to authorise you to draw on the Secretary of the Treasury for a sufficient sum to meet your necessary expences. You are therefore hereby authorised to draw on the said Secretary for any sum not exceeding Five thousan dollars, on account of your outfit and salary as minister, and to call on Thos. Toby and Bro. agents of Texas in New Orleans, or upon the commissioners for negotiating the loan of five millions, to cash your drafts for that amount, out of any funds of Texas in their hands. You will advise the secretary of the treasury of each draft you draw, and by whom cashed.

S. F. Austin
Sec. of State

✦✦✦

ALS. Tx, TLP.

Stephen F. Austin to William H. Wharton

Department of State
Peach point Novr. 22, 1836

Dr Sir,

I send you a tin case enclosing your credentials and instructions as minister plenepotentiary to the United States of America. It contains your commission—a letter of credence to the secretary of State of the United States, and office copies of them—your general instructions—your private & special instructions, and Documents relative to the organization of the Govt. of Texas—I also send you a file of the Texas Telegraph[1] —Please to acknowledge the recipt of them to file in this department—You already have the Declaration of Independence and the constitution.

I herein enclose you, by the orders of the President, authority to draw on the Secretary of the Treasury[2] for any sum not exceeding five thousand dollars and to call on Thos. Toby & Bro.[3] agents of Texas to cash your drafts, or upon the commissioners of the five million loan.

Wishing Mrs. Wharton & yourself a speedy and pleasant passage,

I have the honor to remain Your most obt.

S. F. Austin
Sec. of State

✦✦✦

ALS. Tx, TLP. Extract published in *DCRT*, 1: 141–142.

1. The *Texas Telegraph*, more properly known as the *Telegraph and Texas Register*, was established at San Felipe on October 10, 1836, by Gail Borden Jr. (1801–1874), Thomas H. Borden (1804–1877), and Joseph Baker (1804–1846). The paper, which published the republic's official documents, moved several times. From August 1836 to April 1837 it was published in Columbia; in April it relocated to Houston.

2. Henry Smith (1788–1851), secretary of the treasury, 1836–1838. Smith arrived in Texas in 1827 from Kentucky and became an early advocate of independence. He was provisional governor of Texas from 1835 to 1836 and a member of the Texas House of Representatives in 1840.

3. The Toby brothers of New Orleans (Thomas ca. 1798-1849; Samuel ca. 1810-1852) became agents for the Republic of Texas in May 1836. They were authorized to sell Texas land to raise funds, but sales proved difficult. Texas ended the agreement with the brothers in 1837. Thomas Toby moved to New Orleans from Philadelphia about 1817.

On January 22, 1836, in New Orleans, Commissioners Archer, Austin, and Wharton appointed James Wolfe an agent of Texas with authority to negotiate loans and appoint additional agents (Austin to Wolfe, January 22, 1836, Austin Papers, *3: 312–313). He was named secretary of legation on November 24, 1836. Wolfe was the son of prominent Richmond, Virginia, businessman Benjamin Wolfe, who served for a time as mayor of Richmond. Two of Wolfe's brothers, Udolpho and Joel, were prominent liquor importers in New York, and one, Nathaniel, became a leading attorney in Kentucky, but there is scant information about James Wolfe. According to Jacob R. Marcus,* United States Jewry, 1776–1985, *4 vols. (Detroit: Wayne State University Press, 1989), 1: 29), James Wolfe was the first Jew admitted to law practice in Virginia. Houston replaced Wolfe as secretary of legation with Fairfax Catlett in December 1836, but despite that he continued to represent Texas as an agent.*

James M. Wolfe's Oath of Office as Secretary of the Texas Legation

[November 24, 1836]
Republic of Texas
Brazoria County.

This affiant maketh Oath that he will support the Constitution of the Republic of Texas and will keep all and every Secret which may come to his knowledge whilst acting as Secretary of the mission from the Republic of Texas near the United States of America and will faithfully and diligently render all the aid in his power to the minister Wm. H. Wharton in discharging whatever duties may be assigned to said minister by the abovesaid Republic of Texas.

Sworn to and Subscribed this 24th. November 1836 W. H. Wharton

James Wolfe

✦✦✦

DS. Tx, TLP.

Stephen F. Austin to William H. Wharton with Enclosure

Columbia Novr 25 1836.

Dear Sir

Cols. Hockly[1] and Bee[2] start tomorrow with Genl Santa-Anna for Washington City.

The President confidently believes that much good will result to all the parties concerned by an interview between Genl Santa Anna and the President of the United S. It is very evident that the true interests of Mexico, of the U.S. and of Texas, all demand a speedy termination of the war in this country, and the annexation of Texas to the U.S. Genl. Santa Anna distinctly says that he is satisfied of this fact, and will use all his influence to effect it. He thinks that it is all important he should return to Mexico by Washington City in order to have an interview with the President of the U.S. and he is permitted to do so.

I inclose to you a copy of the secret treaty made with President Burnet. It is still considered a secret, and therefore ought not to be published by any of us—also a copy of the public treaty, you may possibly need them.[3] Copies of them were inclosed to Genl. Jackson by Santa Anna in his letter of 4th July.

There is nothing new except the total loss of the Steam boat Oceana. She sunk yesterday at Brazoria with a full load of merchandize, just from the mouth of the river

Yours Respectfully
S. F. Austin
Sec of State

✦✦✦

LS. Tx, TLP. Published in *DCRT,* 1: 143.

1. George Washington Hockley [vice Hockly] (1802–1854), originally from Philadelphia, followed Sam Houston to Tennessee and then to Texas in 1835. Houston appointed him as his chief of staff when he took command of the Texas army. Houston appointed Hockley secretary of war in 1838 and again in 1841.

2. Barnard Elliott Bee Sr. (1787–1854), from South Carolina, was the brother-in-law of South Carolina governor and avid Texas supporter James Hamilton. Bee later became secretary of war in the Houston administration and secretary of state under President Mirabeau B. Lamar. Bee served as minister to the United States from 1840 to 1841.

3. President Burnet and Santa Anna signed two treaties at Velasco on May 14, 1836, one public and one secret. The public treaty established peace between the warring parties and provided for the restoration of property, the return of prisoners, and the retreat of Mexican forces from Texas. In the secret treaty Santa Anna agreed to "prepare matters" in Mexico so Texas independence would be recognized.

Enclosure: The Public and Secret Treaties of Velasco, May 14, 1836

Public Treaty

Articles of agreement entered into between his Excellency David G. Burnet, President of the republic of Texas, of the one part, and his Excellency Genl Antonio Lopez de Santa Anna, President General in Chief of the Mexican army of the other part:

Article 1st

Genl Antonio Lopez de Santa Anna agrees that he will not take up arms, nor will he exercise his influence to cause them to be taken up against the people of Texas, during the present war of Independence.

2nd

All hostilities between the Mexicans and Texian Troops will cease immediately, both on land and water.

3rd

The Mexican Troops will evacuate the Territory of Texas, passing to the other side of the Rio Bravo del Norte.

4th

The Mexican army in its retreat shall not take the property of any person without his consent and just indemnification, using only such articles as may be necessary for its subsistence, in cases when the owner may not be present, and remitting to the Commander of the army of Texas or to the commissioners to be appointed for the adjustment of such matters, an account of the value of the property consumed, the place where taken, and the name of the owner if it can be ascertained.

5th

That all private property, including cattle, horses, negro slaves or indentured persons of whatever denomination, that may have been captured by any portion of the Mexican army or may have been taken usage in the said army since the commencement of the late invasion, shall be restored to the Commanders of the Texian army, or to such other persons as may be appointed by the Government of Texas to receive them.

6th

The troops of both armies will refrain from coming into contact with each other, and to this end, the commander of the army of Texas will be careful not to approach within a shorter distance of the Mexican army than five leagues.

7th

The Mexican army shall not make any other delay on its march, than that which is necessary to take up their hospitals, baggages etc. and to cross the rivers; any delay, not necessary to these purposes, to be considered an infraction of this agreement.

8th

By Express, to be immediately dispatched, this agreement shall be sent to Genl Vincente Filisola and to Genl T. J. Rusk Commander of the Texian army, in order that they may be apprised of its stipulations, and to this end, they will exchange engagements to comply with the same.

9th

That all Texian prisoners now in possession of the Mexican army or its authorities, be forthwith released and furnished with free passports to return to their homes; in consideration of which, a corresponding number of Mexican prisoners rank and file, now in possession of the Government of Texas, shall be immediately released. The remainder of the Mexican prisoners, that continue in possession of the Government of Texas, to be treated with due humanity, any extraordinary comforts that may be furnished them, to be at the charge of the Government of Mexico.

10th

Genl Antonio Lopez de Santa Anna will be sent to Vera Cruz, as soon as it shall be deemed proper. The contracting parties sign this instrument for the above mentioned purposes by duplicate at the Port of Velasco, this fourteenth day of May 1836—Signed David G. Burnet—James Collinsworth,[1] Secretary of State—Antonio Lopez de Santa Anna—Bailey Hardiman, Sec'y of the Treasury—P. W. Grayson, Attorney General—

Copies from the originals

S. F. Austin
Sec of State

Secret Treaty

Antonio Lopez de Santa Anna, General in Chief of the Army of Operations, and President of the Republic of Mexico before the Government established in Texas, solemnly pledges himself to fulfill the stipulations, contained in the following articles, so far as concerns himself.

Art. 1st

He will not take up arms, nor cause them to be taken up against the people of Texas, during the present war of Independence.

Art. 2nd

He will give his orders, that in the shortest time the Mexican troops may leave the Territory of Texas.

Art. 3d –

He will so prepare matters in the Cabinet of Mexico, that the Mission, that may be sent thither by the Government of Texas may be well received, and that by means of negotiations, all differences may be settled and the Independence that has been declared by the Convention may be acknowledged.

Art. 4th–

A treaty of commerce amity and limits will be established between Mexico and Texas. The territory of the latter not to extend beyond the Rio Bravo del Norte.

Art. 5th

The prompt return of Genl. Santa Anna to Vera Cruz, being indispensable for the purpose of effecting his solemn engagements; the Government of Texas will provide for his immediate embarkation for said port.

Art. 6th

This Instrument being obligatory on one part, as well as on the other, will be signed by duplicate, remaining folded and sealed, until the negotiation shall have been concluded, when it will be restored to his Excellency Genl. Santa Anna; no use of it to be made before that time, unless there should be an infraction by either of the contracting parties—Port of Velasco May 14th 1836—Signed David Burnet—Antonio Lopez de Santa Anna—James Collinsworth, Secretary of State—Bailey Hardeman, Secretary of the Treasury—P. W. Grayson, Attorney Genl.[2]

✦✦✦

Secretarial Copy. Tx, TLP.

1. James Collinsworth (1806–1838), an attorney, came to Texas from Tennessee in 1835. He signed the Declaration of Independence at the Convention of 1836 and served on the committee to write the Texas Constitution. Houston appointed him an aide-de-camp during the revolution. He served as secretary of state for a time in 1836 and was named a commissioner to the United States to seek annexation. In November 1836 he was elected to the Texas Senate and in December of that year was appointed the first chief justice of Texas. He fell, or jumped, from a steamboat in Galveston Bay and drowned.

2. Peter Wagener Grayson (1788–1838) had been a member of the Kentucky legislature before he came to Texas, where he owned a plantation near Matagorda. During the revolution Grayson served as Stephen F. Austin's aide-de-camp. Interim President Burnet appointed him attorney general. With Collinsworth he was sent on a mission to the United States to seek recognition and annexation. Sam Houston named him attorney general, and he was also naval agent to the United States. Grayson was appointed minister to the United States in June 1838, but on the way to Washington, he committed suicide near Knoxville, Tennessee.

William H. Wharton to Stephen F. Austin

On board S[team] Boat Genl Gaines near Natchez,
December 2d 1836

Dear Sir

All of my notes to you have been written under the most disadvantageous circumstances at moments snatched from other pressing business and generally either in a crowd or under the importunities of the person who was to bear to them. This must account both for the manner & matter for I have in no instance had time to reconsider my first impressions or to retain a copy. What I have said here covers advice from the head & heart & as is unavoidable in such cases, much error has crept into my suggestions. When I get quietly seated at Washington I will write more composedly & send you my letters in a fair hand. Whatever I write before getting to Washington must be considered as done en passant & totally unofficial. For fear of forgetting however, whenever an idea occurs I will write if it is with a pencil & on my knee for a table. Should I appear at any time blunt or uncourtly you know me well enough to know it will be unintentional in the broadest sense of the word & sorry indeed would I be if I thought you could for a moment entertain a contrary opinion. I am writing now on a boat which from the power of its engine shakes far more than any I ever traveled on—but I am anxious to mail this at Natchez & you must pardon the scrawl.

In my general instructions you observe that should they refuse to receive me as minister before a recognition, that you have furnished me a commission to act as the Agent of Texas. That commission you neglected to send. It is not among my papers & if you deem it important, send it on immediately. Superscribe all of your letters with these words To be forwarded by the Express mail and they will reach Washington in 5 days from New Orleans. The instructions I am much pleased with. They are ably & judiciously drawn up. Do hurry that act waiving being a Catholic &c &c & also the judiciary act through as fast as possible. I cannot get along without them.

I think I told you last year that after my protest to Genl Jackson against a sale of Texas by Mexico as was supposed to be Gorostiza's business, I had a long conversation with Donnelson[1] (Private Secretary) which I considered at least demi-official in which he said that the U. S. did not recognize the right of Mexico to sell Texas after our declaration of Independence, but that if the US chose to give Mexico a few million for a quit claim just for national character sake, [leaving] at the same time to Texas the arranging of the terms of her annexation, on this state of things Donnelson contended that Texas should not through pride object. I answered him then as I would such a proposition if now made unless you instruct me different, namely let Texas & the U. S. agree upon the terms definitely & then the U S may give Mexico what hush money she pleases. Texas for her part will give nothing but lead. Write me on this subject. Under every disadvantage & in great haste.

I have the honor to be yours &c
Wm. H. Wharton

✦✦✦

ALS. Tx, TLP. This letter was addressed to Stephen F. Austin. A pencil note on the first page, reading "To the President:", suggests that it was forwarded to Sam Houston. Garrison, in *DCRT*, 1:148-149, publishes a similar but clearly different letter to Austin, also written on board the steamboat *General Gaines* on December 2, 1836.

1. Andrew Jackson Donelson [vice Donnelson] (1799–1871), Andrew Jackson's nephew and private secretary. In 1844 President Tyler appointed him chargé d'affaires to Texas. Rumors that Gorostiza had orders to seek the sale of Texas to the United States began about April 1836 (Sam P. Carson to George C. Childress and Robert Hamilton, April 1, 1836, *DCRT*, 1: 76–77).

Peyton Sterling Wyatt to William H. Wharton

Alabama U.S.
6 Decem. 18[36]

Sir,

I have addressed several letters [to you] in the course of a few months past; to which I have [had] no reply. Be good enough to write me by first opp[ortunity] on the subject of Texas.

It will be inconvenient for me to visit Texas again < . . . > the spring; but should a reinvasion take place sooner< . . . > me know and I will be with you forthwith.

My friend Mr. Phelan informs me that he < . . . > at Washington City, and that you regretted not seeing < . . . > in Texas. Sir, I assure you I shall ever regret < . . . >

Since leaving your Country I have been < . . . > in our Creek war in Alabama.

It is not unknown to you I presume that < . . . > most of my Company of Volunteers at Goliad and < . . . > Mission del Refugio. I was on furlough in < . . . > at the time; and was unable to join them before the catastrophe. I am burning to avenge their fall < . . . > shall look for orders from the Government of Texas as my services may be required.

Address your letters to me at Huntsville, Alab[ama] care of Jno. D. Phelan Esqr.

I am, with great respect Your obedient servant
P. S. Wyatt

+++

LS. Tx, TLP. Damaged, with some missing text.

Hostile Indians were among the constant difficulties the fledgling republic faced. Among many other incidents, a large force of Comanches and Kiowas attacked Parker's Fort on the Navasota River on May 19, 1836, killing five persons and tak-

ing five others captive, including Cynthia Ann Parker. A party of Caddoes attacked settlers near Nashville-on-the-Brazos in June 1836, killing two men, then attacked settlers at Little River. There were also reports that Indian representatives met with Mexican officials at Matamoros, where they were encouraged to join Mexico in a war against the Texans.

Stephen F. Austin informed US General Edmund P. Gaines, on July 4, 1836, that the Indians had undertaken "active hostilities on the whole line of the frontier along the upper or San Antonio road." Austin suggested that Gaines place troops at Nacogdoches in order to prevent "an indian war and preserve the tranquility of the U.S. frontier" (Austin to Gaines, July 4, 1836, Austin Papers, *3: 384-385). President David G. Burnet also assured Gaines that Texans would approve the advance of United States troops to Nacogdoches (Burnet to Collinsworth and Grayson, July 8, 1836,* DCRT, *1: 104-105).*

Shortly thereafter Gaines ordered the 4th US Infantry, under Lt. Col. William Whistler, from Louisiana to Nacogdoches as well as six companies of infantry and three companies of dragoons from Fort Towson, Indian Territory. The troops were withdrawn in December 1836, which resulted in renewed complaints from Texans about Indian depredations.

Stephen F. Austin to William H. Wharton

(No. 3)
Columbia Dec. 10. 1836.
Department of State

Honble W. H. Wharton,

Since your departure, Congress has progressed rapidly in completing the details for the organization of all the branches of Govt under the constitution. The greatest harmony and union prevail throughout the country. The Army is rapidly increasing, is well supplied with clothing and provisions, and is better disciplined than it ever has been; for which latter partial improvement we are principally indebted to Adjutant General Johnson, formerly of the US Army.[1]

We have rumours of an invasion by land and water; how far they are true is uncertain; we are however fully prepared to meet them on land, and in a short time expect to be ready for them on sea.

Public anxiety is unabated on the subject of annexation to the United States. The opinion in favour of that measure is much more decisive, if possible, than when you left. It is therefore expected, that you will press that matter with as much earnestness as prudence will permit.

Rumours occasionally reach us of the disposition of the Indians on the northern frontier, to take sides in the war against Texas. The Caddoes are decidedly hostile, and have committed many depredations.

I was assured a few days since, by a person of known veracity, that the Cherokees of the Nacogdoches district, the Caddos, Comanches and all of the small tribes, who were under their influence, except the Shawnees, had actually entered into a combination to join the Mexicans last spring, and were preparing to do so, when they heard of the defeat at San Jacinto. It is therefore of vital importance to the tranquillity of the United States' frontier, that the American troops should be continued at Nacogdoches, and the number increased, rather than diminished. This measure is also evidently required by the obligation of the United States to restrain her Indians from committing hostilities within our territory. You will therefore represent this subject to the Government of the United States, for the purpose of showing the necessity of continuing the garrison at Nacogdoches.

Respectfully Your Most Ob'd.
S. F. Austin
Sec of State

✦✦✦

LS. Tx, TLP. Published in *DCRT,* 1: 149–150.

1. Albert Sidney Johnston [vice Johnson] (1803–1862), of Kentucky, graduated from the United States Military Academy in 1826. He resigned from the army in 1834 and came to Texas in 1836. He was appointed adjutant general of the Texas army on August 5, 1836. President Mirabeau B. Lamar made him secretary of war in 1838. After service with Texas volunteers in the War with Mexico, Johnston rejoined the US Army in 1849. On the outbreak of the Civil War, Johnston became a general in the Confederacy. He was killed at Shiloh.

Stephen F. Austin to William H. Wharton

No. 4
(Duplicate)
Columbia
Dec. 10th 1836
Department of State

Honble W. H. Wharton

It is certainly desirable that Texas should enter the American Union at once and undivided; but should you discover that this condition, if positively insisted upon is likely materially to affect the main object which is annexation; I am directed by the President to say that you are at liberty to waive it and agree to a territorial Government with the necessary guarantees as to a State Govt. so soon as it is petitioned for. This Govt. has too much confidence in the just and liberal principles by which the United States are governed to doubt that full and ample justice will not be done us in every respect.

Should you discover that Mexico is willing to give a quit claim for Texas to the U.S. I am also directed by the President to say that this Govt. will not object to entering the American Union by that means, provided that the leading principles and rights embraced in your instructions of 18th ult. are fully and amply secured to Texas. You will therefore consider yourself invested with discretionary powers as to this particular.

The army and navy of Texas should be provided for in the Treaty of Annexation on such terms as may be considered just and expedient for both parties; you will therefore keep this point in view in the negotiation.

Respectfully, Your most ob'd't
S. F. Austin
Secy of State

P.S. You will by no means omit to exhibit your general instructions of 18th ult to the President and Secretary of State of the United States.

S. F. Austin
Sec of St

✦✦✦

LS. Tx, TLP. Published in *DCRT,* 1: 150–151.

Stephen Hendrickson Everitt to William H. Wharton

Senate Hall
Columbia
Decm 10. 1836

Dr Sir

Every thing here remains perfectly tranquil. Mr [James] Collingsworth fills Your seat. It is useless to say that he fills it with much, very much credit to himself and friend. We shall adjourn in 10 or 12 days haveing done all or nearly all that we ought to do till we hear from You and Your operations. We have sold one league of land on Galveston Island for 50,000 Doll[ar]s to P. J. Menard[1] and associates.

We are looking anxiously for the presidents message[2] as we can tell how things are goeing with by the reading of that document.

[Richard] Ellis will run for Supreme Judge

[Shelby] Corzine[3] will run for District Judge and your humble Servant will run for home. Write to <....> That I <.... remainder of letter missing...>

✦✦✦

ALS. Tx, TLP. Stephen Hendrickson Everitt (1806–1844), a land speculator and merchant, came to Texas from New York. He was a delegate to the Consultation of 1835 and the Convention of 1836. He was a senator in the first five Texas Congresses, until 1840.

1. Pierre J. Menard (ca. 1808–1861), a French-Canadian trader, moved to Texas from Illinois in 1834. He opened a store on the Strand in Galveston and speculated in land.

2. President Jackson's eighth annual message of December 5, 1836, in which Jackson acknowledged the "known desire of the Texans to become part of our system," but stated that the United States would remain scrupulous in maintaining neutrality in the conflict between Texas and Mexico (*Messages and Papers,* 3: 236–260).

3. Shelby Corzine (d. 1839), from Alabama, arrived in Texas in 1835. He was elected to the Senate of the First Texas Congress in 1836, but resigned to become judge of the First Judicial District. He later served on the commission to determine the boundary between the United States and Texas.

Henry Smith

Portrait by William H. Huddle (1847-1892). Courtesy of the State Preservation Board, Austin, TX; Accession ID: CHA 1989.104. Photography by Bill Kennedy, August 31, 1992 (pre conservation).

Henry Smith to William H. Wharton

No.5.
Republic of Texas
Treasury Department
Columbia 14 December 1836

Respected Sir/

I have under this date received information from the Department of State that you were authorized to draw on me for Five thousand Dollars, the amount of your outfit, provided you had not been able to have that amount previously negotiated. And also for the sum of Four thousand five hundred Dollars as Salary, quarterly as it falls due. In order that the necessary means be placed within your control, I have the honor to inform you that David White[1] Esq. of the City of Mobile, has been appointed agent of this government, and will in a short time be in funds sufficient to answer your demands. You will therefore please draw on him with instructions to place the same to the account of this government, of which you will at all times notify this Department, and no failure it is presumed will be apprehended.

With sentiments of regard and consideration I am very respectfully

Your Obdt. Svrt.
Henry Smith

✦✦✦

LS. Tx, TLP.

1. David White (1780–1841) was appointed Texas agent in Mobile on December 10, 1836.

Stephen F. Austin to William H. Wharton

(No 5)
Department of State
Columbia
Dec 14th. 1836

Sir,

In addition to the authority given to you by my letter of 19th ult. to draw for your outfit of five thousand dollars, the President has directed me to authorise you and I do hereby authorise you to draw upon the Secretary of the Treasury for your salary of four thousand five hundred dollars per annum, as it becomes due quarterly, and to call on David White of Mobile to cash your drafts, in whose hands these will be funds amply sufficient for that purpose.

Should you not have succeeded in cashing the drafts, drawn by you under the authority of 19th ult. above referred to, you are also authorised to call on David White to cash those drafts, giving to him in both cases timely notice of the call, and advising the Secretary of the Treasury of each draft you draw and by whom cashed

Respectfully Yr. Most obt.
S. F. Austin
Sec of State

✦✦✦

LS. Tx, TLP.

Stephen F. Austin to William H. Wharton

(No. 6)
Columbia
Dec. 14th 1836
Department of State

I have the honor to inform you that the President, by and with the advice and consent of the Senate, has appointed Fairfax Catlett[1] Esqr Secretary of Legation of the Mission to the U. S. of A. The President therefore directs, that you receive and present him as such to the Secretary of State of the United States[2] that he may be officially known and recognised.

Respectfully Your Most obt.
S. F. Austin
Sec of State

✦✦✦

LS. Tx, TLP.

1. Fairfax Catlett (1812–1843), of Virginia.

2. John Forsyth (1780–1841), of Georgia, served as secretary of state under presidents Andrew Jackson and Martin Van Buren, 1834–1841.

Putnam P. Rea to [William H. Wharton]

New Orleans Decr 14 1836

Dear Sir,

A few days since I made the notice you requested in the letter you left for me as you were on the point of starting for Washington, and I forwarded a slip containing it to the [Washington] Globe and the [National] Intelligencer. I sent those papers also the slip containing the report of your committee on foreign relations—and I send by the Express of today, an editorial article on the subject of annexing Texas, which is intended to be followed by two or three others. Anything, or rather every thing of any interest whatever which comes from Texas can be forwarded by the Exps mail to the Wash[ington] papers above.

You will have opportunity of seeing it. I go body & soul for Texas. Zavala is said to be dead.

We have nothing new today—the P[resident]'s message has not yet been received but is hoped for today.

I am dear sir with high esteem & regard your friend & servant

P. P. Rea

✦✦✦

ALS. Tx, TLP. Putnam P. Rea (ca. 1800–1843), editor of the New Orleans *Commercial Bulletin,* was a vocal supporter of Texas.

The Constitution of the Republic of Texas declared "the importation or admission of Africans or negroes into this republic, excepting from the United States of America is forever prohibited, and declared to be piracy," and the First Texas Congress passed a law on December 21, 1836, imposing the death penalty for anyone convicted of importing slaves from anywhere except the United States (Gammel, 1: 1079, 1257). Even so, it is certain that throughout the 1830s slaves were smuggled into Texas from Cuba.

Stephen F. Austin to William H. Wharton

No. 7.
Republic of Texas
Department of State
Columbia 16th. Decr. 1836

Sir

It has come to the knowledge of this Government, through the channel of common rumor, sustained by the statements of several persons of known veracity, that extensive projects are in contemplation to introduce African Negro Slaves into this country by citizens of the United States in a manner that will equally violate the laws of the United States and the Constitutional provision of this Republic on the subject.

It is intended, as we have been informed, to land said African Slaves, on the sea shore east of the Sabine river or on the east bank of the Sabine, within the limits of the United States and then reship them to this Country, and thus attempt to bring such introduction of slaves under that clause of our Constitution, which admits them from the United States exclusively.

This attempt to evade the prohibition of the African Slave trade, contained in our Constitution[1] certainly will not be sustained by the tribunals of this Republic, but it is desirable, that the Government of the United States should be apprised of such attempts to carry on a piratical commerce by her own citizens through her territory and in American vessels; I am therefore directed by the President, to instruct you to lay this subject before the Government of the United States; and to request its co-operation on the Sabine frontier and in the Gulf of Mexico, to enforce the laws for the suppression of the African Slave trade.

Yours Respectfully
S. F. Austin
Sec of State

✦✦✦

LS. Tx, TLP. Published in *DCRT,* 1: 155–156.

1. Gammel, 1: 1079 (General Provisions, sect. 9).

A navy was essential for the survival of Texas. The republic needed to preserve access to the sea route between Galveston and New Orleans and to prevent the Mexican navy from attacking its shores. The first vessels in the Texas fleet, aside from commissioned privateers, were the schooners Liberty, Invincible, Independence, *and* Brutus, *all acquired in early 1836.*

All four were lost before the end of 1837. After escorting the vessel taking Sam Houston to New Orleans for treatment of the wound he suffered at San Jacinto, the Liberty *was sold in July 1836 to settle bills for repairs. The* Independence *was captured by Mexican warships off the Brazos River on April 10, 1837, while carrying William H. Wharton back to Texas. Wharton and the crew members were eventually able to escape, but the* Independence *became the* Independencia *in Mexican service.*

The Invincible, *which had been built for the African slave trade, encountered the American merchant brig* Pocket *off the Rio Grande in April 1836. Captain Jeremiah Brown prized the* Pocket, *which was carrying military supplies for Mexico and transporting Mexican naval officers, and sent it to Galveston. The* Invincible's *crew was later charged with piracy in New Orleans over the* Pocket *affair. The case was dismissed, but in 1838 Texas agreed to pay the* Pocket's *investors for damages they had sustained. In August 1836 Captain Brown sailed the* Invincible *to New York for refitting. The next month, without authorization, Captain William Hurd also took the* Brutus *to New York for refitting. Both vessels ran up large bills, which led to financial distress and embarrassments, as shown in several letters that follow. Upon returning to Texas both captains were replaced. In August 1837 the* Invincible *and the* Brutus *vessels ran aground off Galveston while engaging Mexican warships and were destroyed.*

Fleming T. Wells to William H. Wharton

New York. Dec. 16.th 1836

Dear Sir,

I am induced by peremptory necessity to call upon your liberality to relieve me from the unpleasant Situation in which I am.

Having been in New York, now, longer that three months, daily expecting some arrangements to be made by which our Vessel would be fitted out, we have to this moment no prospect to be relied upon that it will be done in any short time, if at all.

The consequence of this, to me, is that I have not money to pay even my board bill of Two months with another for clothes which necessity compelled contract on my arrival here, anticipating no difficulty in the sale of the land Scrip, by which funds were to have been raised for the use of Invincible, of this there has been an entire failure

You being the only man to whom I can apply in this extremity with any probably hopes of success for assistance—I beg of you the loan of one hundred and fifty dolls. either upon my own account to be returned immediately on my arrival in Texas according to order, or upon the account of the Government of Texas. This Sum will suffice to release me from the unpleasant situation I am at present. I need not say how very horible it is to be dunned for a board bill without the means to discharge it.

You know when I entered the service of Texas, during this time I have not received one dollar for my services farther than to pay my most moderate expenses, using in the meantime five hundred Dolls. of my own private <. . . . .> thing worse <. . . . .> impose upon the generosity of a friend—and particularly so in this case as I am confident you have to rely upon your own resources for your expenses as the representative of Texas.

But imperious necessity and fearing my inability of discharging what I owe, and the consequent discredit of a failure, are paramount.

I hope you will duly appreciate my situation and extend the aid I have requested for which I shall [be] under infinite obligations, and will not fail to reciprocate in the most grateful manner.

Will you have the goodness to attend to this on its receipt, directing your letter, care of B.S. St. John corner front Maiden Lane Str, New York.

I am Sir, with much Respect & esteem you most Obt. Svt.
F. T. Wells

✦✦✦

ALS. Tx, TLP. Fleming T. Wells (d. 1844), from Orange County, Virginia, was the purser of the Texas Navy vessels *Invincible* and *Liberty*.

Stephen F. Austin to William H. Wharton

No. 8
Department of State
Columbia 19th Decr. 1836

Sir:

Mjr. General Felix Huston,[1] who is at this time commanding the Army, writes officially to the Secy of War, from Camp Johnson on LaBaca,[2] under date of 13th instant as follows: "Traveña (a Mexican) informs me today, that when the Cherokee chiefs were in Matamoros last summer, the interpreter, named Necibio Cortinez, who he says has been much with the Indians, and about Nacogdoches, stayed at his house, and from him he learned, that the Indians had agreed with Urrea to appear friendly with the Texians, untill the Mexicans crossed the Guadalupe, and then they were to march on the frontier with five thousand warriors."[3]

Genl. F. Huston writes that he has confidence in this statement of Travino's and believes it to be true.

I am directed by the President to communicate this information to you, to be used as you may deem expedient, in corroboration of the information heretofore collected relative to the disposition and intentions of the Indians, to join the Mexicans in the present war. I have to inform you that John Woodward[4] Esq has been appointed by this Government, Consul General of this Republic for the Ports of Boston, New York Philadelphia, and Baltimore; and that he is directed to report himself to you, on his arrival in N. York, and apply through you, for a recognition of his Consul Generalship, by the United States Government.

Respectfully your most obt.
S. F. Austin
Sec. of State

✦✦✦

LS. Tx, TLP. Published in *DCRT,* 1: 156.

1. Felix Huston (1800–1857), then commanding the army, had been an avid supporter of Texas in Natchez, Mississippi. In 1836 he and Rezin Bowie (1793–1841) led about five hundred volunteers to Texas but arrived too late to take part in the fighting. President Houston appointed Huston a brigadier general and acting commander in chief on December 20, 1836. When Albert Sidney Johnston was appointed over him, Huston challenged him to a duel and on the fifth exchange shot him in the hip. Huston later established a law practice in New Orleans.

2. Camp Johnson, the headquarters of the army, was on the LaVaca River.

3. "Traveña" and Necibio (Eusebio) Cortinez, an Indian agent, not otherwise identified. Gen. José de Urrea (1797–1849).

4. John C. Woodward was Texas consul general for the ports named from December 15, 1836, to February 6, 1840, when he was dismissed for selling Texas land with defective titles.

Stephen F. Austin to William H. Wharton

No. 9
Department of State
Colombia Decr 21, 1836

Sir

The judiciary of Texas has been fully organised by the passage of the following laws

"An act to establish and organize the supreme court & to define the powers and jurisdiction thereof"

"An act establishing the jurisdiction & powers of the district courts"

"An act organizing the inferior county courts and defining the powers and jurisdiction of the same"

"An act organizing justices courts and defining the power and jurisdiction of the same and also creating and defining the office & powers of commissioners of roads and revenue."[1]

The following persons have been duly appointed and commissioned judges

James Collinsworth *Chief Justice*
Shelby Corzine *Judge of 1st Judicial district*
Benjamin C. Franklin[2] 2d do
R. M. Williamson[3] 3d do
J. W. Robinson[4] 4th do

elected by joint ballot of both houses. The chief justice & the district judges form the supreme court.

I have only time to give you the above outline by this opportunity, as the said laws & appointments were not all completed until to day—will send copies of the laws by the next opportunity.

Respectfully your most obt
S. F. Austin
Sec of State

✦✦✦

ALS. Tx, TLP.

1. These laws, all passed in December 1836, are in Gammel, 1: 1139–1144, 1201–1206, 1217, 1258–1271.

2. Benjamin Cromwell Franklin (1805–1873), a Georgia attorney, came to Texas in 1835. He fought as a private at San Jacinto. He resigned from the court on November 29, 1839, and opened a law practice in Galveston.

3. Robert McAlpin Williamson (1806?–1859) was admitted to the Georgia bar before he settled at San Felipe de Austin in the 1820s. Williamson was a delegate to the Consultation and participated in the Battle of San Jacinto.

4. James W. Robinson (1790–1857) arrived in Texas from Indiana in 1833. He was a delegate to the Consultation and lieutenant governor of the provisional government. Robinson served in the army at San Jacinto. He resigned from his judicial position in 1840 to open a law office in Austin. In 1850 he left Texas for California.

Stewart Newell to William H. Wharton

Philadelphia Dec. 21st 1836

Dear Sir

Permit me to congratulate you upon your arrival again amongst us and in the appointment of yourself to treat with the government of the U. States, upon the affairs of Texas. I think you will find the people much pleased and we trust your labours will be short and I think will be successful unless some political question may be started in Congress by which a short session may be disapated in idle debate and nothing be done.

I trust however this may not be the case and that Texas will receive her share of attention and her independence be recognised and I here beg leave to say that as far as it was practicable to do so the condtions of the appointment I had the Honor to receive from Genl Austin and yourself has been complyed with but am sorry to say that little was done the feeling in a pecuniary way being rather Anti-Texian but I have succeeded in inducing a number of them to leave this City for Texas and have now formed a Company of 24 of our most respectable and wealthy Merchants in this City to enter into operations under a Charter if it can be obtained from the Government of Texas.

That I think would be of great advantage to Texas and the Company and should be pleased to have you join them after I have an opportunity of submitting the prospectus.

I expect to leave Philada for Texas in a few days and will endeavor to see you previous to leaving in the meantime wish to ~~state~~ name to you the importance of Texas having an Agent located in the City's of Baltimore Philada. and New York clothed with full power to make contracts for the Government of Texas under advices from the government. The want of such has been very great in this City and I really believe had such an appointment been made here much might be done. I have had many offers made me to sell Military Equipments and to buy lands but having no authority to act have always declined acting. Captain Berbeck[1] of the Texian Army has been in Philada for several days and has visited me every day. His purpose was to obtain a conveyance for Men from this place to N. Orleans or Texas, upon a Letter of credit from Messrs Tobys, of N. Orleans. He tells me he left the Letter signed by President Burnett and yourself in the hands of Messrs Tobys, and received thiers in exchange but owing to the difficulties of these gentlemen during the last Summer thier Letter will be of little service in the way he wishes. I have called with him upon those Gentlemen who are personally acquainted with Messrs Tobys, but they decline acting upon thier Letter but I think if an Agent was appointed for this City and a Shipping or Commission Merchant could be had to accept of it that the Captain could have his views obtained and should you be authorised to make such an appointment and inform me if agreeable to you I would endeavor to furnish you a person who is responsible and competent and should be pleased to hear from you by return of Mail if possible upon the subject.

Our acquaintance being but short on your former visit to this City and my being now about to depart for Texas there to ask certain privileges to be granted to some of my friends who I trust by thier Acts may prove themselves friends of Texas I feel it a duty owing alike to the Gentlemen I now represent to the Government of Texas and to my self to afford you as the representative of that Country the opportunity that so favorably offers of knowing what I deem important since knowledge of myself and those I represent and will take the liberty of referring you to Hon. J. B. Sutherland, Hon. M. W. Ash, Hon. Jos. R Ingersoll[2] all now at Washington Members of Congress and to the first named as to the Company alluded to and thier responsibility &c. and wishing you success in your Mission and enjoyment of Health.

I am Sir Your Obt. Servant,
Stewart Newell

+++

ALS. Tx, TLP. Stewart Newell (d. 1891) was a key figure in the Philadelphia Friends of Texas, which encouraged emigration to Texas and raised funds to support orphans and widows of the revolution. Newell was also a land agent in Velasco and Sabine by 1838. He was US Consul at Velasco, 1837–1840, and at Sabine, 1843–1845.

1. Wilhelm Christoph Frederick Bernbeck [vice Berbeck] (1802–1837), immigrated to the United States from Germany in 1831. He was in New Orleans in 1834, enlisted in the Texan army and was a veteran of the Battle of San Jacinto.

2. All three were members of Congress from Pennsylvania. Joel Barlow Sutherland (1792–1861) was a Jacksonian in the Twentieth through Twenty-Fourth Congresses, 1827–1836. Michael Woolston Ash (1789–1858) was a Jacksonian in the Twenty-Fourth Congress, 1835–1836. Joseph Reed Ingersoll (1786–1868) was an anti-Jacksonian and a Whig in the Twenty-Fourth through Thirtieth Congresses, 1835–1848.

James M. Wolfe to Unknown Recipient

Washington City Decr 23d 1836

Dear Sir

I have just received communications from New York informing me that the Texian vessels (Brutus and) Invincible are detained for debts contracted by the commanders Brown and Hurd[1] to the amount of Twenty thousand dollars or thereabouts and am instructed by Mr. Wharton to inform you of the above facts.

The Communications addressed to Mr. Wharton from New York have been transmitted to the Secretary of State of Texas and directed to your care at New Orleans and when they arrive be pleased to forward them on. The vessels will not be released without the advance of nearly half the amount.

I have the honor to be Sir yr. Obedient Servant
J. M. Wolfe

✦✦✦

ALS. Tx, TLP.

1. Jeremiah Brown, originally from Rhode Island, came to Texas in 1830. He captained a merchant schooner, worked as a pilot on the Brazos River, and ran a tavern at Velasco before joining the Texas navy. He was captain of the Texas navy vessel *Liberty* before taking command of the schooner *Invincible.* William A. Hurd (d. 1838) had commanded the Texas navy schooners *San Felipe* and *Liberty* before he was given command of the schooner *Brutus.* He was relieved of command in April 1837 following the return of the vessel from New York. Brown was relieved as well.

Samuel May Williams to William Wharton

Baltimore 23rd Decembr 1836

My Dear Sir,

My time of yesterday having been absorbed in attending to the Brig Flight[1] now loading at the point for Texas, I was prevented from writing to you as intended.

I have made arrangements with my brother Henry H. Williams[2] to furnish funds from time to time as you may require them. You will therefore draw upon him for Five hundred dollars when ever you think proper; and when I am favored with a personal interview, which I hope can be in a few days, we can then arrange the for different amts you may want, and also the probable times at which they will be wanted. My Brother did not get the note you addressed to him, which was the reason you did not see him when you passed thro this place.

If you have the time please drop me a line and inform me of what impression the Old Roman's message[3] has made in Washington; as also that made upon your own mind relative to it.

Altho it is not what I hoped for, still I flatter myself with a hope that recognition will be carried thro the Congress.

If you find it inconvenient to draw upon this place, let me know, and I will have the money remitted.

Present me to Col Wolfe and accept assurances of my cordial esteem.

Respectfully yr friend & St
Saml. M. Williams

✦✦✦

ALS. Tx, TLP. Samuel May Williams (1795–1858) as a young man worked in his uncle's commission house in Baltimore and as a supercargo on a merchant ship to South America. He came to Texas from New Orleans in 1822 and gained employment as a translator and clerk for Stephen F. Austin. In 1834 Williams established a mercantile firm in partnership with Thomas F. McKinney (1801–1873). Their firm provided considerable financial support to Texas. Samuel Williams, along with his brother, Henry, were well connected with the Baltimore shipbuilding community. In 1838

Williams was commissioned to negotiate a $5 million loan in the United States for the purchase of ships for the Texas navy.

1. Williams purchased the *Flight* in Baltimore to carry men and cargo to Texas. On its first trip, however, the *Flight* ran aground and broke up in San Luis Pass off the southwest coast of Galveston Island.

2. Henry Howell Williams (1796–1873), brother of Samuel May Williams, owned a commission house in Baltimore and provided financial support to Texas. He took over management of the McKinney and Williams business and between 1838 and 1845 lived in both Galveston and Baltimore.

3. In a special message on December 21, 1836, President Andrew Jackson provided Congress with extracts of reports he had received from Henry M. Morfit (1793–1865), whom he sent to Texas in 1836 as a special agent to investigate whether the republic could sustain itself. Morfit sent twelve reports (in Senate Document 20, 24th Cong., 2d Sess., Serial 297), which did not support immediate recognition. In his message Jackson said that "prudence" dictated that the United States should not recognize the Texas independence until it was beyond question that the new republic could sustain itself (*Messages and Papers,* 3: 265–269).

Wharton and later Texas diplomats received many letters inquiring about missing relatives, requesting government appointments, and seeking information about the availablity of land and opportunities for success in Texas.

George Reber to William H. Wharton

Lancaster Dec 23rd 1836

Dear Sir

The great interest which is felt by the people of this country in behalf of Texas and the means which you have had of satisfying their curiosity by your residence in that country will be my apology for troubling you with a few inquiries. Is the climate a healthy one? And what inducements would an attorney have to settle in Texas at this time? I have no doubt that an expose from you of the true condition of the country and the prospects which it holds forth to the different pursuits of men would hasten the emigration of many industrious and enterprising people. Many look upon Texas as having a climate similar to

New Orleans which has become a terror to our people, and many persons labour under the belief that it is the theater only of the desperate. Correct this impression and Texas will soon be crowded with good citizens.

It would be well to give an estimate of the probable expense of emigration from Cincinnati as this deters many. I hope that you will give me some answers to my inquiries in relation to climate ~~and~~ the prospects of attorneys and the expense of getting from N Orleans to Texas. It was my intention to have written to Mr. Senator Ewing[1] from this state and request him to make the above inquiries, but upon reflection have concluded to address you personally.

Yours respectfully
George Reber

✦✦✦

ALS. Tx, TLP. George Reber (1808–1878) remained in Ohio and served one term in the Ohio House of Representatives in 1848.

1. Thomas Ewing (1789–1871) was an anti-Jacksonian, then a Whig, in the US Senate, 1831–1837.

Lorrain Thompson Pease to William H. Wharton

Hartford Decr 24 1836

Dear Sir

Seeing your arrival at Washington announced in the last evening's papers I embrace this early opportunity to congratulate you on the honor of being the first minister plenipotentiary from the country of your adoption to your native country.

Knowing as I do both your zeal & ability to serve the country which you represent I feel that I ~~can~~ may also justly congratulate that country on the character of its representative here.

You will probably recollect, that in our journeying together I could not easily forbear an expression of my admiration for your country, which a then recent visit, had inspired me. This alone would very naturally have lead me to take a deep interest in its welfare. The 18 months which have intervened have been an eventful period for Texas and aside from the domestic occurences which have bound me indissolubly to country, would have served greatly to increase the interest that I had previously taken in its welfare.

My second son[1] was one of the few of Fannin's[2] command who escaped the massacre, but escaped only to die in the arms of his Elder brother and leave his bones to be decently interred on the beach at Velasco. The Elder I hope is still living. His last letter to me was dated 15 Sept in which he proposed to write again soon. His long silence has given me no little anxiety & his mother already heart stricken at the loss of our dear son is greatly alarmed for the fate of the other. If you can give us any intelligence in regards to my son E. M. Pease who was for sometime Secretary of the General Counsel you will much oblige his anxious parents. Whether he was in health or otherwise at your departure from Texas & if in health, how he was employed.

I shall avail myself of the privilege which our brief acquaintance may seem to justify by addressing you again & more at large in relation to the affairs of Texas which my extreme solicitude for my son now incapacitates me from doing.

Excuse this hasty scrawl as I had but 10 minutes to write without loosing todays mail.

With great respect I remain your most obedt servt

L. T. Pease

NB Please address me at Enfield Hartford Co Ct

✦✦✦

ALS. Tx, TLP. Lorrain Thompson Pease (1788–1848), of Enfield, Connecticut, came to Texas with his son Elisha (1812–1883) in 1835. Lorrain returned to Connecticut, but Elisha remained in Texas. He participated in the Battle of Gonzales in 1835. He was secretary of the General Council of the Provisional Government and participated in writing the constitution at the Convention of 1836. He later developed a law practice at Brazoria, served in the Texas legislature after annexation, and was elected governor in 1853 and 1855. During Reconstruction General Phillip Sheridan appointed him governor, a post he held from 1867 to 1869.

1. Lorrain T. Pease (1815–1836) was taken prisoner at Goliad. He escaped the massacre but subsequently died of his wounds.

2. Colonel James Walker Fannin Jr. (1804–1836) arrived in Texas in 1834 and settled at Velasco. He took part in battles at Gonzales and Concepción. Fannin and most of his men were executed by order of Santa Anna at Goliad, following the Battle of Coleta.

James Treat to William H. Wharton

New York Decr 24th 1836
Saturday 1. P.M.

[e]xp[ress] mail.
My friend Wharton:
Dr. Sir

I had this pleasure a few days since covering Letters of Introduction for Mr Weaver,[1] and was happy to learn by a letter, subsequently received from the latter, that he had already made your acquaintance, & also, that of Mr. Williams.[2] Altho' I have not the pleasure of a line from you (owing no doubt to your many occupations,) yet I have a letter from Mr Williams, written at Baltimore & one from Mr Weaver at Washington, both dated 22d & received this morning. I have also seen the Special Message, which I had not anticipated so soon, and, hardly know what to think of it. In fact, it seems almost out of the question, to understand, either the views, intentions or manouvres of this Govmt. in regard to the Mexico & Texas question, at least, we here at this distance, are quite at a loss, tho' you who being on the spot, may understand it quite clearly. If we are to judge from the two messages, nothing is to be done towards recognition, the present Session, or until the next battle is fought & further proof thus Exhibited, that you can sustain your selves against Mexico & her millions? is this so? or is it understood that any action is to be had through Either House of Congress? The latter, is difficult, if opposed by the administration. Well, what then? is the U States to go to work and see if they can acquire the cession direct from Mexico, as the Easiest way of settling the question, and most likely to succeed with the Mexican Govmt? or, is every thing to be left in Status quo, and subject to such movement as Van Buren,[3] may adopt after 4th March? If this latter, it appears to me your Govmt. are to go to work on their own hook at once: and put themselves in a State of defence by Land & Especially by Sea, and work out your own Salvation, without any regard to the U States, & when you have sustained yourselves another year, &, thrashed the Mexicans in another campaign; then you may also dictate your own terms, or refuse to annex unless you obtain your own terms. I should like to know, what general plan is to be anticipated, or adopted, for on it depends in my opinion, much, very much, as regards the fate of your country.—will you tell me something about these matters? will you in other words enlighten us for we are all in the dark. If you are coming this way to spend New Years, you can tell us all about it. If not you must give us pen & ink for It. I send you [New York] Courier & Enquirer of to day with the news from Mexico—also send one to Williams, address[e]d at Washington; and another to Baltimore. I further send one to Mr Weaver, to whom I wrote yesterday, and requested him to shew it to you. The new Brig Libertador Mexicano 4th July so call[e]d sailed from Tampico 5. Nov. convoying 4 sail of coasters down to Campeachy; so it appears they will not venture onto the coast of Texas, until the other Brig arrives (last advices left her at Key West) & then you will I fear be blocked up, unless you get your Small fleet together, and beat them. You must remember that if you conquer capture, or defeat their fleet, it is Equivalent to defeating their 2d army, for the latter will nev[er] go into the country, if their navy is Either beaten, or shut up in port. I would make any & Every Effort & any sacrifice to increase the navy & prevent any blockade by sea. If you can do this, and drive them into port Even, you will be more likely to obtain a recognition, than in any other way. Excuse my scrawl I am much hurried. Why will not you & Saml. M. Williams run over here & see us? I hope you can and will fix on some mode of getting away these vessels.

S. Swartwout[4] requests comp[limen]ts & would be glad to shake you by the Hand, as always.

obt Servant & friend
Jas. Treat

✦✦✦

ALS. Tx, TLP. James Treat (d. 1840), a New York land speculator connected with Samuel Swartwout, was an early advocate of Texas annexation to the United States. President Mirabeau B. Lamar sent Treat to Mexico as a special agent in 1839, and he died on the return voyage to Texas.

1. This is mostly likely William Augustus Weaver (1797–1846), of Virginia, who served in the US Navy from 1813 to 1824, and who afterward worked in the State Department as secretary to the commission adjusting the claims of Spanish citizens in the United States and as commissioner to Mexico from 1834 to 1840.

2. Either Samuel May Williams or his brother Henry Howell Williams.

3. Martin Van Buren (1782–1862), elected president in 1836.

4. Samuel Swartwout (1783–1856) was US Collector of Customs for New York from 1829–1838. He was an open and enthusiastic supporter and fundraiser for Texas. He was later accused of embezzling over $1 million from the customs office.

Edward Willoughby Kenny to William H. Wharton

December 27th 1836
Old. Va.
Hardiman Co[un]ty

Sir

The undersigned hopes you will pardon the liberty he takes in addressing the following.

My step son, a Mr John Hoskins[1] left home in September was a year for the purpose of going to K.y. He went through Nashville, at which time, I think I saw from the news papers you were there. In the June previous he was in K.y., and if I mistake not became acquainted with you in some of the towns of that state.

In our conversations he spoke of you, and the cause in which you were engaged. I have thought it probable, that being a well wisher to the success of the Texian Cause he went from Nashville as a Volunteer. If you have any knowledge of a Gentleman by that name, about 22 years of age, well educated, of Gentlemanly address, spare made, you would confer a favour on his mother who is devotedly attached to him, and whose absence makes her miserable, by answering this, and also oblige his friends and connexions.

I remain your's very respectfully, and wish you success in the cause of the Texian Republic.

Edward Willoughby Kenny
P. Office
Middleburgh
Hardiman
West Ten—

Mirabeau B. Lamar

Portrait by William H. Huddle (1847-1892). Courtesy of the State Preservation Board, Austin, TX; Accession ID: CHA 1989.106. Photography by Eric Beggs, August 13, 1993, post conservation.

✦✦✦

ALS. Tx, TLP. Edward Willoughby Kenny was born in Ireland and, at age twenty-one, emigrated to Virginia. He moved his family to Hardeman County in 1830 and to Memphis in 1837, where he went into the commission business with the firm Ander, Carr, Walker, and Company.

1. John Hoskins, not otherwise identified.

Clement P. McKennie to William H. Wharton

Charlottesville, Va. Dec 27, 1836.

Dear Sir,

I take the liberty of writing you a few lines, which I hope you will excuse. I am anxious to remove to Texas as soon as I can make preparations to do so, provided I hear of an opportunity of getting pleasantly situated in that delightful country. We have heard so much of the best lands being monopolized by New York & other large land companies, that I am almost led to fear that the actual settler would be compelled to locate himself on inferior lands or to pay a high price to those companies. It is in relation to these matters that I am desirous of obtaining information from an authentic source, for the benefit of myself & friends. You will therefore very much oblige me, if your engagements will permit, if you will have the goodness to communicate to me such information as you may consider useful to one wishing to emigrate to your country. What quantity of land is it probable that the present government will grant to settlers? At what price? What is the probable price of land in the settlements, somewhat improved? On rivers? What is the extent of the supply of good water? Are springs or wells most used? My object is either to engage in the mercantile business, or planting. Please give your opinion of the relative advantages of the two pursuits. Say at what location you believe the former might be prosecuted with advantage. I will not trouble you with numerous & long inquiries as the kind of information that would be useful to me, would naturally occur to you & I trust you will find it convenient to comply with my request. I feel an ardent friendship for Texas, & admiration for those noble spirits who have bravely fought in the defense of her liberties. She must conquer—she must be free. At all events I am willing to risk my all in the adopted country of the Houston's, the Austins, the Archers, the Lamars,[1] the Rusks, and others; some of whose names delicacy forbids me to mention in this place. I beg that you will favor me with an answer as early as convenient.

With sentiments of the highest esteem, yours very truly

C. P. McKennie

✦✦✦

ALS. Tx, TLP. Clement P. McKennie (ca. 1798-1856) published the *Central Gazette,* the first newspaper in Albemarle County, Virginia, from 1820 to 1834. About 1834, McKennie opened a bookstore near the University of Virginia campus.

1. Mirabeau Buonaparte Lamar (1798–1859) was a Georgia newspaper publisher when he came to Texas in 1835. He was at the Battle of San Jacinto and was among those who called for the execution of Santa Anna. Lamar served as vice president of Texas, 1836–1838, and as president, 1838–1841. As president, he opposed annexation to the United States, implemented a forceful Indian policy, and supported Yucatan's rebellion against Mexico. Later, in the 1840s, Lamar supported annexation by the United States. He was a soldier in the War with Mexico and was US minister to Nicaragua and Costa Rica from February 1858 to May 1859.

George Lincoln to William H. Wharton, with Enclosures

Worcester. Mass. Dec. 28. 1836

To the Hon. William H. Wharton, Minister Plenipotentiary from the Republic of Texas.

The subscriber[,] son of Levi Lincoln of Worcester,[1] in the State of Massachusetts, now in the 20th year of his age, humbly & respectfully solicits the appointment of Midshipman in the Navy of the Texian Republic. We beg leave to state that he has long anxiously desired to make this application, that he has firm health, & a vigorous constitution, capable of enduring any hardships to which he may be subjected, and a devoted purpose of fidelity to the service, which should he be honored with the appointment he humbly trusts would lead him to every effort in his power to discharge satisfactorily his dutys to the government of his then adopted Country. He also begs leave to state that he has had three years experience at Sea in the Merchant service of this Country, & in that time has made two voyages to the East Indies & home by way of Europe, for the result of which he would refer you to the copies of letters of recommendation which he has received & which are appended to this letter.

The first from Capt. Sever[2] with whom he was a year, & the last from the Hon. S. C. Phillips,[3] a member of Congress from this state. And he will also refer you to the files of the Navy department in Washington for some recomendations which he sent on in the year 1833, Aug. 12 when he made application for a birth in the Navy of the U.S.—as my father is now in Washington attending Congress I must beg of you not to say any thing to him about this application, unless you can give me the appointment, or until you send me a warrant, & even then I should prefer to inform him myself as although I mentioned to him before he left home, that I had an inclination to make this application, he seemed to have some objections, but which I think can be easily overruled. The danger of losing my letters of recommendation, must be my apology for sending you the Copies.

I remain your humble and Obedient Servant,
George Lincoln

✦✦✦

ALS. Tx, TLP. George Lincoln (1816–1847) did not receive an appointment in the Texas navy. He was an army captain during the Mexican War and was killed at the Battle of Buena Vista.

1. Levi Lincoln (1782–1868), a prominent attorney and figure in Massachusetts politics. He was governor of Massachusetts from 1825 to 1834 and member of the Twenty-Third through Twenty-Seventh Congresses from 1834 to 1841 as an anti-Jacksonian and a Whig. He was US Collector of Customs at Boston, 1841–1843.

2. James Warren Sever (1797–1871) studied law in the office of Levi Lincoln. From 1820 until 1835, he was in the employ of the shipping house of Thomas H. Perkins of Boston and captained vessels in the East Indian trade.

3. Stephen Clarendon Phillips (1801–1857), a Salem, Massachusetts, merchant, was a representative in the Twenty-Third through Twenty-Fifth Congresses, 1834–1838.

Enclosure:
Copy of James Warren Sever to Stephen Clarendon Phillips

Boston, July 19, 1836

Dear Sir,

Understanding that my young friend Mr. Lincoln is about making an application to you for imployment, it gives me much pleasure to say that from the uniform propriety & regularity of his conduct while with me during a years voyage to India, I have the utmost confidence in his disposition to meet any confidence which may be placed in him. His habits are wholly unexceptionable under circumstances where most young men would have erred.

His best recommendation is his unwillingness to be idle & a determination to rely upon his own resources is the best pledge that he will prove himself active, persevering, & confidential in any imployment which you may have it in your power to offer him. Personal obligations to his father & a strong interest in his success, must be my apology for thus addressing you.

Very respectfully your Obt. Svt.
Signed James W. Sever

Enclosure:
Recommendation by Stephen Clarendon Phillips for George Lincoln

Salem. July. 22. 1836.

To the foregoing letter from Capt. James W. Sever which I recommend to the consideration of any to whom it may be presented as a testamonial of a Shipmaster of the highest respectability, it gives me pleasure to add that the opinion expressed by Capt. Sever in favor of Mr. Lincoln was confirmed by Capt. Gillis[1] (now deceased) who commanded the Ship Equator in which Mr. Lincoln performed his last voyage in the capacity of Clerk as I understand from several sources. Without being able to speak of Mr. Lincoln from any personal acquaintance I have no doubt from the information which I have obtained by inquiring of others that he is well fitted to perform the duties of assistant Supercargo or clerk or of an officer of a Vessel, & that he wants only a little experience to be entirely qualified to take charge of a <document torn> Vessel & Cargo. In respect to his character & habits, a<document torn> as his talents and education, I believe that he will prove <document torn> self worthy of full confidence & that he will not fail to give satisfaction to his employers.

Signed, S. C. Phillips

✦✦✦

1. Gillis, not otherwise identified.

Thomas W. Faulkner to William H. Wharton

New York
Decr. 28th. 1836

Sir

A stranger I hardly know how to address you or in what language to beg a favor of you but feeling that from the high office now held by you your heart must incline with friendly feelings to one wanting an opportunity to distinguish himself but wanting friends also (unless he can call you one) must submit to fate and spend the prime of life in fruitless endeavors to obtain that which would enable him to end his life in comfort & ease. This situate permits me Sir to ask you to obtain if possible a commission in the Texan Army or Navy for me and rest assured Sir I will always endeavour by every act in future to merit the kind consideration of the person who so highly benefits me. I am Sir by birth an Englishman 5 feet 11 inches high & well made and never had any illness in the course of the 23 years I have been an inhabitant of this lower World. By your acceeding to my request therefore you would not be amenable to the laws of the United States and would make a fellow creature comparitively happy.

Hoping you will give me the opportunity to distinguish myself in the pursuit of Honor & Glory

I beg leave to subscribe myself Your Obedt & Grateful Servt

Thomas W. Faulkner
152 Franklin Street

✦✦✦

ALS. Tx, TLP. Thomas W. Faulkner, not otherwise identified.

Following the Battle of San Jacinto, Sam Houston needed medical treatment for a wound in the ankle. On May 15, 1836, he sailed for New Orleans on the Flora, *which was escorted by the Texas navy schooner* Liberty. *In New Orleans, Texas Secretary of the Navy Robert Potter (1799–1842) relieved William Brown (d. 1838, the brother of Captain Jeremiah Brown) of command of the* Liberty *and replaced him with Captain George Wheelwright. The* Liberty *incurred $7,000 worth of repairs and supplies but was unable to pay for them. Robert Triplett provided a $5,000 loan, which was insufficient, and the vessel was seized for nonpayment of its debts, which totaled more than $10,000. In July the vessel was sold. Henry Carleton led a legal effort to recover the vessel but was unsuccessful.*

Henry Carleton to William H. Wharton

New Orleans 29 Decer. 1836

Sir,

As whatever concerns Texas will be regarded with interest by you, allow me to forward you the enclosed statement of a cause pending before the Parish in this City, by whose process the schooner Liberty is now held under seizure.

Though the points are not fully state[d] yet the nature of the defense may be well understood. I have but little doubt of success on the appeal before the Supreme Court, and as little, that the judgement of the Parish Court will be against me.

I have the honor to be very respectfully
Your Obedient Servant
Henry Carleton

✦✦✦

ALS. Tx, TLP. Henry Carleton (1785–1863), the US attorney in New Orleans, was a fervent supporter of Texas.

Richard Mentor Johnson to William H. Wharton

House of Represents.
Dec 29th 1836

My Dear Sir,

I have rd your favour. It would give me pleasure to see you morning 10 oclock or evening when you are well enough.

I shall not fail to do every thing, in my power for Texas. I think a short time will bring every thing to a favourable issue. It is out of my power to take the lead in any measure for want of time &c &c.

Sincerely your friend
Rd. M. Johnson

✦✦✦

ALS. Tx, TLP. Richard Mentor Johnson (1780–1850), of Kentucky, had a long political career as a member of the US House of Representatives and the US Senate, 1807–1837, first as a Democratic-Republican and then as a Jackson supporter. He was vice president of the United States during the Van Buren administration, 1837–1841. Johnson was credited with killing the Shawnee leader Tecumseh during the Battle of the Thames in 1813.

Andrew Janeway Yates to William H. Wharton

Confidential
New Orleans Decr 29, 1836.

Sir

I arrived in this City on Saturday last in pursuance of my instructions from the Govt of Texas, as Commissioner to negotiate the loan of Five Millions of dollars under the law of Nov. 18 of the Congress of Texas.[1]

Since my arrival I have learned that Santa Anna, contrary to the expectations of many has proceeded direct to Washington City, with Almonte[2] who was appointed the Comr of the Mexican Govt to establish the Boundary line between that Country and the United States, and as there is a strong probability of that question being settled in such a manner as to include Texas within the limits of the United States, it has occurred to me that an arrangement might be made for a negotiation of so much of said loan as will be necessary for the necessities of Texas from the Government of the United States. It would be impossible to negotiate the loan, or any part of it in this City and perhaps even in this Country except at a very great discount, until after a negotiation of the Independence of Texas, by the Govt of the United States, and a consider a loan on the Bonds of the Govt at 30 years, bearing an interest of 10% per annum, much too great a sacrifice for the Country to make, if she should be in any manner annexed to the Union. Under these circumstances, and without presuming that the subjects of property in the public lands of Texas, & the liquidation of her debts will be agitated in any negotiation which may take place, I have thought proper to address you before taking any decided step in the matter and request of you to ascertain whether a loan of Two Millions of dollars could not be obtained from this Government, ostensibly perhaps, from some individuals, so that the United States may have it under her control. I shall forward the Bonds from this City to Columbia to be executed in two or three days, & will wait with anxiety an answer from you here.

I brought out some dispatches for you from the State Department, which were mailed on my arrival here, and I presume they contain the instructions you desired in relation to the importation of slaves, as I was assured should be done.

I remain Sir
very respectfully yours
A. J. Yates

✦✦✦

ALS. Tx, TLP. Andrew Janeway Yates (1803–1856), an attorney originally from Connecticut, arrived in Texas in 1835. He was appointed commissioner in order to assist the efforts of Archer, Austin, and Wharton in the legalities involved in loans and purchases for Texas. After the revolution he lived in Liberty and Galveston. In 1851, he relocated to San Jose, California.

1. "An Act to Authorise the President to Negotiate a Loan on the Bonds of the Government not Exceeding Five Millions of Dollars," Gammel, 1: 1092–1093; Austin and Wharton to Yates, May 9, 1836, *Austin Papers,* 3: 350–351.

2. Juan Nepomuceno Almonte (1803–1869), a diplomat, had made an inspection tour of Texas in 1834 and was taken prisoner with Santa Anna after San Jacinto.

He traveled with Santa Anna to Washington. He served as Mexican minister to the United States from 1841 to 1845. He later supported the French intervention in Mexico and died in Paris.

Lorrain Thompson Pease to William H. Wharton

Enfield Ct Jany [Dec.] 30 1836

Dear Sir

Your valued favor of the 27 Inst has just come to hand. It finds me rather severely indisposed having been confined to my room the last two or three days, but I already feel the influence of its cheering intelligence, which has relieved my family from distressing anxiety. In the last letter from my son which bore date the 12 Sept he promises to write again shortly. Since that we had not heard a syllable from him, and as he is usually a punctual correspondent, his silence has given rise to the worst apprehensions. The gloom spread around us by the intelligence of the death of his brother, has served probably to increase & magnify our fears.

I hasten to comply with your request, in forwarding you a copy of the Connecticut preamble & resolutions on the subject of an acknowledgement of Texian Independence.[1]

Being at some distance from the seat of government I could not readily obtain a certified copy from the office of the secretary of state. I have therefore been compelled to send you a slip cut from a Newspaper.

You suggest the expediency of attempting to procure a reinstruction from the Legislature now in Session. After the late message of the President, there would be too much danger of a failure, and a failure, you will see, might, If our members were so pleased to construe it, be deemed equivalent to a revocation. The matter therefore stands much better as it is. The instructions having been passed at the last stated session & sent by their order to our delegation in both Houses of Congress for their guidance, and the present session of the state Legislature Being only an extraordinary session, of the same members who passed the instructions, assembled now for special & not for general objects, an omission to act again on the same subject cannot be tortured into a revocation of any former act. An attempt therefore to procure the passage of reinstructions, might mar, while it could not mend, what has been well done.

You can readily suppose that the great mass of members of our state Legislature which is composed of more than two hundred persons, of course not all of them men of the highest grade of intelligence and situated as they are at such a distance from the scene, really know little about the affairs of Texas and that the interest they felt in the matter could scarcely be in an equal ratio with their knowledge. Public attention here would scarcely have been called to the subject but for my influence with a single press whose circulation is more extensive than any other but yet not general through the whole state. This single press I had taken care to supply with original communications & other matter such as appeared to me best calculated to awaken the attention & sympathy of the public in behalf of a cause which presented strong claims to the support of the philanthropic friends of liberty.

It was by the efforts of a few of my warm personal [friends] in the Legislature several of whom were also the acquaintances and friends of my son who is in Texas, that the instructions were originated & pressed through <. . .> at the last session. They fortunately met with no opposition from any member of the dominant party and that from the other side having been made to assume a party character tended rather to aid their passage than otherwise. Should the subject now be brought up again the late message of the President, I forsee, would be presented as a bugbear to deter the timid among my political friends from to[e]ing the mark as we yankees say, at any rate with the foregoing facts before you, you can Judge whether my fears of an unfavorable result are not sufficiently well founded.

Acknowledging myself as I do perfectly identified in feeling with the people of Texas, I shall not hesitate to communicate without reserve to the Representative of that country at Washington any & every species of intelligence in my possession which may appear to me calculated to aid him in the object of his mission or such as he can use in forming an estimate of its probable result, trusting entirely to his discretion to receive as confidential such things as his judgment may point out. I am in habits of correspondence with the members of our own delegation in Congress and have taken some pains to draw from them the general feeling there in regard [to] Texas, and to ascertain whether it is more or less favorable now than during the last Session.

They inform me that so far as they can judge the members are less inclined to recommend the acknowledgment of the independence of Texas, now than they were at the close of the last session. You and I know that timidity not to say cowardice is the characteristic of an American Legislature, state & national, that they have forever been found lagging in the rear of public sentiment that whenever they have acted a bold & manly part It was because, they were driven to it by public sentiment, too loudly & unequivocally expressed to be longer disregarded.

That a large majority of the people of the US would at once acknowledge the independence of Texas, and receive it into the American Union I have not a doubt, and I have as little doubt that Congress will refuse to do either the present Session. Very many of those who well know that their constituents would not only approve of the measure but really demand it at their hands, will now shelter themselves under the late message, glad to find any shelter to escape the performance of a duty which requires a little manly courage.

Courage which is really as necessary to make a good Legislator as a good General has unfortunately not been deemed so by the people of this country and our Legislative Halls have too often therefore been found the receptacles of cowards.

Whether you came with very confident expectations that Congress would take any steps in your favor the present session I know not but feeling as I do a warm interest in the success of your mission as well from a friendship to your country as for yourself I have thus taken the liberty to express my apprehensions & the ground of those apprehensions that nothing will be done the present Session.

I pray however that I may be mistaken
and remain yours truly,
L. T. Pease

✦✦✦

ALS. Tx, TLP.

1. The Connecticut legislature passed a resolution on May 27, 1836, instructing its state senators and requesting its representatives in Washington to vote for the recognition of Texas independence. The resolution is published in the Washington, DC, *United States Telegraph*, January 6, 1837, with an editorial by the editor urging Congress to recognize Texas.

John Stouffer to William H. Wharton

Baltimore decbr 30 1836

Sir,

Excuse the liberty of an afflicted Father, who has had the misfortune to have lost an fond and affectionate son in the Texian Cause, Luit. Henry S. Stouffer,[1] who died at Velasco on 10 August last. Not having been advised of the particulars of his disease attendance and death as wished I have taken this liberty to apply to you, presuming that probable you war there at the time it being the seat of Government, and may have known him personally or something of his death. If so, will thank you to advice me by return of mail particulars in generally of him, his sickness, how long sick, sufferings, attendance of medical and otherwise, how he died and interment and property left. I understand he died at the house of Mr Hotchkiss inn Keeper Velasco.

My son Entered the Texian Services in January or February last as Luitnent of a Volunteer Compan from Newport Kenty. under the Command of Captn. Sherman[2] of that place. He corresponded with me regularly untill 20 July last, date of his last letter, he was engaged in the Battle of Jacinto.

Please inform me what he may be entitled to in Land and pay from the government, and how it is necessary for his heirs (which I presume I am his legal one) to proceed to obtain his rights and when that can be obtained.

Your answer by mail will confer a favour to his afflicted Father and your hum obt servnt

Jno Stouffer

✦✦✦

ALS. Tx, TLP. John Stouffer, not otherwise identified.

1. Henry Stouffer (d. 1836) was a veteran of the Battle of San Jacinto.

2. Sidney Sherman (1805–1873) organized and equipped a company of volunteers at Newport, Kentucky. He commanded the left wing of the Texan army at San Jacinto. He later established the Buffalo Bayou, Brazos, and Colorado Railway Company.

Thomas Jefferson McKaig to Henry Alexander Wise

Cumberland [Maryland] Decr. 30th 1836

My Dear Sir

If you have not got so far the start of an old school-mate in this vain world and will stop a moment in your rapid flight I would a word with you. Some ten years have rolled by since you and I were "loud babbling o're our books" at Washington Pa. and many a change no doubt has come ore the spirit of our dreams, but with me the memory of times that are past are pleasant. We have taken different roads in our passage through this world. You, like Rienzi the last of the Romans, thundering in the ears of corruption to save a sinking state,[1] with an intellect, gigantic and brilliant ascending in honors rugged path, I ca[l]mly treading the quiet scenes of domestic life to look on and admire. I wish by the way some time when you throw your gloves off, if it suits, you would dress off our miss representative Frank Thomas of revolutionary memory.[2] But enough of this "go ahead" the people look to you and Bailie Peyton[3] as much as to any two men in the nation.

I recd a letter a day or two ago from Washington Pa. from a younger brother, I have at College,[4] who writes me he is appointed debater for the Union L[iterary] Society to discuss the following question "Is the aid and encouragement now being afforded to the Texans in their struggle for independence by <u>citizens of the United States</u> justifiable by the law and comity of nations and consistent with the treaty of amity and neutrality which exists between the United States and Mexico." He writes me the discussion will create great interest in Washington, the more particularly because a company of some 60 of their young men are now in Texas and that he is totally destitute of the information necessary to maintain the affirmative of the question. He can of course get there all he wants of international law, but I presume from the wording of their question they intend taking the broad ground of the justice or injustice of the war on the part of Texas, whether it be such a struggle as ought to enlist the sympathies of the friends of rational and civil liberty. He has the affirmative: To discuss which he wants the political history and present condition of Mexico. He wants the date of the revolution in Mexico. The different generals who have risen and fallen since then, the date of our treaty with Mexico and indeed the treaty itself. The date of the suppression of the constitution of 1824 in Mexico and the rise of St. Anna, and the resistance of Texas with their reasons for resistance. It occurs to me that all the information required could be obtained from a pamphlet published some time ago by Mr. Austin, and from a small volume intitled "Recollections of the revolution in Mexico."[5]

Would it be asking too much of you to endeavor to procure Mr. Austin's pamphlet and some old newspaper in which the treaty between Mexico and the U. States was published. And if the little volume spoken of can be procured to ask Mr Templeman to get it and send it by Capt. Thruston to <u>me</u>.[6] I have no doubt Col Wharton the Texan minister, if applied to, could and would furnish the information asked. I feel a great interest in the matter for divers good reasons, say 17 good reasons, the first is that I think the Texans are right, and I think that is enough without the other 16.

I did hope to have seen you in Washington this winter but my professional business called me to Baltimore this fall before the meeting of congress, and I do not know that I shall get time to go down again. Take care of yourself this winter. I was firmly of opinion that endeavours were made in a certain quarter last winter to have you <u>Killed off</u>, but thank God they will have to get other mettle than little Bynum.[7] John C. Mitchel,[8] one of our school fellows was a candidate last fall for a seat in our legislature but the Vanites defeated him. He is a very worthy citizen, and a young man of some promise. Let me hear from you if possible, occasionally at any rate, and make my respects to Mrs. Wise,[9] and accept the assurance of my highest consideration.

Yours &c
Thomas J. McKaig

✦✦✦

ALS. Tx, TLP. Thomas Jefferson McKaig (1804–1882), an 1826 graduate of Washington College, was among the most successful lawyers in western Maryland, representing the Baltimore and Ohio Railroad for thirty-nine years. He served terms in the Maryland House and Senate. Henry Alexander Wise (1806–1876) graduated from Washington College in 1825. He attended Henry St. George Tucker's law school in Winchester, Virginia, and was admitted to the bar in 1828. Wise served six terms in the US House of Representatives, Twenty-Third through Twenty-Eighth Congresses, 1833–1844, as a Jacksonian, a Whig, a leader of John Tyler's "Corporal's Guard," and a Democrat. From 1844 to 1847, he was US minister to Brazil. He was governor of Virginia from 1856 to 1860. During the Civil War he was a Confederate brigadier general.

1. The reference is to Cola di Rienzi (ca. 1313–1354), a Roman of common birth, who urged the people to reclaim their former glory. In 1347, he led an uprising that overthrew the corrupt nobles and assumed the title of Tribune. Lord Byron, in *Childe Harold's Pilgrimage,* celebrated him as the "last of the Romans . . . the forum's champion, and the people's chief."

2. Francis Thomas (1799–1876) represented Maryland in the Twenty-Second through Twenty-Sixth Congresses, 1831–1840, as a Democrat, and the Thirty-Seventh through Fortieth Congresses, 1861–1868, as a Unionist and Republican. He was governor of Maryland, 1841–1844, and US minister to Peru, 1872–1875. In 1836 Thomas led an unsuccessful effort to block the election of state senators in an effort to force the call of a state constitutional convention. Those involved were labeled revolutionaries.

3. Balie [vice Bailie] Peyton (1803–1878) represented Tennessee in the US House of Representatives, initially as a Jackson supporter in the Twenty-Third Congress, 1833–1834, and then as a Jackson opponent in the Twenty-Fourth Congress, 1835–1836.

4. The only identified brother of Thomas J. McKaig is William Wallace McKaig (1806–1880), who graduated from Washington College in 1829. He was an attorney in Ohio from 1831 to 1839 and entered practice with Thomas J. McKaig in Maryland in 1839.

5. Austin's "An Address Delivered to a Very Large Audience of Ladies and Gentlemen in the Second Presbyterian Church, Louisville, Kentucky, on the 7th of March, 1836" (Lexington: J. Clarke, 1836).

6. Possibly George Templeman (d. 1852), a Georgetown, DC, bookseller, 1831–1852. Charles Mynn Thruston (1792–1873), a West Point graduate and regu-

lar army officer until 1836, when he became a farmer in Cumberland, Maryland.

7. Jesse Atherton Bynum (1797–1868), a North Carolina Jacksonian and Democrat in the Twenty-Third through Twenty-Sixth Congresses, 1833–1841.

8. John C. Mitchell [vice Mitchel] graduated from Washington College in 1825.

9. Ann Eliza Jennings Wise (ca. 1809–1837), the daughter of a minister, whom Wise met while a student at Washington College.

Stephen F. Austin died on December 27, 1836, in Columbia, Texas. Since becoming secretary of state in October, his rented living quarters and office had been what its owner referred to as "shed room," without a stove or a fireplace. In December a norther blew in, and Austin took ill. Physicians, including Branch T. Archer, administered opium and tartar emetic and applied a blister to his chest. Not surprisingly, these did not help. At 11:30 in the morning Austin spoke, saying "The independence of Texas is recognized! Don't you see it in the papers? Doctor Archer told me so!" With that effort he became unconscious and died within a half hour (Gregg Cantrell, Stephen F. Austin: Empresario of Texas *[New Haven: Yale University Press, 1999], 363–364). With Austin's death, Attorney General J. Pinckney Henderson was appointed secretary of state. One of his first letters to Wharton informed him that Memucan Hunt would join him as a representative of Texas in Washington.*

James Pinckney Henderson to William H. Wharton

Columbia, Texas
Decer 31st AD 1836

Dr Sir

It gives me pleasure to introduce to your acquaintance my friend Genl Hunt[1] with whom I doubt not you will be much pleased. He is a

Memucan Hunt
Daguerreotype by Matthew Brady, ca. 1844-1856. Courtesy Library of Congress Prints and Photographs Division, Washington, DC 20540. LC-USZ62-109855

gentleman of great chivalry high character and intelligence and has been appointed by the President Minister Extraordinary to act in conjunction with you at Washington. This step was deemed necessary owing to the fact of the complete organization of the Government since your departure by the passing of the Judiciary Laws and election of the Judges in pursuance thereof by Congress. I hope and expect you will act in the most perfect harmony & concert in all of your intercourse with the Government of the US. in furtherance of your mission.

I am with the greatest Consideration and esteem your obt sevt
J. Pinckney Henderson

✦✦✦

ALS. Tx, TLP. James Pinckney Henderson (1808–1858), a lawyer from North Carolina, arrived in Texas with a group of volunteers in June 1836. In November 1836 Houston appointed him attorney general and secretary of state upon Austin's death. Henderson became minister to England and France in 1837. He returned to Texas in 1840 and began a legal practice at San Augustine. In 1844 Henderson and Isaac Van Zandt negotiated a treaty of annexation with the United States, but the treaty was defeated in the Senate. After Texas became a state, Henderson was elected its first governor. He led Texas troops in the War with Mexico. Henderson served in the US Senate from November 1857 until his death in Washington on June 4, 1858.

1. Memucan Hunt (1807–1856) had been a planter and businessman in North Carolina and Mississippi before arriving in Texas in June 1836. Hunt continued as commissioner and minister to the United States until June 5, 1838. He served as secretary of the navy from December 1838 to May 1839 and as the Texas representative on the US-Texas boundary commission in 1839. He was inspector general of the army, adjutant general in the Somervell Expedition in 1842, and saw brief service in the War with Mexico. Hunt served one term in the Texas legislature in 1852 and in 1853 was appointed United States commissioner to settle the southwestern boundary.

James Pinckney Henderson to Memucan Hunt

Republic of Texas
Department of State
Columbia Decr 31 1836

Sir

The following instructions are given you as a general guide by which you are to be governed in order to affect the important objects of your mission. You have received your commission as Minister Extraordinary of Texas[1] to the United States of North America together with other papers necessary to show the perfect organization of the Government of this Republic &c and fearing that some difficulties may arise in relation to your reception as Minister previous to the recognition of the Independence of this Republic by the Government of the United States, you have been furnished with seperate credentials authorizing you to urge this desirable object as Agent of this Republic, in which event you will act in concert with The Honble. Wm. H. Wharton the resident Minister or Agent of this Republic near the Government of the United States, but should no difficulty arise in relation to your reception as Minister, and you should be received as such you will then act in concert with the Honbl. Wm. H. Wharton the resident Minister Plenipotentiary and will be governed or guided in your negotiations by the instructions already given to that Honble. Gentleman by the late Secretary of State, together with this letter which contains instructions for you and he jointly; founded principally upon facts arising out of the more complete organization of this Government since the departure of Mr. Wharton for the United States.

You will discover by the instructions above alluded to that the principal objects of your Mission are First: The recognition of the Independence of this Republic, Second: The annexation of this Country to the United States either as a seperate State to be on equal footing with the other States of the Union, or as a Territory with the right to admission into the Union as a State when she can number a sufficient amount of population to entitle her to admission according to the laws of the United States. You will therefore proceed to the Government of the United States at Washington City with as little delay as possible where you will confer and act in conjunction with the resident Minister of this Republic The Honble. Wm. H. Wharton and in all your intercourse with that Government you will doubtless use the utmost frankness and candor. You will urge the recognition of the independence of this Republic upon the ground that it is so de jure and de facto. So far as regards the right of Texas to declare herself Independent or the sufficiency of the reasons upon which she founded her declaration of Independence, it is very clear that no other Nation has the right to enquire; This position has in all cases upon

James Pinckney Henderson

Protrait by William H. Huddle (1847-1892). Courtesy of the State Preservation Board, Austin, TX; Accession ID: CHA 1989.032. Photography by Perry Huston, September 22, 1995, post conservation.

which the Government of the United States has heretofore acted been acknowledged but from such an enquiry you will not find it necessary to shrink, and your own knowledge of the causes together with the ~~conditions~~ reasons contained in the instructions heretofore given to the resident Minister at Washington will be sufficient to satisfy so just and liberal a Government as that with which you will have ~~the honor~~ to negotiate should any be required; Therefore it occurs to me that the only point upon which the Government of the United States will require of you to satisfy it, is whether Texas is Independent de facto—has established a regular organized Government in all its parts—and is capable of sustaining itself. In addition to the evidence of these facts already furnished the Minister resident at Washington, you have been furnished with evidence to show that the Judiciary has been regularly and completely organized since the departure of Mr Wharton for that Government. The Supreme Court consisting of a chief justice and the Judges of the Superior or Circuit Courts as his associates: the District or circuit courts consisting of a Judge for each circuit or District, and the county or inferior Courts consisting of a chief Justice in each county all have been organized by the late Congress of the Republic and the Judges of each elected and commissioned and are now prepared to hold their several courts so soon as the time shall arrive when Congress have declared they shall hold them respectively; for the evidences to show that the other constituent parts of this Government are organized and in full operation you are refered to the documents and instructions heretofore furnished to the resident Minister. To this end it may not be unimportant to show with what unanimity and good feeling the late Congress of this Republic acted, and the harmony which prevailed throughout, between it and the Executive also the entire confidence which prevails throughout the whole Country in the several departments of the Government, upon this point it will not be difficult to satisfy the Government to which you go that there is no danger of the permanancy of this Government being affected by internal dissentions; another fact bearing upon this point may well be mentioned which is that of two of the three Gentlemen who were candidates for the Presidency having been appointed to two of the most important offices in the Cabinet, and all acting now with the most perfect harmony and good faith, as regards all other facts bearing upon this point you will find the Instructions alluded to above amply sufficient.

Should the Government of the United States have recognized the Independence of Texas previous to your arrival at Washington, or should it be done during your Stay there in your capacity as Minister Extraordinary, you will then with the resident Minister urge the second object of your Mission—The annexation of Texas to that Government.

In addition to the reasons given in the former instructions you may urge it on the ground of the very great commercial advantages as well as the Naval strength which it would give to the United States, for in the event of [the refusal of] that Government to receive this Country into the Union either as a State or a Territory it may become necessary for Texas to form a Treaty of Amity and Commerce with England or some other European power which would forever and entirely preclude the people of the United States from enjoying any of the benefits resulting in Texas from the richness of her soil, commerce &c &c. These reasons may be very forcibly impressed particularly upon the Representatives of the Northern States from whom we may expect to meet the greatest opposition because should Texas be attached to the United States the immense consumption of those articles principally manufactured in the Northern States will more than compensate for the additional strength which its annexation will add to the political influence of the South, the great and abundant supply of the raw material from this Country will reduce the price which they will have to pay for the same and at the same time keep it at a more uniform price; thus preventing the great fluctuations as frequently occurring in the United States to the Distress and ruin of thousands; as things now are in the United States a partial failure one year will raise the price of the raw material much above its intrinsic ~~value~~ or ordinary value, the next it will be suddenly reduced by an abundant crop, but open as this Country would do an immense territory for the production of cotton; land the richest and most productive in the world, these fluctuations would not occur as no failure which could ordinarily happen would visibly shorten the supply, on the other hand should the Government of the United States refuse to admit this country into the Union &c &c Texas would in all probability in order to gain immediate wealth strength and respectability be induced to form a treaty with England by which all the advantages of commerce wealth and strength would be forever lost to the United States and important advantages given to a Power on her Southern border which already confines her on the North.

In ~~addition~~ a national defensive point of view it is all important to the United States that she should possess this country, with it, she might rest satisfied to see Cuba the key of the whole West Indies together with that whole chain of Islands in the hands of any other one power. The immense forest of the best live oak in the world which are to be found in Texas would enable the Government at a reduced expense to build and keep up a Naval power superior to that of any European Nation, she could in sight of the forests of live oak build launch and protect her navy which would enable her to keep possession of the whole ocean bordering on South America and the West Indies, but take from the United States these advantages and add them to England or any other power and it would hang like an Incubus upon her prosperity.

You may expect perhaps [to] meet with some opposition to the annexation of Texas to the United States from that portion of the States which is in favor of abolition or opposed to slavery so far as it regards Slavery in Texas; it cannot seriously be made an objection to our annexation because it will not be increasing the number of slaves in the World as none are imported here from Africa or any other country except the United States the Constitution of Texas forbids it and a law passed by Congress punishes any violation of it with death. In the event that there should be doubts entertained whether a treaty made with this Government for its annexation to the United States would be ratified by a constitutional majority of the Senate of the United States you are instructed to call the attention of the authorities of that Government to the propriety and practicability of passing a law by both houses (in which it would require a bare majority) taking in this country as a part of her Territory, this law could be passed (provided Congress has the power to do so) based upon the vote of the people of Texas at the last election but in framing such an act great care should be used in order secure all of the rights of Texas and its citizens as fully as you are instructed to have them attended to in any treaty which may be made if such an act is passed you can give that Government the fullest assurances that it will be approved by this Government and people but inasmuch as this is rather a novel position you will speak of it with great prudence and caution.

It is desirable under any and all circumstances that the United States troups now stationed near Nacogdoches should remain in that position, the position which they now occupy is one [of] the most favorable to promote the great object of watching and keeping the different Indian Tribes from committing hostilities upon the frontier of the United States and should the Independence of Texas be acknowledged or should no steps be taken towards it, still the great regard which this Government and the people of Texas have for the Government and people of the United States will induce this Government to afford any and every facility in its power to secure to them peace and prosperity.

Intelligence but recently received from Matamoras states that negotiations have been carried on successfully ~~with some of these Indian tribes~~ the Cherokees east of Naches to commence hostilities against the whites as soon as they are informed of the approach of the Mexican Army upon Texas.

The withdrawal of the American Troops stationed at Nacogdoches, from that vicinity, would operate as an inducement to the Indians to commence aggressions upon the Inhabitants, you will therefore urge this upon the consideration of that Government in the most impressive manner.

The President desires that you should renew the assurance of the very high regard and attachment which this government and the people entertain for the Government and people of the United States, and the distinguished person at its head.

J. Pinckney Henderson
Acting Secratary of State

✦✦✦

LS. Tx, TLP. Published in *DCRT,* 1: 161–165.

1. Henderson to Forsyth, December 31, 1836, *DCRT,* 1: 165–166.

W. W. McCoy to William H. Wharton

Shelbyville I[ndian]a Dec 31st 1836

Sir

A company is being raised to join the Texian Army. They will not be able to leave before the 15th or at earliest the 10th of February. Upon what terms will we be received? And what equipage will be necessary?

You will please give all the particulars that I may be able to inform the men upon what terms they may expect to ingage in the service of the Republic.

Your obt Serv
W. W. McCoy

✦✦✦

ALS. Tx, TLP. W. W. McCoy, not otherwise identified.

James Pinckney Henderson to William H. Wharton

State Department
Columbia Texas
December 31st 1836

Sir

Yours of the 2nd Instant[1] has been received by this department and the credentials for you as agent of Texas have been made out and forwarded to you by Genl Hunt to be used by you in the event of the Government of the United States refusing to receive you as minister. Genl Hunt has been furnished with the like credentials. He has also been commission[ed] Minister Extraordinary to act in connexion with you the Resident Minister Plenepotentiary. To him additional intructions for you both have been given to guide you in your negotiations. I am directed by the President to say to you that Mr Wolf of whom you speak has no claims upon this Government as the Secy of Legation has been appointed and provided for.

You will doubtless join with the whole nation in lamenting the death of its founder Genl Stephen F. Austin, who departed this life on the 27th Instant. He was interred with military honors. In his death the Country has sustained an irreparable loss.

That your own good health may long continue is the sincere wish of

Yours With The Most profound respect & esteem
J. Pinckney Henderson

✦✦✦

ALS. Tx, TLP. Published in *DCRT,* 1: 161–165.

1. Wharton to Austin, December 2, 1836, *DCRT,* 1: 148–149.

James Collinsworth to William H. Wharton

Quintana 31st Decr 1836

Dear Sir

Our congress you will have been duly notified has adjourned. A government is now completely organised capable of "transacting and performing the duties & obligations of an Independent government."

General S. F. Austin you will also have heard is dead. He was interred two days ago at Mr. Perry's.[1] Genl Rusk is to be Secretary of State and Fisher[2] who was a member of the house Secretary of War. Corzine, Williamson, Franklin and Robinson were elected circuit Judges. I was elected Chief Justice beating Judge Ellis tolerable easy. I would give you the other appointments but as both Journals and news-papers will be regularly forwarded to you it is unecessary. Dr Archer is very much dissatisfied with that part of the Presidents Message relating to Texas, I view it in a very different light. A recognition of our Independence this winter is Sanguinely looked for and that of annexation sincerely hoped but much less expected. Should you be able to achieve both you will be entitled to and receive a nations gratitude. Your brother's health is better than when you left here.

Commend me to Mrs W. and believe your friend and Ob't Serv't
Jas. Collinsworth

P.S. I hope soon to hear from you.

✦✦✦

ALS. Tx, TLP.

1. James Franklin Perry (1790–1853) was born in Pennsylvania and migrated to Potosi, Missouri, where, in 1824, he married Emily Austin Bryan (1795–1851), Stephen F. Austin's widowed sister. In 1831 they moved to Texas and established Peach Point Plantation near Brazoria, where Stephen Austin also made his home. Perry was the administrator of Austin's estate.

2. William S. Fisher (d. 1845) came to Texas from Virginia in 1834. He represented Gonzales at the 1835 Consultation and took part in the Battle of San Jacinto. He was appointed secretary of war on December 21, 1836, and served in that office until November 13, 1837. He later participated in the Somervell Expedition and commanded the disastrous Mier Expedition. Taken prisoner by Mexico, he was released in 1843.

Richard Royster Royall to William H. Wharton

Matagorda Jan 1, 1837

Dear Sir

I have thought proper to publish an offer of my services as General Agent for the selecting, locating and perfecting titles to land in Texas and for the transacting of all business connected with the Land Office.[1]

I have taken the liberty of giving your name as a reference permission to have done which I should have wished to receive had time permitted; I hope however it may meet your approbation, and trust that at some future time I may be enabled to reciprocate the obligation your assistance will confer upon yours.

Very respectfully
R. R. Royall

✦✦✦

ALS. Tx, TLP. Richard Royster Royall (1798–1840) came to Texas from Alabama in 1832 and established a plantation at Matagorda. He was a member of the 1835 Consultation.

1. "An Act to Establish a General Land Office for the Republic of Texas," Gammel, 1: 1276–1284. Houston vetoed the bill, which he felt was premature, but Congress, on December 22, 1836, passed it over his veto. Even so, the president declined to open land offices.

Thomas Jefferson Chambers to William H. Wharton

Cincinnati January 1st. 1837

Dear Sir,

I am still detained here waiting for my artillery and the execution of various orders for supplies for the use of the army. The creation of an army out of nothing without the aid and countenance of the government, I have found to be a difficult and tedious operation. But perseverance overcomes everything. I am at length able to set a day for moving towards Texas; and you may rely upon it, that I will not again leave it or the army until the war is terminated. I shall start by the 10th Feby. by which time I shall have all my arrangements completed; and never did a lover rush to the arms of the yielding object of his devotion with greater rapture than I shall to the army. It seems to me that I have been bound in the U.S. by some supernatural influences, which I have been unable with all my efforts to overcome. Each successive day has presented some new difficulty, or something to be done, which has seemed to me to be more useful to our country, than lying idle in an inactive camp. But it is said the enemy is again about to invade us, and I will go ready or not. I rejoice at it, and I trust in Heaven I may soon have an opportunity of meeting him. And I hope ere long we shall repay all their visits, by knocking in person at their own doors.

I forgot to mention to you, before we parted at Maysville, the necessity of not divulging my views upon Matamoros and the castle of San Juan de Ulua. The success of the movement, when made, will depend upon its being covered by the most profound secrecy.

What is the state of our affairs at Washington? Will our independence by recognized? Shall we be annexed to the U.S.? I feel great solicitude upon these subjects, and I should esteem it a particular favor, if you would write me to Louisville.

I hope we shall be much freer in our intercourse than heretofore. Allow me to assure you that a frank interchange of thoughts with you upon the affairs of our country would afford me very great pleasure

Please present me to Mrs. Wharton. I hope that repose from the fatigues of her journey has restored her to health.

I have the honor to remain sincerely you friend and obt. svt.

T. Jeff Chambers

P.S. As I came up the river from N. Orleans last spring on board the steam boat Homer, I had the pleasure of becoming acquainted with Miss Margueritte Preston, sister of the Senator from S. Carolina.[1] If you should meet her, please recall that circumstance to her recollection, with an expression of my most respectful regard. She was the first countrywoman from my native state, I met after a ten years' absence, and she was pleased to express the warmest sympathy in our cause; and you may imagine what a lasting impression the kind expressions of a countrywoman so lovely and beautiful, were calculated to make upon the memory, at such a dark period of our affairs. Say to her that I hope she will continue to cherish the same noble sentiments in our favor, and that she will use her influence to destroy the effects of the senseless views of the executive of S.C. gov. McDuffie,[2] and if I live through the storm of war now gathering upon our borders, I will thank her in person.

Chambers

✦✦✦

ALS. Tx, TLP. Thomas Jefferson Chambers (1802–1865) went to Mexico from Alabama in 1826. In 1829 the Mexican government appointed him surveyor general of Texas. Chambers recruited volunteers in the United States for Texas, but they did not arrive in Texas until after the Battle of San Jacinto. He unsuccessfully sought several political offices. He was murdered in Anahuac.

1. Chambers refers to Margaret [vice Marguerítte] Preston (1818–1852), sister of Senator William Campbell Preston (1774–1860), who represented South Carolina in the Twenty-Third through Twenty-Seventh Congresses, 1833–1842.

2. In his 1836 message to the South Carolina legislature, Governor George McDuffie (1790–1851) opposed US support for Texas, maintaining that it might lead to a war with Mexico, which might seek the aid of a European power, and potentially result in a servile insurrection in the South. Even if most Texans came from the United States, they were mostly "mere adventurers" who had voluntarily expatriated themselves. *Niles'* 51 (December 10, 1836): 229–230.

Samuel May Williams to William H. Wharton

Baltimore 2d Jany 1837

Dear Sir,

On my arrival at this place last evening, I recd with other letters, one from our friend Treat of the 29th in which he says "Mr Sayre[1] has just call'd to say that Capt. [Jeremiah] Brown informs him that several parties who have claims on the Sch[oone]r Invincible have expressed a willingness to take scrip for their claims, say Ship Chandlers bill $1200—sail makers $600 borrowed money <u>$3000</u> in various ways in all say (for I do not pretend to be exact) some 5500 can be satisfied with scrip. Then sales for cash can be made for the balance of her wants; The question to me was would I give up the necessary scrip (out of the 51 sections recd from Sayre) for this arrangement? To which I replied that I did not feel myself authorized to assume any distinction in the matter of the Vessels a disposition of the scrip &c &c." I wrote Mr Treat last night and said to him that if he had not considered himself as authorised to act in the disposal of the scrip for the release of the Invincible, under the joint letter written by you & myself—that I authorised him to adjust the matter and have the Schooner prepared for sea immediately. Treat expresses much anxiety to have me proceed directly to that place, and my own judgement inclines me to the opinion that I ought to go on immediately. Possibly various benefits might result, certainly no harm. I would unhesitatingly proceed to N[ew] York were the S[team] Boats running—but I like not pounding in a stage, if however I make up my mind to go on [I] will inform you. Should I determine to go I shall send you five hundred dollars by Mr Munroe[2] who will go to Washington tomorrow

Treat says "The Castle of <u>San Juan de Ulloa</u>, was surrendered by the <u>Spaniards</u> to the <u>Mexicans</u>, either late in Novem[be]r or early Decem[be]r 1825. I think about 25 or 28th Novem[be]r. A friend who was in Mexico thinks early in Decem[be]r. Should the very day be important for you to know, I may be able to ascertain for you." This completely accords with my own recollections of the affair. It was from 14 to 15 months after the publication of the Constitution.

The letters rec[eive]d by my brother from Texas for me were only as late as 3rd Novem[be]r nearly three weeks anterior to your departure. They contain nothing of which you were not apprised before you left.

If any thing transpires that interests the prospects of our Country I will thank you for a line. My brother presents his respects.

Truly & Respectfully yr obt St
Saml. M. Williams

✦✦✦

ALS. Tx, TLP.

1. Charles D. Sayre (1799?–1856?), who came to Texas from New York in 1831, was among the founders of the Brazoria Insurance Company. He later owned a sugar plantation and sugar mill in Brazoria County.

2. Munroe, not otherwise identified.

Samuel May Williams to William H Wharton

[Baltimore]
Tuesday Morning 3d Jany 1837

My Dear Sir,

Please find enclosed Five Hundred Dollars in Bank Notes, which I send not as evidence that I am going to New York as intimated in mine of yesterday, but fearing you may be in want and I shall be detained here a day longer to get off the Flight.

Be good enough to ask Mr Cochrane[1] what will be the cost of a 12 or 18 pounder upon his principle, and also to inform you where one can be made. My brother has an idea of fitting out a vessel if such a gun be procured. Also ask Mr Cochrane if such a gun can be made in his absence. Henry says that it is better to give $3000 for a gun of that description. The length of time it would require to cast and prepare the Gun is also important.

Truly & sincerely yours
Samuel M Williams

✦✦✦

ALS. Tx, TLP.

1. John Webster Cochran [vice Cochrane] (1811–1873), of New Hampshire, had invented a breech-loading rifled cannon with a revolving cylinder that held multiple shells.

Fleming T. Wells to William H. Wharton

City of New York. Jan. 3d. 1837

Sir,

Your letter of the 1st. ult. was this day recd, and I am instructed by Capt. Brown to inform you that there is no vacancy for a midshipman in schooner Invincible, there being at present a full complement.

I am Sir, With much Respect And esteem your obt. svt.
F. T. Wells

✦✦✦

ALS. Tx, TLP.

Thomas Green to [William H. Wharton]

Rich[mon]d. 4th January 1837.

Dear Sir,

I had promised myself the pleasure of seeing you again, before this time, but may be deprived of that gratification a week or two longer. Apart from the events which render your country a subject of so much interest, I have been very glad to renew the friendly intercourse that subsisted during our short acquaintance in Washington and New York.

Allow me the pleasure of being the medium of your forming an acquaintance with our Senator in Congress—a particular friend of mine,[1] to whom I beg you will hand the enclosed letter. I know he would be glad to make your acquaintance and I feel assured, it will be the source of much pleasure to you both.

I am with great regard Yr. friend & obt sevant
Thos. Green

✦✦✦

ALS. Tx, TLP. Thomas Green (1798–1883), an attorney, practiced in Richmond, Virginia, and Washington, DC.

1. Virginia's US senators at this time were William Cabell Rives and Richard E. Parker. It is not clear to which of them Green refers.

J. C. Rogers to William H. Wharton

University of Va.
4th Jany 1837

Sir—The notice given in the papers of your arrival & recent departure from Texas, has induced me to address you this letter. And my apology for the intrusion is the anxiety I feel to hear from my brother W. H. Rogers. A member of your Congress, & who I have heard rumered was likely to die.[1] Supposing you to have known him, or at least to know if this report be true or false, I ask of you all the information in regard to him and to the circumstances, in your possession. By giving of which you will confer a lasting favour on

your unknown friend & obt. Sevt.
J. C. Rogers

✦✦✦

ALS. Tx, TLP. J. C. Rogers, not otherwise identified.

1. W. H. Rogers, not otherwise identified. He was not a member of the Texas Congress.

Stewart Newell to William H. Wharton

Philadelphia Jany. 5/3~~6~~7

Sir

Upon your arrival at the City of Washington I addressed a Letter to you requesting to know your views as to the appointment of a General Agent for Texas in Philadelphia and having been long impressed with the necessity of such an agent being required. I had spoken to Mr. James Patton[1] a Merchant of this City to know if he would accept of the appointment if such an one was offered him he told me he would and he can be recommended as a Gentleman who is well and favourably known as a Merchant now engaged in the Shipping and Commission business and I know of none so well calculated and adapted to the Office named and if no other benefit was derived to Texas from the appointment it would increase the number of her friends and add some little in her favour by being properly represented in our Commercial City. My family having continued so unwell I shall be obliged to leave them in Philada. and proceed in a few days to Texas alone and should be pleased to receive your answer to my enquiry as early as possible and if not asking too much also to hear from you what is the prospect of a recognition during this Session of Congress

I have the Honor to be Your Most Obt.
Stewart Newell

✦✦✦

ALS. Tx, TLP.

1. Possibly James Patton (1756–1845), an Irish immigrant and successful Philadelphia merchant.

James Treat to William H. Wharton

New York, January 5th 1837,
Thursday night 9 o clk #

My dear Sir,

Your valued favour of the 26th of Ulto, was duly received & should have had earlier reply, and I may add would have had but for my continued indisposition, during the whole of the present and part of the past week, and under which I am still labouring. I can very well conceive that your labours & occupations must be great & incessant, & that you have but little leisure to devote to your casual correspondents, even were you in good health.

I have not recd the Morfit report you sent me, tho' I got one from Mr. Weaver. As regards the vessels of war, Brutus & Invincible I have done with other friends all I could do, as my letters to You & especially to S. M. Williams will shew, I could not, however do all I could wish. Mr Sayre placed the Brutus in a situation to go to sea, tolerably well provisioned and Equippd, and I presume she sailed yesterday evening, or this morn[in]g, if the Ice, would permit. Not having seen Mr Say[r]e or anyone else, to day, cannot say certainly. Will endeavour, to ascertain in the morni[n]g & let you know. I received your line address[e]d to Capt Hurd, enclosed to me by Mr Williams & immediately sent it to him at Sayres office, & presume he received it, tho', not having seen him since, am not certain. I also noted your requests at foot of Williams letter address[e]d to Mr Swartwout & myself. Another additional reason for my late silence is, & has been that, I was assured, that yourself & Williams would both be here. This was stated by Capt Allen,[1] & also by Hurd & [Jeremiah] Brown, tho' not to me directly, yet thro' Sayre.

This report I was perhaps the more ready to believe, because, I wished it, and because I had suggested to you (& to Williams more especially) that, I thought, you could run over here, between Christmas and New Years; probably without any detriment, to your affairs in Washington, and by comparing notes, and as we used to say Talking up matters & things, you might do some good even here. Again, I had written often to Williams & Weaver & often, if not always with request that you should see the letters, and being moreover sick, alone, and much annoyed, with my own affairs. Hard money times, & the interruption of the Holiday days, & excessive cold weather, altogether, have placed me for 10 days nearly Hors' du combat. I had also hoped that my affairs, might have enabled me to run on to the Capital to see you, but even this, has been prevented by all the circumstances above related & many more, not enumerated. Still, & after all, our needle here is always faithful to the Pole. We go for Texas & if possible (which Heaven grant) for recognition this session. We continue to do all we can, & tomorrow, I shall give to the Courier & Enquirer Hamilton's[2] & Poinsett's speeches[3] (sent me by the latter) to make use of. You should eye them there also. They are of the right character, I think. St. Anna at Louisville 25th must now be at Washington. You must manage to make all you can out of him. What that may be, you must be able to judge for I am in the dark about the real object of his visit. Excuse this scrawl. I write at the bedside of a very sick child &

am more than half sick myself. Will add anything there may be tomorrow. Yours &c

Jany 6th Friday 2 pm. Here you have my scrawl of last night, and well I gave it to you, for this morning I should not been able to have devoted more than just enough to say a few words. I am happy to say that the Brutus went to sea last night at 5 pm by steam, and luckily got through the ice. I have not seen Capt Allen, but intend to call this evening. It appears he has been examining into the state of the Invincible &c, and I learn this morng that Mr Williams was expected here last night, but not having arrived, presume he will be here to day. I had ho[ped] you would have come with him, but presume not, or I should have heard of it. I am pleased to learn that the Legislature of Kentucky are about passing some favourable resolutions in relation to the recognition of Texas independence.[4] This at least will be an offsett to the McDuffie story.

Your letter was received by Capt Hurd before his departure, so I have learned this morng from Capt Taylor.[5] I am again suffering martyrdom from my teeth, which all but kill me.

Yours &c in haste,
James Treat

✦✦✦

ALS. Tx, TLP.

1. John M. Allen (d. 1847), a Kentuckian who had served in the US Navy, came to Texas in 1830. He had been a member of the Tampico Expedition of 1835 and was at the Battle of San Jacinto. Allen commanded the privateer *Terrible* in 1836. That same year, David G. Burnet sent him on a recruiting expedition to the United States. He later became mayor of Galveston.

2. In response to Governor McDuffie's message to the South Carolina legislature, Senator James Hamilton's report, which was adopted by the Senate, denied that Texans were "mere adventurers." They were, the report stated, defenders of liberty against the tyranny of Mexico's central government and like South Carolinians defenders of slavery against "fanaticism." *Niles'* 51 (December 31, 1836): 277. James Hamilton (1786–1857), of Charleston, had been a member of Congress from 1821 to 1828. He was governor of South Carolina from 1830 to 1832. He became an early supporter of Texas.

3. In his "Remarks of Mr. Poinsett in the Senate of South Carolina on the Subject of the Recognition of Texas," Poinsett said that the "interests of the whole Union, and especially of the South, required that Texas, if once separated from Mexico, should be

annexed to these United States" (*Washington Globe*, February 11, 1837). Joel Roberts Poinsett (1779–1851), of Charleston, was the first US minister to Mexico from 1825 to 1830. He became secretary of war in the Van Buren administration in 1837.

4. "Preamble and Resolutions on the Subject of the Recognition of the Independence of Texas by the People of the United States," January 24, 1837, urging the recognition of Texas independence when it might be done without violating treaty obligations or the national honor. *Acts of the General Assembly of the Commonwealth of Kentucky, December Session, 1836* (Frankfort: A. G. Hodges, 1837), 353.

5. Thurston M. Taylor (b. 1785), of Maryland, who resigned from the US Navy in 1836 to enter Texas service.

Samuel May Williams to William H. Wharton

Baltimore 6th January 1837

dear Sir,

Business having detained me at this place longer than I expected, has afforded me the satisfaction of receiving yours of yesterday for the contents of which please accept my thanks.

My Brother H. H. W. in conjunction with myself are of opinion that Mr. Cochrane should at once be engaged to make the 12 pounder refered to in yours, and therefore wish you to engage him to have one immediately made, for which we will be perfectly willing to pay <u>Twelve hundred dollars</u> if on trial it cannot be made for <u>One thousand.</u> The money shall be ready by the time the Gun is, provided it shall be necessary to make prompt payment. On the subject of the 4 pounder, we think it too small for sea service, but it would be inimitable for a field piece, and if Mr Cochrane would sell it on a credit of 4 or 6 months, would like to buy it, for the Govt. being persuaded that they would be pleased to have the Gun.

I have this morning a letter from Toby dated 29th Decemr. in which he encloses to me, a communication on the subject of the seizure of the Liberty in New Orleans. The ground taken by Carleton in the defence, is that the Liberty being a national vessel was not liable to seizure. I have taken the Communication to the Patriot office and it will appear this evening Toby further says that if the lower court decides against them, they have no doubt but the Supreme Court will decide in their favor. He has sent one to Treat to be published in New York, and recommends that it should appear in the Globe. Will send you one of the papers so that you may have it published.

I regret that your afflictions continue to interfere with your business and your comforts. I hope you will soon be releaved from them.

Very truly & sincerely yrs,
Saml. M. Williams

✦✦✦

ALS. Tx, TLP.

Branch T. Archer to [William H. Wharton]

Velasco Jany 7th, 1837

Dear Friend.

In our publick relations, nothing of interest has occurred since you left us, save the chartering of the Railroad, navigation, & Banking company.[1] This company is composed of sixteen member: Genl Green[2] & myself have taken the liberty to introduce you as one.

You can accept or decline as m[a]y best comport with your feelings and interest. The Genl. will be with you in twenty five, or thirty days, he will take with him, all the papers connected with the association, on which you will be able to determine for yourself. In any event, I trust you will give to the company all the aid in your power; as I am satisfied you cannot fail to see the incalculable advantages that must accrue, to this infant republick, by the introduction of five million of dollars at this time.

That amount of capital would enable us at once, to develope the resources of this fine country, and at the same time, furnish us, with the sinews of war. In a few days, I shall leave for the army where I shall probably remain several weeks. Should any matter of interest transpire in that quarter you shall hear from me.

Your headman, and my friend Duglas[3] has had the misfortune to lose his wife. He has poor fellow, my most earnest sympathy for I have never seen any man black or white, more seriously affected by a similar loss. He desires to be remembered to yourself, and his mistress, with earnest prayers for your speedy return.

Should you want the two thousand dollars, on the first of March I have directed my friend Doct Stone[4] to raise them for you. You will see him in Washington and can make such arrangements, as I have no doubt will be satisfactory.

Present me most respectfully to Mrs. Wharton & son & accept for yourself the best wishes of Your Friend & svt.

B. T. Archer

✦✦✦

ALS. Tx, TLP.

1. "An Act to Incorporate the Texas Rail Road, Navigation, and Banking Company," December 16, 1836, Gammel, 1: 1188–1192. The company was given rights to connect Gulf ports by canal, construct railroad lines, and establish a bank once it subscribed twenty percent of its stock. The company failed because it proved unable to sell enough stock.

2. Thomas Jefferson Green (1802–1863), originally from North Carolina, attended the United States Military Academy and afterward became a planter in Florida. He was related by marriage to the Whartons. Green came to Texas in 1836 and was appointed a brigadier general in the Texas army. In 1842 he took part in the Somervell Expedition, was captured, and held at Perote prison in Mexico, from which he escaped. Green returned to the United States and moved to California in 1849.

3. Duglas, not otherwise identified.

4. Dr. G. M. Stone, of Richmond, Virginia.

Thomas H. Pitts to William H. Wharton

Loretto [Virginia] Jany 8. 1837.

Dr Sir,

In the Washington Papers I have noticed your arrival at the seat of Government, as minister from the Republic of Texas—a circumstance that afforded me much pleasure having sincerely cherished the warmest sympathies toward the heroic population of a sister Republic in their laudable & patriotick efforts to establish their independence.

The brave people of Texas have not only my best wishes for their success, but I am anxious to repair to the scene of operations, & can carry with me me about twenty young men willing to engage in the service, but have not the means of defraying their expenses—

If any aid in this way can be obtained we will, with the least possible delay repair to the Young Republic & cheerfully engage in the common cause. Were I able, I would not hesitate to make the necessary advances, but being Poor can only throw in my might, which shall be cheerfully contributed.

Respy
Thos. H. Pitts

P.S.
I can produce the necessary testimonials that I can be confided in
Thos. H. Pitts

✦✦✦

ALS. Tx, TLP. Thomas H. Pitts, not otherwise identified. There is no record that he served with the Texas army.

Henry H. Williams to William H. Wharton

Baltimore January 9 1837

Dear Sir,

I am in receipt of your esteemed favour of the 7th addressed to my Brother or myself. My Brother left on Saturday morning last for New York with the view & hope of dispatching the Brutus & Invincible & he will probably be back by the last of this week. I am fearful that there will not be much Scrip in my Brother's hands for sale after dispatching the vessels at all events it will require, a greate deal more than he now has to carry out his plans independant of the Carbines on Mr. Cochranes pla[n]. I wrote to New York to ascertain what 200 guns could be had for they answer from 60 to 70 $ each according to the finish with one circle and for each additional circle $6. I have in my hands scrip for twenty five Sections of Land and I shall be glad if you can arrainge to pay for the cannon ordered in Scrip at 50¢ per acre although I had hoped the Scrip would have been up to 75¢ per acre, I have howe[ver] refused to sell at 50¢ except for cash there is now so small an amount I would keep the whole myself If I could raise the money as I feel confident I could resell it at a very large advance in a short time.

The Government ought to give Scrip sufficient to fit out two good vessels. Built for the Express purpose of being armed with Mr. Cochranes cannon. Two such guns with 30 men each would be more than a match for the 14 Guns on Brigs Built for the Mexicans service & would not cost more than one third of the money.

The Government of Texas will I think find it impossible to raise money by a lone unless at enormous sacrifice. But I am anxious to see the commissioners are here & understand what they wish to do respecting the addition of a naval force. Cochranes Pattent guns will change the mode of naval warfare & smaller vessels will be substituted for the large ones, at least it will be so with regard to Mexico, as they will not probably even hear of the improvement this century.

Yours Very Truly
Henry H. Williams

PS. I have no doubt S. M. Williams would enter into a contract with Mr Plumber[1] for security of his located lands for the guns & give him <. . .> fine lands at much less Price than they can be bought for in Texas.

✦✦✦

ALS. Tx, TLP.

1. Plumber, not otherwise identified.

George Lincoln to William H. Wharton

Worcester [Massachusetts]. Jan 10th. 1837

Sir,

I have received the two letters which have been sent me from Washington, dated Jan. 1st and 6th, & in answer to the last have to say, that the risk of going to Texas a stranger & alone, & of throwing myself upon the clemency of entire strangers, as the authorities there are to me without letters to them is great, almost to great, for I sacrifice a prospect & situation in the Merchant Marine of this Country which fiew enjoy. But I should be willing to sacrifice my situation here for a good prospect in the Texian Navy—as my inclinations are all & always have been Naval.

I have made up my mind to go if you can do me the favour of writing & sending me some letters to the authorities there & any documents which will be likely to advance my interest & views there. Without something of the kind it would be to rash in me to go. You can get my history, character, & qualifications from Mr. S. C. Phillips a member of Congress from Salem, Massachusetts. I shall go immediately after the reception of your answer to this, if you see fit to grant my request. With a fervent prayer to Heaven to watch over & protect the interests of our then common Country I close & remain

Very respectfully your Obt. Svt.
George Lincoln

✦✦✦

ALS. Tx, TLP.

Thomas Toby and Brother to William H. Wharton

New Orleans 10 Januy 1837

Sir

The Sch. Julius Caesar & Col Fanin reached here yesterday, by them we have dates to 31 ulto

No letters for you have been received by us & if there were any were probably placed in the Letter Box. If so they will not reach you til some time after this. We shall address the Executive & request all letters sent to us & shall forward them by the Express mail. We wrote Mr. S. M Williams sending him an extract of a letter from Vera Cruz, shewing the public state of the Country &c, which we recommend him publishing in the Globe.

By an arrival from Matamoras we have received the account of 3000 troops being stationed there & 4000 men at Saltillo the greater part Convicts. The Schooner *Correo* arrived at Matamoras loaded with floating Brigs & Provisions, calculated for their operations against Texas. Bustemente[1] had arrived at the City of Mexico which had created much excitement & many Generals had been arrested who were in favor of the federal Govmt.

The troops at Matamoras had heard of Santa Ana's release with great rejoicing.

We have been informed that Col. Austin was dead. We were aware of his being very sick.

Yours in haste,
Thomas Toby & Bro

✦✦✦

ALS. Tx, TLP.

1. Anastasio Bustamante [vice Bustemente] y Oseguera (1780-1853), a physician, entered the army in 1808. He became president in 1830. Santa Anna led a revolt against Bustamante in 1832 and forced him into exile. Bustamante returned to Mexico in 1836 and assumed the presidency in April 1837. Santa Anna deposed him again in 1841.

Benjamin Chew Howard to William H. Wharton

Jany 10th. 1837.

My dear Sir

Would it be agreeable to you to have an interview with the Committee on For[eign]. Aff[air]s. of the House? and if so, would it be convenient to do so on Thursday morning?

If you reply in the affirmative, I will call for you at 11 o'clock.

Respectfully yours
Benjn. C. Howard

✦✦✦

ALS. Tx, TLP. Benjamin Chew Howard (1791–1872) represented Maryland as a Jacksonian in the Twenty-First and Twenty-Second Congresses, 1829–1833, and in the Twenty-Fourth and Twenty-Fifth Congresses, 1835–1839, in which he was chair of the Committee on Foreign Affairs.

Randolph Ross to Willam H. Wharton

Lynchburg Va. Jany 10th 1837

Sir,

The position which you occupy in relation to Texas connected with the solicitude I feel for her success, are circumstances which has given rise to the presumed liberty in forwarding to your charge accompanying letters, the one to my son,[1] who from the last information 30th Octr. was acting as aid de camp to your Genl. Felix Huston, the other to the President of yr. Republick, who is an old acquaintance & I have much reason to believe our mutual friend. being desirous that those letters should have the most safe & speedy passage within my reach & not being sufficiently advised as to the mode or manner of conveyance without the limits of the United States is my apology in presuming this trespass on you.

Not having the pleasure of personal acquaintance with you will explain why these letters are made [to] pass to you through the Hon William C Preston.

From the elevation of Genl Houston to the Presidency of yr. state, up to the period of President Jackson's message I had every confidence that our governmt. wd not only give to you as the representative of Texas a welcome, but an official reception, but judging from that message refering to Texas, I have but too much reason to fear that my fond expectations has not been realized. To be advised of my error wd afford sincere pleasure, from this you will infer & correctly so, that you have the best wishes of every heart for the successful achievement of your mission in every particular. indeed from the men[a]cing attitude of Genl. Bravo & the reasoning & conclusions of [the] message alluded to, I feel ready to ask in what manner the humble friends of Texas can best serve her.

The two letters mentioned you will observe I have left to the favour of yr direction except the names.

With due respect please believe me yr most obt & Hbl. Sevt

Randolph Ross

P. S. 15th. Since closeing the foregoing letter, has come under my observation the restoration of Santa Anna to his liberty & the reasons which influenced the measure as set forth by my son John M.[2] of Natchez in his letter to the Editor of the Natchez Courier of the 21st ult. The policy appears to me well founded & from which I gather some hope in the nearer approach of Texian independence & Texian annexation.

R.R.

✦✦✦

ALS. Tx, TLP. Randolph Ross (b. circa 1784), not otherwise identified.

1. Reuben Ross (d. 1839) was Huston's aide from August 1836 to June 1837.

2. John M. Ross, not otherwise identified.

Edward R. Gibson to William H. Wharton

Jan. 11th, 1837

Sir,

The bearer of this Mr. Gaither[1] is a young man who is about publishing something in relation to Mexico & Texas. He wishes an introduction to you with some reference to that subject.

Very respectfully I remain your Most obt. Sevt

Edward R. Gibson

✦✦✦

ALS. Tx, TLP. Edward R. Gibson, not otherwise identified.

1. Gaither, not otherwise identified.

James Pinckney Henderson to William H. Wharton, with Enclosure

Columbia Texas

Jan 12th 1837

Dr Sir

You will find inclosed herein additional instructions for yourself and your colleague the Honble M. Hunt but upon a different subject from those already given.

Since the adjournment of Congress nothing has transpired of importance. We have heard that the Mexicans were concentrating their forces at Matamoros for the purpose of an immediate invasion of Texas; which was for some time believed by Genl Felix Huston and consequently created some anxiety in the army and uneasiness amongst the Citizens. The truth of this report we never did believe in the Cabinet at least so far as regarded their intention of <u>invading</u> Texas, but all necessary preparations for having the Militia in the field have been made, nothing has been heard for some time calculated to induce the belief of their approach nor do I expect soon to hear it confirmed. Genl Houston has gone to the Army to reorganize. Genl Rusk who has been appointed to fill the vacancy occasioned by the death of Genl Austin has not yet arrived at the seat of Government. I have not seen your brother for some days he is absent up the Brazos River. The whole country is quiet and full confidence appears to reign in the minds of all, in the Government. As soon as we can have them printed (which will be in a few days) I will send you a copy of the most important acts of Congress. Be pleased to remember me kindly to Mrs. Wharton and also to Genl Hunt if he has arrived. And accept for yourself my best wishes and Highest regard.

J. Pinckney Henderson

✦✦✦

ALS. Tx, TLP.

Enclosure: James Pinckney Henderson to William H. Wharton and Memucan Hunt

Columbia Texas
Department of State
January 12th 1837

To the Honbl Messrs Wharton & Hunt

I am directed by the President to instruct you to enter into a negotiation with Genl Santa Anna before he leaves the City of Washington for an exchange of prisoners.

So far as regards the manner time and place of the exchange you of course must be the Judges as this must be done to suit as near as possible the convenience of both governments.

The terms of the exchange will be those which universally govern such transactions that is for all Texians who are now prisoners of war in the hands of the Mexican Government and who shall hereafter be discharged by that Government. So shall a like number of Mexican prisoners of war according to rank be discharged by this government, and as regards the expense heretofore incurred by either government for keeping the said prisoners and that which shall accrue in the exchange you are instructed either to settle now or leave it for subsequent negotiation. It is however desirable that the exchange should be made as soon as practicable and if such an exchange can be agreed upon at this time with Genl. Santa Anna and he should be favourably received in Mexico it will facilitate this very desirable object.

You will doubtless communicate frequently and fully to this Department your progress in your mission.

J. Pinckney Henderson
Acting Secy of State

✦✦✦

LS. Tx, TLP. *DCRT*, 1: 174.

Peter Wagener Grayson to William H. Wharton and Memucan Hunt

Department of State
Columbia [January] 13th
1837

Sirs

The Secretary of State being confined today from indisposition I am instructed by the President to inform you, that since the date of the last communications made to you on the subject of Indian aggressions on the Brazos, fresh inteligence has been received by him of further outrages having been committed in the eastern part of Texas in the neighbourhood of the Naches, within a few days past; two men of a small party having been killed there, by the Caddoes and their associates as it is supposed.

The President instructs me to say that he entertains no doubt the Indians have been emboldened to the perpetration of these aggressions, by the withdrawal of the United States Troops from this Side of the Sabine, and he consequently thinks that their immediate return is urgently demanded to prevent the further Occurrence of Similar enormities.

He has undoubted information of the course now being constantly practised by the Indians bordering on Red River; which is to make incursions upon those districts of Texas which are most defenceless, for the purpose of Stealing Horses and other property, and bearing them off to places of Security near, and it may be too, within the Territory of the United States,

A large number of fine American horses have lately been seen tied out, near to Red River, which there is no doubt had been stolen by the Indians from the Citizens of Texas.

These incursions besides being attended with robberies of every kind, are but too often signalized by the more deplorable consequences of murder and bloodshed.

It is hoped that the government of the United States moved by the present undoubted signs of disaffection and disorder on the part of their Indians, and of those bordering on their territory, will feel the propriety at the earliest moment of interposing, within the confines of Texas, a military force of Sufficient respectability, to restrain the excesses complained of, as it is certain that they can in no other manner effectually enforce the peacefull behaviour of their Indians, and thus discharge their treaty obligations they are under in this respect.

I have the honor to be, yr obt St.
P. W. Grayson
Atty Genl

+++

ALS. Tx, TLP.

Unknown to William H. Wharton

New York 13. Jan:
1837

Dear Sir,

I have been watching with an anxiouse eye, the political events of Texas, for the last two years, with a hope that it[s] concerns might become tranquil, and that eventually, I should be enabled to establish a permanent interest there.

When you, Col: Austin and Mr. Archer, were here last year, I was introduced to you at the American Hotel by Mr. Sibel.[1] As I conversed mostly with Col: Austin; I cannot expect you will distinctly recollect me at this time. The object of my visit there was, to see if any arrangement could be made, by which Negroes could be introduced into Texas from the West Indian Islands? Since then, I have seen a Copy of the Constitution of the Republic of Texas, which declared that "No free person of African desent shall reside permenently in the Republic without the consent of Congress."[2]

If Congress would give that consent, thro' the means of special Commissioners to be created by law for purpose, or authorise Justices of the Peace, or any of the Judges of higher courts to give the needful consent, I could within four months, take in to Texas from one of the West Indian Islands, several hundred of free Negroes, as Apprentices for a term of ten and fifteen years. The value of such an establishment, you can as well, and no doubt better, appreciate than myself.

I have written to several influential Gentlemen in Texas, urging them to endeavour to get the Texian Congress, at its present Session; to take immediate measures to appoint persons to give the consent required by the constitution; and now would ask of you the same favour: I am fully persuaded that Texas has little to fear from her Mexican enemies, and that ere long, all will be peace and security there. You are extensively acquainted there, and intimately so, with her best interest, and should be glad, if you would use your influence to have Congress pass the law giving its consent to the introduction of <…remainder of letter missing…>.

✦✦✦

Incomplete letter. Tx, TLP.

1. Sibel, not otherwise identified.

2. Gammel, 1: 1079 (Section 9 of the General Provisions of the Texas Constitution).

Joseph Eggleston Segar to William H. Wharton

Richmond, Jany 14th. 367

Sir:

I shall take it as a favour of no small magnitude, if you will furnish me with all the information of the present condition & prospects of Texas—such facts, in particular, as it would be suitable to urge in behalf of a proposition, in the Virginia Legislature, to instruct its senators to vote for the recognition of Texian Independence. If I can be satisfied that it is proper for the government to interfere at this time, it is possible the proposition may be brought forward here by myself or some one else—provided we find, upon enquiry, there will be a prospect of success. Please consider this communication as entirely confidential.

With my best wishes for the cause of your home country,

I am, Sir, Very Resply Yours &c

Jos Segar

✦✦✦

ALS. Tx, TLP. Joseph Eggleston Segar (1804–1880), a lawyer, was a member of the Virginia House of Delegates, 1836–1838, 1848–1852, and 1855–1861. Segar was elected several times to Congress as a Unionist during the Civil War but, except for the period between March 15, 1862 and March 3, 1863, was denied a seat.

Henry H. Williams to William H. Wharton

Baltimore Jany 14th 1837

Dear Sir

I am this morning in receipt of a Line from my Brother Saml which says that he is confined to his bed with a sever Billious attack at the U States Hotel Philadelphia. He hoped to be able [to] leave his room in three or four days, & wished me to inform you of his Illness.

From the hand writing, I should judge he was very ill & I regret exceedingly that I am so situated that I cannot go on to Philad at once.

I hope you will drop him a line & let him know how things go with you in Washington.

Very Respectfully your obt Servant
Henry H. Williams

✦✦✦

ALS. Tx, TLP.

James M. Wolfe to Unnamed Recipient

Washington City January 14th 1837

Sir

I am directed by Mr. Wharton, to state that he recd your last favor this morning and he directed me to enclose to you the within letters one to the President of Texas another to the Secretary of the Navy[1] and the other to Commodore Hawkins.[2]

Yrs &c
James M. Wolfe

✦✦✦

ALS. Tx, TLP.

1. Samuel Rhoads Fisher (1794–1839), from Pennsylvania, came to Texas in 1830 and settled at Matagorda. He was a member of the Convention of 1836 and signed the Declaration of Independence. He was secretary of the navy from October 28, 1836, until his death on March 14, 1839. He was briefly suspended from office in October 1837 but was reinstated by the Texas Senate.

2. Commodore Charles Edward Hawkins (1802-1837) served in the US Navy until 1826 when he resigned and joined the Mexican navy. In 1836 he obtained a commission in the Texas navy and was given command of the *Independence*. He was later given command of the entire navy.

Despite a less than encouraging response to his July 4, 1836, letter to Andrew Jackson, Santa Anna, with his aide and translator Juan N. Almonte, left Texas in the custody of George W. Hockley, Barnard E. Bee Sr., and Major William H. Patton on November 26 for Washington, DC, to meet with the president. The party made its way overland to Plaquemine, Louisiana, where they took passage on a steamboat up the Mississippi and then up the Ohio. By Christmas they were in Louisville, and from there they continued by road to Lexington and Wheeling. The travelers arrived in Washington on January 17, 1837. The two generals talked, and Jackson had the Mexican leader to dinner, but no understanding between them emerged on Texas. Jackson provided the US Navy vessel Pioneer *for his return to Vera Cruz, which he reached on March 1, 1837. Back in Mexico, Santa Anna renounced the promises he had made at Velasco.*

Barnard Elliott Bee Sr. to William H. Wharton

Wheeling Va
Saturdy Mg.
14 Jany, '37

Dear Sir,

We have at last reached Wheeling! And altho we leave it this mg., yet as we do not travel at night, you must not expect us before Tuesday or Wednesday! The Gen'l is quite well, and rejoices to think he will really arrive at Washington, before the end of the year! We all rejoice to hear of the improved health of Gen'l Jackson. Remember me to Mrs. Wharton.

I am with regard respectfully Yours
Barnard Bee

✦✦✦

ALS. Tx, TLP.

George Lincoln to William H. Wharton

Worcester, Jan. 16, 1837.

It is not yet quite time to receive the answer of my last letter to you, but I was induced to write this from having received a letter from Capt. Brown stating that a recommendation from you would insure me the situation which I want. If you have not already written the letters for me to take on I shall be very much obliged to you if you will, & will not loose any time about it, as I probably shall leave in about 8 days, and if you have written you need not take any further notice of this & I will take this opportunity of thanking you for the kind interest which you seem to have taken in my behalf.

Your humble & Obt. Svt.
George Lincoln.

✦✦✦

ALS. Tx, TLP.

Jeremiah Brown to William H. Wharton, New York

New York, Jan th 17. 1837.

Dear Sir,

I Received your short note from Washington City Dated December 29th—

From the purport of the same, and your sanguine way of wrighting I was in hopes before this I should [have] been Ready to have been afloat, but it is not the case as yet. You also wrote me to keep my officers and crew in good spirits in as much I have Endevoured to do so—but the Task is a hard one, they are not in their Eliments. You must be aware a Sailor on Shore without money—(I will Leave it to you to make the Comparison.) but this is not the thing myself. With all the officers beloning to the Invincible are anxious to be afloat and rendering servise to our Country, and your attention and capability in Rendering that servise in conjunction with S. M. Williams is Expected and will be greatfuly Receivd.

My Dear Sir, as a friend as I hope I can, as formaly call you do your utmost to get me away, and as far as my feble Efforts can avail you shall Ever find a friend and Servt.

in Your Obt Servt
J. Brown

The Brutus sailed last Thursday week. Mr Williams is sick in Philadelphia—Capt Alen is married.

✦✦✦

ALS. Tx, TLP.

Edward Milford to William H. Wharton

American Hotel
New York 18 Jany 1837

Respected Sir,

As this Establishment has always been regarded as the Head Quarters of the friends of Texas in New York,[1] I should be obliged if your influence could be used with the Gentlemen accompanying General Santa Anna to bring him here, should the General visit New York. Our accommodations are now very extensive and furnished in a manner suitable for visitors of distinction.

When your Excellency again visit New York, I shall be glad to retain apartments for your accommodation beforehand.

Believe me very respectfully Your obedient servant
Edwd Milford Esq

✦✦✦

ALS. Tx, TLP. Edward Milford, not otherwise identified.

1. Milford's American Hotel was at 235 Broadway.

James Treat to William H. Wharton

New York, January 19th. 1837.
Thursday noon

My Dear Sir,

I had the pleasure 6th Inst, since which I have nothing from you direct, tho', I frequently hear of you, thro' various channels, and am well aware of your unceasing efforts, to bring about a recognition of your Independence during the present Session, and therefore, know your time is constantly occupied, in these all important matters. A moments leisure, and improved health (neither of which have enjoyed much since New Years) enables me to write you today, and tho' I have nothing of moment to advise, yet wish to remind you that neither you nor your cause is forgotten by me. I should [have] written you more frequently, but for reasons already given, and also were it not for the fact, that up to the date of your arrival at Washington & to the present time, I have been in correspondence with Mr Williams & Capt Weaver, with whom I knew you conferd daily & to them, have given all the information I had of interest from time to time. Swartwout, who went on some time since, must also have conferd fully with you, and aided you all in his power—& I knew you saw daily the Courier & Enquirer which contains the latest & most correct information from N. Orleans & from Mexico, & being well acquainted with the sources of its information, informd. Capt Weaver that the statements in that paper might be generally relied upon. I have sent you Specially several numbers and requested Hoskins[1] to do Daily, which I presume has been done. Day before yesterdays Courier, contains some interesting information, which I sent you, and shall also send you that of today, both going to shew, the entirely confused state of Mexico, dissatisfaction of a great portion of the people, & the great probability of an immediate revolution. I have also sent occasionally papers to Mr Walker[2] of the Senate. I also enjoined upon a Dr Batonin[3] to see you thro' Mr. Weaver to whom he had letters of introduction. This Gentleman came from Vera Cruz in the last packet, and was to have been in Washington, during the last week, having been delayed in Baltimore by loss of his baggage. I well knew that his information plainly & frankly given to Mr Forsyth & Genl Jackson, would produce a very favourable effect on your affairs, and therefore requested Capt Weaver to introduce him to you that you might both confer with him, and apply the information obtained where it would be most advantageous &c &c. I hope the result has equalled my expectations, and to infer from the tenor of my letters from Mr Williams, Still at Phila. & to whom I write today in reference to the Invincible &c, &c, &c. I am happy to perceive by the movements, calls for information and resolutions of both Houses, that much interest is felt in & out of doors in relation to your independence & when I heard the other day a further message was in preparation for congress on this topic I argued favourably; I also saw with pleasure the bearing of Mr Weaver's review: Hoped for some good from St. Anna's arrival & finally have brought myself to believe you will Succeed. I await Mr Swartwout's return tonight with much interest to learn further particulars & details. I sent you yesterday a Star of Tuesday, containing Breckinridges Letter on Texas & Recognition, message,[4] &c and tho' it bears hard on the President & Van B[uren]. yet there are some new & singular views taken of the question. I could only obtain 1 number. When you see it, you can judge how far it can be made available, with some persons, in the discussion. I have been trying to get Hoskins to take up the matter, and make an article by certain Extracts from Morfits Report and also from the Report to the Senate of So. Carolina by Gov. Hamilton & Mr. Poinsett, having furnished him with the above papers, and he has promised me to do so but then his many occupations and the crowded state of his columns have thus far prevented. I shall continue to urge it upon him, until done. I am sorry circumstances will finally prevent Mr W[illiam]s from coming to New York a thing we have all been Expecting for 2 or three weeks—I shall do all I can, to relieve the Invincible under the advice & direction of Mr Williams, as he requests me—tho' cannot until I can ascertain the views of claimants, say whether they will take Script or not. I perceive Mr Almonte is with you and presume Gen S Anna also. It is stated (I know not how correctly) that he is coming here to Embark. Of the policy of this measure I cannot judge, not knowing his or your general views, or objects. I should think however that his departure hence for V. Cruz as stated should be duly weighed before carried into Effect and I suggest to you whether it will not be best, for him to remain at all Events, until the issue of the question soon to be decided by congress in relation to recognition. If the recognition is carried, then certain things might be done or if not a different course might be the better policy. This is conjectural however; as I said before being in the dark about the arrangements, objects, plans of accomplishing them &c &c I cannot well judge—see Courier & Enquirer of Tuesday and today for latest news from the South and most authentic. I am expecting Ann Eliza from Vera Cruz every day—to have sailed from 25th Decr. to 1st Inst. She will doubtless bring interesting intelligence, of which I will promptly advise You.

Very truly & cordially yours
James Treat

✦✦✦

ALS. Tx, TLP.

1. Edwin Hoskin [vice Hoskins], the commercial and foreign editor of James Watson Webb's New York *Courier and Enquirer.*

2. Robert J. Walker (1801–1869), US senator from Mississippi, 1835–1845, was a leader in the movement to recognize and annex Texas to the union.

3. Batonin, not otherwise identified.

4. Perhaps James Douglas Breckinridge (d. 1849), a Louisville, Kentucky, attorney and former member of Congress (1821–1823), but the letter is not found.

R. P. Waller to William H. Wharton

Fredericksburg Va Jany. 20th '37

Dear Sir

I take advantage of your present residence in Washington to make some enquiries in regard to my relation Edwin Waller[1] in behalf of his father and other relations—Where is he now living, what is he doing, did he lose any of his negroes & was he in the battle of San Jacinto? I congratulate you on your new appointment as well as your country for the justice in her selection. I was afraid from the tone of the Presidents message this would not find you in Washington but as the appearance of Santa Anna at the Capitol will probably make some change in the aspect of affairs I have since thought you would await his arrival & further advice from your government. If the affairs of Texas could have been as far advanced at the last session, her recognition would have been certain but such is the extreme jealousy of the north of the growing strength of the South that they will never add the possibility of an increase, and I am thinking the power behind the throne (V[an]. B[uren].) has infused into the old man notions contrary to the feelings & principles that have heretofore governed him. I am still in bad health from chronic Bronchitis but my physician assures me I am recovering—unless this state of health prevents me I still have in view the establishment of a press in Texas to be conducted upon a scale to claim patronage both there and in this country. I would be glad to have your opinion of such an establishment. I am sorry I could not have remained in Texas during the revolution but a morbid & deranged state of health disqualified me for any thing & even indisposed me reflect seriously for myself. I frequently think of the kindness & hospitality of yourself & Mrs W. to me while I Staid in Texas. I remember it as I always shall with the liveliest gratitude. I hope your engagements will permit you to answer this soon—on account of Edwin if none other I pray you to answer it as soon as convenient.

I am respectfully your friend &c

R. P. Waller

P. S. Where is John [Wharton]—was he in the San Jacinto battle & in what capacity—did you lose any property?

W

✦✦✦

ALS. Tx, TLP. R. P. Waller is probably Robert Page Waller (1791–1872). The Wallers were a prominent Virginia family.

1. Edwin Waller (1800–1881), originally from Virginia, emigrated to Texas from Missouri in 1831. He took part, and was wounded, in the fight between Texas Anglo

colonists and a Mexican force at Velasco in 1832. Waller was a member of the 1835 Consultation and the Convention of 1836, where he served on the committee that drafted the Texas Constitution. He was the first mayor of Austin and was chief justice of Austin County, 1844–1856. He represented Austin County at the secession convention of 1861.

Memucan Hunt to William H. Wharton

New Orleans 20th Jany. 1837

Dear Sir,

I have been appointed by his Excellency the President of the Republic of Texas associate Minister Plenipotentiary, near the Govt of the U. States, at Washington. I feel honored at bearing this honorab[le] relation to my adopted country, as the associate of one whose character and ability is so well fitted for th[is] distinguished station. Allow me to hope and believe, that the utmost harmony and good feeling will be cherished between us during our associate relations. I seize the earliest oportunity to inform you of my arrival here, and to state that I will be with you as early as practicable. I have additional instructions, to those already furnished you, from our government.[1]

I have the honor, to be, with the most distinguished consideration,

your mo. obt. svt
Memucan Hunt

✦✦✦

ALS. Tx, TLP.

1. See letters included earlier in this collection: Henderson to Hunt, December 31, 1836, and Henderson to Hunt, January 12, 1837.

James Pinckney Henderson to William H. Wharton and Memucan Hunt

Department of State
Columbia, Texas
January 21st. 1837.

To the Honble Messrs. Wharton & Hunt

It again becomes my duty to instruct you upon the subject of Indian hostilities in Texas, which may extend in future so far as to disturb the peace and safety of the people of the United States in violation of the Treaty concluded between the Government of the United States and the Republic of Mexico on the __ day of ___ A.D. 183_.[1]

It is desired by the President that you should continue to urge the propriety on the part of the Government of the United States of stationing a sufficient number of Regulars in the vicinity of the Town of Nacogdoches to keep the several tribes of Indians in subjection and prevent their commencing of hostilities on the whites, as they know no distinction of Territory and if they once commenced hostilities in Texas it inevitably will extend to the citizens of the United States. You can assure the Government of the United States that this Government has the fullest assurance and the most satisfactory evidence of which the nature of the case will admit that the cherokees and their associate Bands have undertaken to assist the Mexicans in overrunning and destroying the citizens of Texas. That they formed a treaty with Mexico during the last summer at Matamoras by their chiefs and head Men by which they engaged to pretend friendship to the whites until the Mexicans Army by their next invasion shall have reached the Gaudilupe River at which time they are bound to commence hostilities against the people of Texas in the east so as to prevent them from joining the main Army.[2]

General Urea paid the said Chiefs at that time one thousand dollars in money and presents and at the same time gave them a draft in New Orleans for five thousand dollars to be paid in arms and amunition. These Indians have also undertaken to unite with them in the war; the Northern Indians, as well as those of the Praires, many of these Indian Tribes inhabit that region of country bordering on the waters of Red River and the United States so that that the safety of families living on the borders of Texas, but in the United States must necessarily be exposed to their cruelties in the event of their commencing hostilities.

You are also instructed to say that the Caddos doubtless encouraged by the said treaty have already committed several murders; that about two months since they murdered Captn Beaston and several persons who were in company with him on the Gaudaloupe River.[3] It is also reported to this Government from undoubted sources that the Caddos have within the last two weeks cruelly murdered a family about thirty miles north of Nashville consisting of an old man, his wife and seven children and about the same time killed two men who belonged to the rangers in that region;[4] This intelligence reached the Executive by express on yesterday, urge the propriety to the Government of the United States of immediately stationing at least five hundred men at or near Nacogdoches; As this request is made by the Government de facto of Texas and its consent given to the measure, the Government of the United States will be fully authorized in this cause. By the law of Nations our Government is not bound to look beyond the powers in possession of the Government with which it acts—it need not inquire who ought to be in power but who de facto has the administration of the Government at the time of action, If however the Independence of Texas is acknowledged by the time you receive these instructions it will remove all difficulty upon this point but let not this event cause you to relax your exertions to effect this desirable object.

Your own perfect knowledge of the situation of the Country and the great danger to be apprehended from these Indians will of course enable you to make use of many arguments to persuade the Government of the United States of the necessity of adopting the course recommended.

Receive the assurance of the high regard and esteem which the President and people of Texas entertain for the President and people of the United States.

Yours With Great Respect &c
J. Pinckney Henderson
Acting Secy of State

✦✦✦

ALS. Tx, TLP. Published in *DCRT,* 1: 177-178.

1. The writer left blank space for the insertion of the date. Article 33 of the US-Mexico Treaty of April 5, 1831, obligated the countries to "by all means in their power, maintain peace and harmony among the several Indian nations who inhabit the lands adjacent to the lines and rivers which form the boundaries of the two countries" and to "restrain, by force, all hostilities and incursions" by Indians living within their boundaries (*Treaties,* 3: 544–556). The whole treaty is at pp. 599–640. Article 33 appears at pp. 622–623.

2. According to the correspondent of the New Orleans *Commercial Bulletin* in Matamoras on July 1, 1836 (published in the *Telegraph and Texas Register,* August 16, 1836), fourteen or fifteen chiefs met with General Urrea and Colonel Ugartechea in June to discuss joining the Mexicans in a war of extermination against Texas.

3. On September 21, 1836, Collin Beason [vice Beaston], Leander Beason, and Maxwell Steel were attacked by about forty Indians just after crossing the Guadalupe near Gonzales. Collin Beason and Steel were killed; Leander escaped (*TTR,* October 4, 1836).

4. Accounts involving conflicts between whites and Indians are often confused. The event described as occurring thirty miles north of Nashville-on-the-Brazos bears likeness to an attack on Fort Parker, near the headwaters of the Navasota River, on May 19, 1836, in which five persons (including "Elder" John Parker) were killed and five (including Cynthia Ann Parker) were taken captive. An attack did occur near Nashville on January 9, 1836, in which three persons were killed and two taken captive. On January 7, 1837, Texas Rangers under the command of George Erath engaged Indians at Elm Creek, near Little River, and two Rangers were killed.

Will K. Hill to William H. Wharton

New Orleans 21st Jany. '37.

Dr Sir

I take the liberty of recommending to your kind attention and consideration my friend General M. Hunt, whom you will perceive has been appointed by the President of Texas your associate minister plenipotentiary near our government.

He is a gentleman, and a scholar, and moreover the unwavering and zealous friend of Texas, and will be found coopperating with yourself in the promotion of all things for the benefit of his adopted Country.

I am now waiting the arrival of your brother John A. Wharton who is expected here dayly, with whom I have business, as soon as he arrives, I shall pursue my Journey to Texas.

Wishing you health, happiness and success in the cause you are engaged—

I am dear Sir your friend & very humble Servt.

Will K Hill

+++

ALS. Tx, TLP. Will K. Hill, not otherwise identified.

Henry H. Williams to William H. Wharton

Baltimore Jany 21st 1837

Dear Sir

I have just recd the inclosed slip by Express mail from New Orleans it may be of service to have it inserted in the [Washington] Globe,

I regret exceedingly to lern of the death of General Austin.

Yours in haste
Henry H. Williams

Sunday Morning

Since I wrote the above I have received a letter from my Brother, dated Columbia, 24 December, containing a certifficate of Scrip in The Texas Rail Road Navigation & Bank Co, as it is possible you may not have received letters so late I anex the names of Stock Holders S M Williams 1/16 J K Allen 1 A C Allen 1 Henderson 1 J & J Collingsworth + 2 Walter C White 1 Mos[e]ley Baker 1 T F McKinney 1 Archer 1 Wharton's 2 Green & his Brother 2 Christy 1.[1] Each sixteenth being 3100 Shares of 100 each, I fear this Co. is got up on too large a scale to go into successful operation for some time to come.

Yours H. H. W.

+++

ALS. Tx, TLP.

1. John Kirby Allen (1810–1838) and Augustus Chapman Allen (1806–1864) came to Texas from New York in 1832. Augustus Allen purchased the schooner *Brutus* in New Orleans and sold it to the Texas navy at cost. The Allens paid the cost of fitting out the vessel. The brothers engaged in many business enterprises, particularly land speculation. In 1836 they purchased land on Buffalo Bayou, established the town of Houston, and convinced Congress to locate the capital there. They also invested in Galveston property. Moseley Baker (1802–1848), the founder and editor of the Montgomery, Alabama, *Advertiser,* moved to Texas about 1833 or 1835. He was a member of the 1835 Consultation and fought in the revolution. As a member of the First Texas Congress, 1836–1837, he sought the impeachment of President Houston. He was also a member of the Third Texas Congress, 1838–1839. Thomas Jefferson Green had five brothers; it is unclear which of the brothers is referred to here.

Andrew Janeway Yates to William H. Wharton

22d Jan 1837

Dear Sir,

Your favor of the 9th instant came to hand by due course of Mail, and as we are anxiously looking for the communication of the arrival of Santa Anna at Washington City, I was surprised you said nothing about it.

You will see in the [New Orleans Commercial] Bulletin about the 15th a piece on the subject of annexation of Texas by a Treaty with Mexico, signed "Philo Texas," the course pursued by the president is full of mystery and disappointment here, and the credit of the Nation suffers materially under it.

Col. Minard[1] has not yet arrived in this City. I look for him daily, but until his arrival I cannot leave for the North.

Gen. Hunt passed through here yesterday on his way to the North, as Envoy Extraordinary but what his extraordinary Mission he has, I did not know.

Please address me in your next at Augusta Georgia.

I remain very respectfully, & truly yours

A. J. Yates

✦✦✦

ALS. Tx, TLP. There is no indication of where the letter was written.

1. It is not clear if Yates refers to Pierre J. Menard or his cousin Michel Branamour Menard (1805–1858), also an emigrant from Canada, Indian trader, and investor in Galveston property.

Samuel Swartwout to William H. Wharton

New York Sunday 22nd Jan 1837

My dear Col.

At ten oclock the night before last I reached home and found my wife and daughter well.[1] Mrs. S put into my hands your kind letter of the 8th inst. for which I desire you to accept my thanks, altho I had before heard its contents from you in Washington. The mails of yesterday from N. Orleans brought us the unhappy news of the death of our mutual friend Col Austin. I assure you, my dear Wharton, that I feel this misfortune not only as a friend of Texas, but as a personal friend of the deceased. I had imbibed the highest opinion of Col Austin's character and amiable qualities and I assure you that I feel his death as a personal calamity. His worth is remembered here and cherished by all those who had the pleasure of his acquaintance.

I am most anxious to hear the results of Santa Anna's interview with Genl. Jackson & your opinion of it. Get your Independence acknowledged & then to the Devil with the Mexican Brute. I am not disposed to be cross, but I am in a damnable hurry to have your country acknowledged free & Independent. I have the Globe of this morning or rather of yesterday received this morning, but don't see it yet. If you can say any thing to encourage us, do so my good friend. I have read "Jefferson" & find he understands his subject well & treats it like an independent patriot—You will succeed—nothing can prevent it, but V[an] B[uren]'s friends—And, if they do what should be their fate? But say nothing of me in relation to them—If they <u>dare</u> they will defeat you, so look out for them. Let Mr. Walker at them and Mr. Benton.[2] They can do you great good in that quarter.

I presume that Santa Anna is the byson of the day or rather the blood-hound or Tyger of the hour. I dare say he is treated with attention & Almonte also—Let me hear about them. If you are too lazy & Col Wolf will take the trouble, I will acknoledge his kindness in the most respectful terms.

You speak of coming on home with Mrs Wharton & your son[3]—That you must certainly do, but not a step, my good friend, until we have arranged matters to your satisfaction first in Washington. Don't show your ugly face here until you can produce the parchment at the same time. Besides Mrs. W. need not stir a foot until she can come in the steam-boat line, which will be after the 4th of March. Present my respectful compliments to Mrs. Wharton and Col Wolf and believe me most sincerely and always yours

S. Swartwout

✦✦✦

ALS. Tx, TLP.

1. Swartwout was married to Alice Ann Cooper (1789–1874); their daughter was Mary Colden Swartwout (1820–1864).

2. Thomas Hart Benton (1782–1858), US senator from Missouri in the Seventeenth through Thirty-First Congresses (1821–1850) and a member of the US House of Representatives in the Thirty-Third Congress (1853–1854). Benton later opposed the annexation of Texas and a Texas boundary that extended to the Rio Grande.

3. John Austin Wharton (1828–1865) studied law and established a successful law practice at Brazoria, in addition to owning a plantation. He served with the Eighth Texas Cavalry (Terry's Texas Rangers) and rose to the rank of major general. He was killed by George W. Baylor in Galveston during a quarrel.

John Fisher to William H. Wharton

New York Jany 23, 1837

Sir

Altho not personally latterly, but formerly slightly acquainted with you which may have passed your remembrance, I take the liberty as one who has some little feeling and interest in Texas to address this communication to you with regard to the Sch[oone]r Invincible. I have been waiting here since shortly after her arrival at this place, calculating to return in her and at the same time have an opportunity of intercepting one of the Brigs built in Baltimore having previously ascertained they would be good & lawful prizes, I have lost frequent opportunities of returning to Texas but owing to its being reported from time to time that Mr. Williams would be here with the necessary means to defray the expenses of this vessel, I have been flattered with the prospect of getting off immediately. Upon your arrival at Washington I calculated something would be done immediately, if a proper representation of the situation of the Vessel had been made, but as nothing has been done and as I believe but few if any attached to the Vessel know what is intended to be done—Will you if you know anything relative to it give me such information as you can or as you may deem it prudent to give me, as soon after you receive this as will suit your convenience.

Respectfully yr obt svt
Jno. Fisher

address me care
13 St John corner Maiden Lane & Front Street

+++

ALS. Tx, TLP. John Fisher (1800–1865) arrived in Texas from Virginia in 1832 and settled in Gonzales. He signed the Texas Declaration of Independence on March 2, 1836, but returned to Virginia in 1837.

Samuel May Williams to William H. Wharton

Philadelphia 23d. January 1837

My Dear Sir,

On the 17th inst. I was favored with yours of 15th. forwarded to me from Baltimore by my brother H. H. Williams. I was truly gratified at the contents, and thank you for it. Had I been able to communicate any thing pleasing relative to the Invincible, I would earlier have acknowledged its receipt, but from day to day have I waited under the hope that on the subject of that Vessel I might to be able to give you some pleasing information. But still clouds and darkness hang over her.

The flattering prospects presented in your letter relative to the recognition of our Independence afforded me so much true satisfaction that I communicated the contents to our friend Treat in New York—I trust in God that your exertions will be crowned with success. And assure you that I fondly hope they may be—first for the general good that will be produced—and second that you may be permitted to bring about that desirable want as a just recompense for your exertions and perseverance—to which I will add my fond hope that in a political point it may yield you a golden harvest of public opinion at home.

I have recd through Mr. Treat the documents accts and vouchers of the expenses of the Schooner Brutus settled by Mr. Sayre and paid by him $8,338 30/100 which with the 4500$ advanced by Treat, Swartwout and others, and the interest will cause her expenses in N. York to exceed $13,000. Mr Sayre also paid on a/c of the Invincible $1206 76/100—and there remains to be paid for her $6857 12/100 of this about $2750 can be paid in Scrip and the balance must be cash or short City paper interest added—Added to which in order to send her to sea; for advance to officers, shipping a crew provisions &c $4,700 is required of which from 1,000$ to $1500 can only be paid by Scrip the balance cash—so that the prospect at the present stands thus $11,551 is now required of which $7,300 must be cash—Treat informs me that at the present there are no purchasers out doors for scrip. Yet expresses as his opinion that a recognition will produce them—unless purchasers of scrip could be found in that place, or in some other, promptly, I assure you that at the moment there is no hope of sending her off, for I cannot at this time raise the amount of cash necessary for that purpose; consequently some time more must elapse before that desirable and all paramount object can be effected. But you may rest assured that no exertions or contrivances on my part shall be wanting to produce it as speedily as for me is possible.

I have a little project on foot here for the sale of 80 Sections ($25,600) one tenth cash the balance 6 & 9 months. And though they are good men who talk of making the Company still they are shy and of course I cannot look upon the matter yet as certain—I have good hopes, and nothing more.

I have letters from Texas up to 24th Decemr. they are business letters and of course do not contain any political matters, every thing going on well, and all appear in good spirits. You of course have advices equally late and of a different tenor, so that you are well apprised of the particular state of things at home.

For two days I have been unhappy on acct of the information of Austin's death—I may be permitted to lament him for he was the truest and best friend I ever had. I wish he could have been spared long enough to have seen the Country for which he has undergone so much, and toiled so arduously—declared and acknowledged free and Independent.

I trust my brother H.H.W. has attended to your monied wants. You can treat him with the same freedom and confidence that you would me in that particular.

I am pleased to learn that Mrs Wharton is with you and in the enjoyment of good health. but regret that Waller was indisposed. I trust he is restored and that you are all blessed with good health. Please present me kindly to Mrs W and accept assurances of my esteem.

Truly and sincerely yr obt St
Samuel M. Williams

✦✦✦

ALS. Tx, TLP.

John Parvin to William H. Wharton

New York Jany 23d 1837

Dear Sir

I take the liberty, which please excuse of writing to you in regard to a claim which I conclude I have on the government of Texas for services rendered by my brother William,[1] who left his residence at Perry Houston Co., Geo. in Novr 1835 & joined a company from that place under the Command of Capt. Ward.[2] They arrived in Texas in the early part of December, was formed into a battalion & Capt Ward elected Colonel, when my brother came under Capt Winns[3] Company

& acted as Secretary to him which probably entitled him to more pay than a private.

It is hardly necessary to say what was the fate of Col Ward & Fanning & their men as they are fresh in the breast of every man interested in the cause of Texas—By a law passed at Washington the lawful heir of those fallen in battle are entitled to 640 acres of lands as Bounty also by a law passed at San Phillipe, a single man was entitled to a third of a League—In regard to the proper mode of making my claim I ask for your advice As I am the only surviving Brother of William & have all his letters to corroborate my statements, some of which are written in Texas while [o]n Camp duty I trust it will prove all sufficient. Any information [y]ou can give me will much oblige

You ob Serv
John Parvin
303 Pearl St

✦✦✦

ALS. Tx, TLP. John Parvin, not otherwise identified.

1. William Parvin (d. 1836), not otherwise identified.

2. William Ward (d. 1836) organized the Georgia Battalion of Texas volunteers in November 1835 in Macon. On their arrival in Texas, the unit was incorporated into Col. James W. Fannin's command as the Georgia Battalion of the First Regiment of Texas Volunteers. Most of the men were killed by orders of Santa Anna at Goliad on March 27, 1836.

3. James C. Winn (d. 1836).

Thomas Toby and Brother to Samuel May Williams, with Enclosure

New Orleans 24 January 1837

Dr Sir,

Herewith we hand you Copy of a letter received yesterday the latest date from Tampico.

It is from a friend of the writers who promises to give us what is passing in Mexico as far as he can obtain information. His views correspond with ours & we do not believe Texas has any thing to fear from Mexico.

Our last dates from Texas, everything was very quiet. The trade is encreasing, two vessels sailed last night for the Brazos. Genl Hunt left a few days ago for Washington & will or ought to reach there about 5 Feby. The Caroline has just arrived bringing dates to 20 Inst. Nothing new all was tranquil.

Vy Repectfully, Your Obt. Servants
Thomas Toby & Bro.

P.S. W. C. White[1] requests us to say your family are all well as he made particular inquiry about them—

✦✦✦

ALS. Tx, TLP.

1. Walter C. White (d. 1837), a merchant at San Felipe de Austin.

Enclosure: Unattributed and Unsigned to Thomas Toby

Tampico 7 January 1837

Dr Sir

The Aft[ernoon]. shall send up to St Louis Potosi the first mail day. The news of Santa Annas release is far from being pleasing intelligence to Mexico and there is not any convention with the Government of the U.S. that he may enter into on his part, that will be fulfilled. Bustamente his mortal enemy, has arrived from Europe and is in Mexico—here we have about 1200 men in good condition, destined nowhere now, I should suppose. The General in Command[1] is Santa Annas greatest enemy and here he would be received at the cannons mouth. Bravo[2] is still at Monte Rea, where he is now likely to remain. Santa Annas release will probably put the whole Country in a bloody revolution and as things stand now there is nothing at present to fear to the parties that somewhat interest you. I do not think it likely that I shall be here very long, so that there is no occasion to write. The Mexican Navy appears to be laying up as ordinary at Vera Cruz. Business pretty fair & 700.000 $ expected in five or six days, from 2 to 300.000 of which will come by the Sch[oone]r Cora and Danl H. Miller. From what I can learn I think in the end everything will turn out better than you expect, however I will be better able to inform you of the prospect a little later.

Unattributed and Unsigned. Tx, TLP.

1. José de Urrea (1797–1849) had opposed the withdrawal of Mexican troops from Texas after Santa Anna was captured. He took command of the Mexican army on June 6, 1836.

2. Nicolás Bravo (1786–1854), from a Creole family in Guerrero, took part in the revolution against Spain. He replaced Urrea as the head of the Mexican Army of the North.

Oliver Hill Prince to William H. Wharton

Athens Ga January 24. 1837

Dear Sir

I wrote to a friend in the senate to enquire whether you had arrived at Washington; & if you was there, for him to inform me if he knew, how long you would probably remain. Soon after the letter was mailed, I saw your arrival announced in the papers, & in due time my correspondent answered me to say that you would probably remain till the end of the session. I hope your stay may be prolonged beyond that time, if not as the minister of an <u>acknowledged</u> Republic as I could wish (however faint the hope may be) still on some other business public or private. For in that event I would arrange to take Washington in my way as I go Northward with my family in the spring; and thus not only have the opportunity of seeing you & Mrs Wharton myself, but secure to my wife the long desired, and scarcely hoped for pleasure of again embracing her cousin.

Please let me know whether there will be any prospect of seeing you there in the latter part of April or early in May. And any information you can give us of our friends in Texas, will be most gladly received.

I have written to them repeatedly, and have <…> fears that several of my letters have failed to [re]ach their destination.

Finding at last a <…> undoubtedly safe, I <……..> (if you [wil]l <…>

<…remainder of page damaged by water and disintegration…> enhanced if possible by the various dangers & trials of her eventful

life. Please to tell her that if she has forgotten me as she probably has, I have a better memory old as I am: that is to say, I remember her as she then was—a child. I hope to see whether I can recognize the grown woman.

Very respectfully sir Yr obt Servt
O. H. Prince

PS. I enclose this in a letter I am writing to Colo W. C. Dawson[1] member from this state of the House of Rep. I recommended you to make his acquaintance if you have not already that pleasure. It will not only be a pleasure, but probably an advantage. He is in for the ~~next Congress~~ two sessions of the next congress, and I know of no person there whose debonair manners, active habits and long experience in the bearings and temper and under currents of legislative bodies, may stand you in better stead; particularly after he shall have had time to extend his acquaintance.

✦✦✦

ALS. Tx, TLP. Oliver Hill Prince (1782–1837), a lawyer from Macon, Georgia, was elected to the US Senate in November 1828 and served until 1829. He gave up the practice of law in 1830 to become editor of the *Georgia Journal*. He died in a shipwreck off the coast of North Carolina.

1. William Crosby Dawson (1798–1856), an attorney from Greensboro, Georgia, served in the US House of Representatives as a states'-rights advocate and a Whig in the Twenty-Fourth through Twenty-Seventh Congresses, 1835–1842, and in the US Senate as a Whig in the Thirty-First through Thirty-Third Congresses, 1851–1854.

Fleming T. Wells to William H. Wharton

New York. 24. Jan. 1837

Dear Sir,

Through the liberality of some of our friends we are enabled to lay before [you] a more favourable account of the state of our affairs, than was rendered to Mr. Williams last week.

General Austin's Map of Texas with Parts of Adjoining States . . . from the Observations of of General Téran of the Mexican Army by Henry S. Tanner. Published in Pocket Map Texas; Philadelphia, 1840. Compiled by Stephen F. Austin with engineers John and William W. Warr, Philadelphia. 28.5" x 23.3".

Salem. July [illegible]. [illegible].

To the foregoing letter from Capt James W. [illegible] which I recommend to the consideration of any to whom it may be presented as a testimonial of a Shipmaster of the highest Respectability, it gives me pleasure to add that the opinion expressed by Capt [illegible] in favour of Mr Lincoln was confirmed by Capt Willis (now deceased) who commanded the Ship [illegible] in which Mr Lincoln performed his last voyage in the capacity of Clerk, as I understand from [illegible] sources. Without being able to speak of Mr Lincoln from any personal acquaintance I have no doubt from the information which I have obtained by enquiring of others, that he is well fitted to perform the duties of assistant Supercargo, or Clerk, or of an officer of a Vessel, & that he wants only a little experience to be entirely qualified to take charge of a Vessel & cargo. [illegible] respect to his character & habits, as well as his talents and education, I believe that he will prove himself worthy of full confidence & that he will not fail to give satisfaction to his employers.

Signed — S. C. Phillips

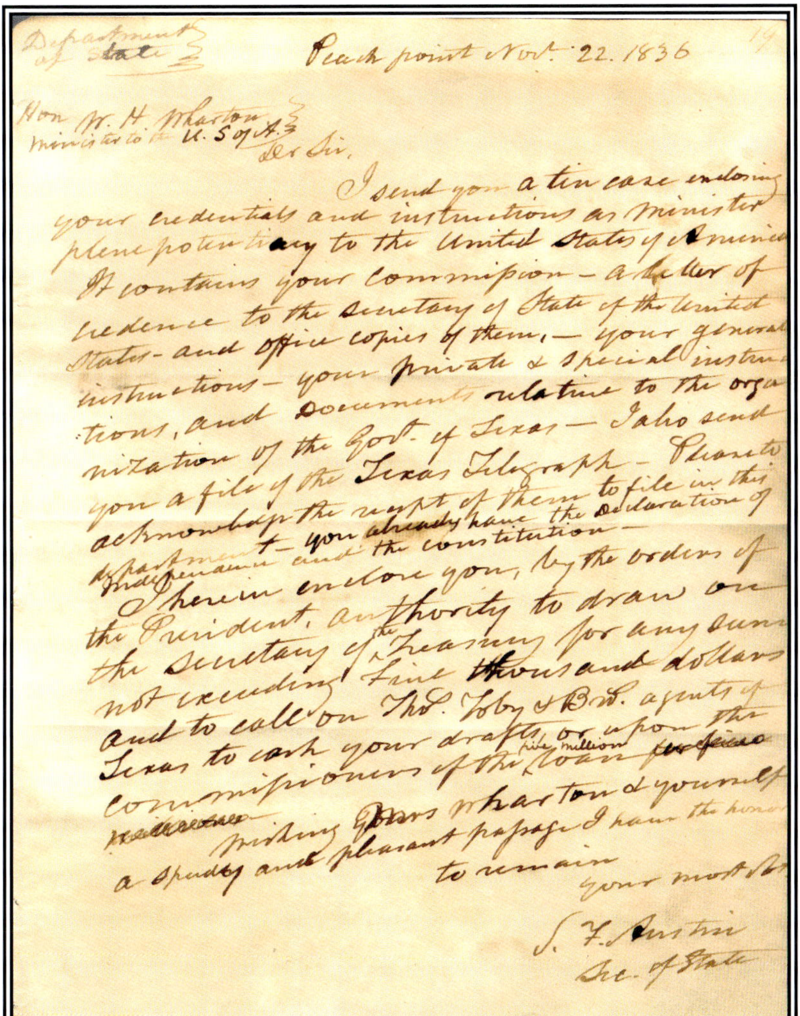

Department of State

Peach point Novr. 22. 1836

19

Hon W. H. Wharton
Minister to the U. S. of A.

Dr Sir,

I send you a tin case inclosing your credentials and instructions as minister plenepotentiary to the United States of America. It contains your commission – a letter of credence to the Secretary of State of the United States – and office copies of them, – your general instructions – your private & special instructions, and documents relative to the organization of the Govt. of Texas – I also send you a file of the Texas Telegraph – Please to acknowledge the receipt of them to file in this department – you already have the declaration of independence and the constitution –

I herein inclose you, by the orders of the President, authority to draw on the Secretary of the Treasury for any sum not exceeding five thousand dollars and to call on Thos. Toby & Brs. agents of Texas to cash your drafts or upon the commissioners of the five million loan

wishing Mrs Wharton & yourself a speedy and pleasant passage I have the honor to remain

Your most obt. Sr.

S. F. Austin
Sec. of State

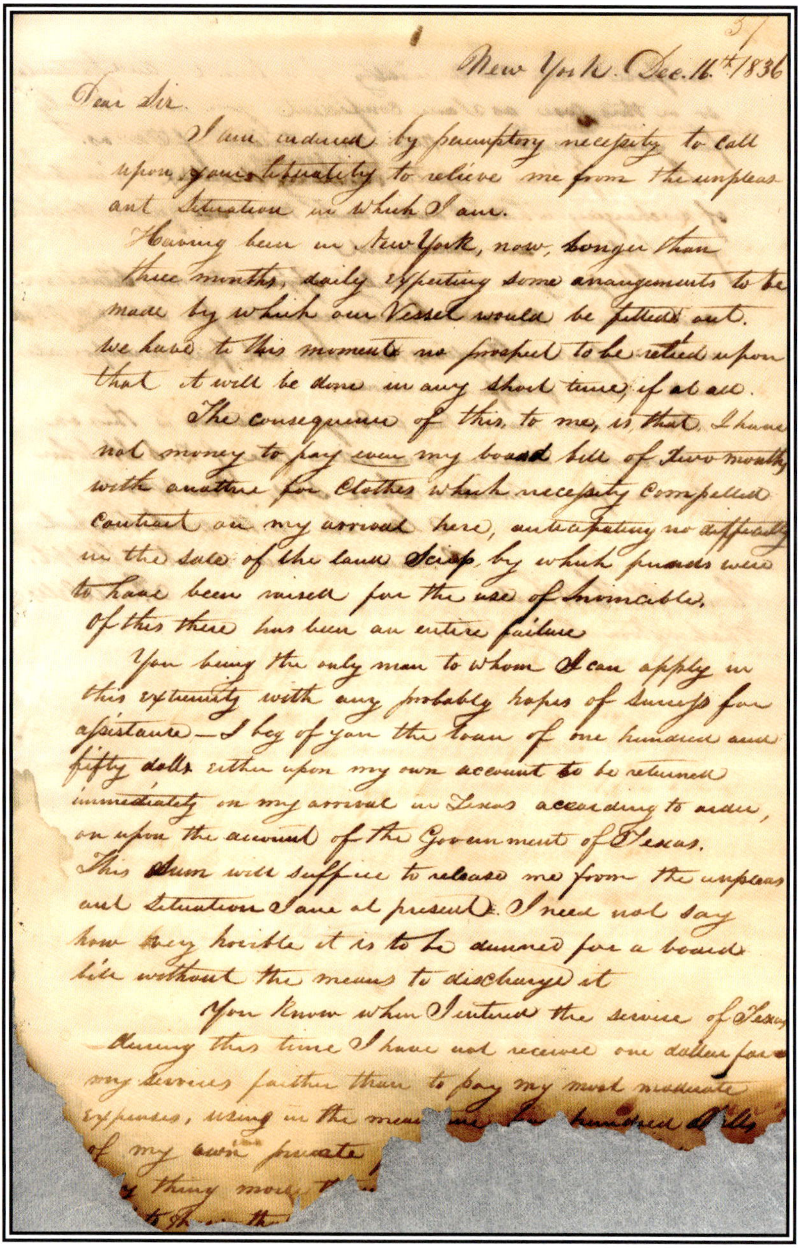

37

New York Dec. 16th 1836

Dear Sir

I am induced by peremptory necessity to call upon your liberality to relieve me from the unpleasant situation in which I am.

Having been in New York, now, longer than three months, daily expecting some arrangements to be made by which our Vessel would be fitted out. we have to this moment no prospect to be relied upon that it will be done in any short time, if at all.

The consequence of this, to me, is, that I have not money to pay even my board bill of two months, with another for Clothes which necessity compelled contract on my arrival here, anticipating no difficulty in the sale of the land Scrip, by which funds were to have been raised for the use of Invincible. Of this there has been an entire failure

You being the only man to whom I can apply in this extremity with any probable hopes of success for assistance—I beg of you the loan of one hundred and fifty dolls either upon my own account to be returned immediately on my arrival in Texas according to order, or upon the account of the Government of Texas. This sum will suffice to release me from the unpleasant situation I am at present. I need not say how very horrible it is to be dunned for a board bill without the means to discharge it

You know when I entered the service of Texas. During this time I have not received one dollar for my services farther than to pay my most moderate expenses, using in the mean [illegible] hundred Dolls of my own private [illegible]

[illegible] thing more [illegible]

[illegible]

impose upon the generosity of a friend - and particularly so in this case as I am confident you have to rely upon your own resourses for your expenses as the representative of Texas.

But imperious necessity and fearing my inability of discharging what I owe, and the consequent discredit of a failure, are paramount

I hope you will duly appreciate my situation and extend the aid I have requested for which I shall under infinite obligations, and will not fail to reciprocate in the most grateful manner.

Will you have the goodness to attend to this on its receipt, directing your letter, Care of B. S. St. John Corner front Maiden Lane Sts, New York,

I am Sir, with much Respect
& Esteem Your most. Obt. Svt.
H. T. Wiles

Hon. W. H. Wharton
Washington City D.C.

Old Va.
Hardiman Co.

The Hon. William H. Wharton,

Sir

The undersigned, hopes you will pardon the liberty he takes in addressing the following—
My Step Son, a Mr John Hoskins left home in September was a year for the purpose of going to K.y. He went through Nashville, at which time, I think I saw from the News papers you were there— In the June previous he was in K.y. and if I mistake not became acquainted with you in some of the towns of that State.
In our conversations he spoke of you, and the cause in which you were engaged— I have thought it probable, that being a well wisher to the success of the Texian Cause he went from Nashville as a Volunteer. If you have any knowledge of a Gentleman by that Name, about 22 years of age, well educated, of Gentlemanly address, spare made, you would confer a favour on his Mother who is devotedly attached to him, and whose absence makes her miserable, by answering this, and also oblige his friends and connexions.

I remain yours very respectfully, and wish you success in the cause of the Texian Republic

Edward Willoughby Kenny

December 27th 1836
P. Office
Middleburgh
Hardiman
West Ten.

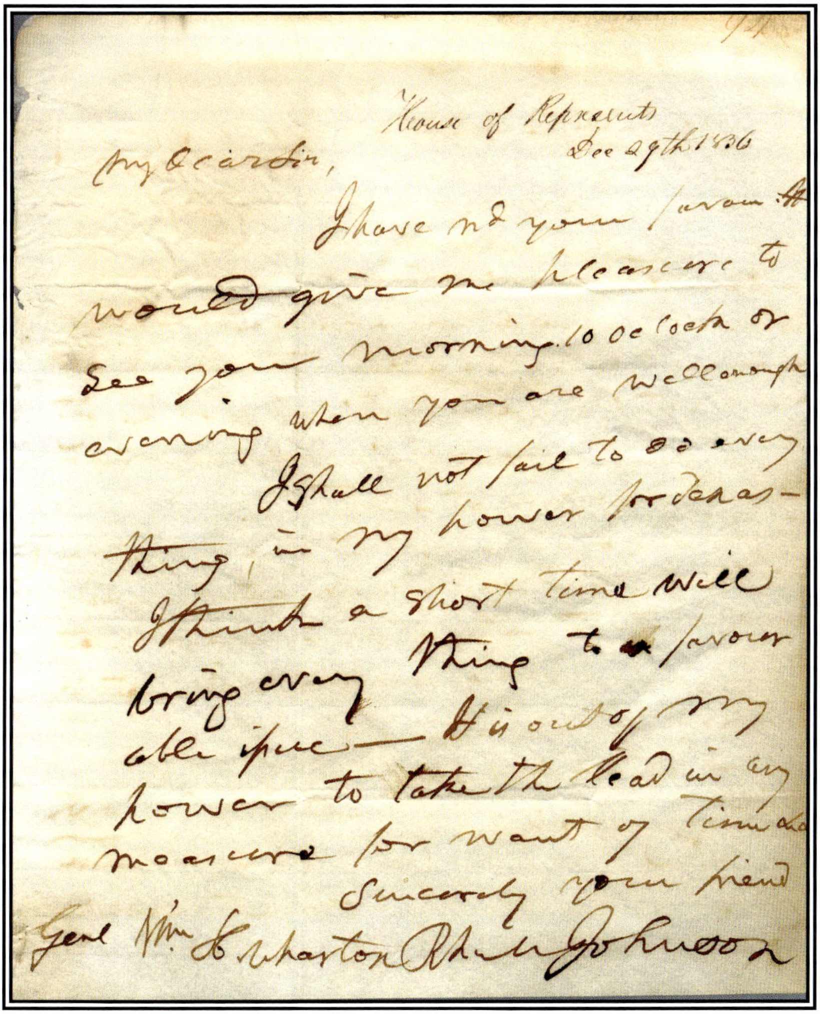

House of Represents
Dec 29th 1836

My Dear Sir,

I have red your favour it would give me pleasure to see you morning 10 oclock or evening when you are well enough

I shall not fail to do every thing in my power for Texas-

I think a short time will bring every thing to a favour able issue— It is out of my power to take the lead in any measure for want of time &c

Sincerely your friend

Genl Wm H Wharton Rh M Johnson

373

Waterloo N.Y. 1837 March 23d

Sir I transmit to your honoralbe consideration the followin draft of a ball as invented by myself it is calculated for the distruction of shipping and fortifications of all kinds. You will observe on the right end a spring which is let into the end and covered with a cap so that it is inclosed and protected by the cheeks on either side and by the cap on the end. the [illegible] that is marked No 1st is hung on a pivit and shuts down in no 2d and when discharged from a cannon is thrown as I as you see ~~the~~ The end marked No 3 is calculated to strike first and when it penetrats to ~~the~~ spring number 1st it explodes the ball being filled with powder it destroys what ever it hits and thus renders your enemies at your mercy I have a model now made and having shown it to several they unanimously concur in the belief of its successful operation If you should concur in the same opinion and will let me know it, and can give me any incouragement of a station in your Navy or Army it shall be at your command as well as myself

Yours respectfully

W. F. Delano

I am instructed by Capt. Brown to give you the following additional information—

That $4500 of the Invincible' bill can be discharged by Land Scrip at .50 cents. That Mr. Augustus Whitlock[1] a responsible man, and to whom about $1200 of the above Amt. is due, agrees to pay the other bills of the Invincible Amounting to about $2000 that can be discharged by paper at 4 mos.—and further to supply provisions necessary to fit out Amounting to about $1500 provided that double the Amt. of Scrip is placed in his hands as collatteral Security (for the last two Amts) until sufficient scrip can be sold to pay them or they are otherwise discharged.

There is also a prospect that about $2000 of scrip can be sold for cash, upon this however you must not rely. Thus you see the debts of the vessel at least can be discharged provided you authorize the arrangement above stated.

We address ourselves to you and expect you to attend to us—upon your exertions rests our only dependence. Mr Williams does not even favour us with a reply to our communications. We consequently reasonably conclude he does [not] interest himself in the matter as he has not aided us heretofore.

Mr. Treat is not authorized to sell a less Amt. of Scrip than is sufficient to refit the Invincible completely. Neither is he authorized to afford us the common necessaries of life. We have confidence in you to believe that some aid will be afforded to effect our relief, and hope you say definitely what you can do for us. That you have arduous duties of another and more important character to attend to we are well aware, and much regret the necessity produced as we conceive by the inattention of others, that drives us to interfere with your other duties by imposing upon your own business.

I am Sir, with much respect and esteem your most Obt. Svt.

F. T. Wells

✦✦✦

ALS. Tx, TLP.

1. Augustus Whitlock, not otherwise identified.

Henry Percy Brewster to Waddy Thompson

Eagle Island, Texas
Jany 24th 1837

Dear Sir

Isolated as we are here, and cut off from almost every source of correct information, I have presumed to trespass upon your time with a few lines. The deep anxiety which we all feel in the course of the United States in regard to the affairs of Texas, and the receipt a few days ago of the message of Gov McDuffie and the special message of Gen Jackson, makes the absence of correct and full information in regard to public feeling and opinion in the United States in relations to our cause painfully unpleasant. And I know of no one to whom I could appeal with such a certainty of obtaining correct general information as yourself.

Your warm and zealous efforts in our cause are known to all here, and deeply appreciated by them.[1] We are all utterly at a loss to conceive the causes which could have wrought such a revolution of sentiment in the mind of Gen Jackson, in regard to the recognition of our Independence. The general opinion is that it was owing to the unfavorable report of the secret agent sent here by him. This agent however before leaving here assured several gentlemen, that his report would be favorable in every respect; a few thousand mexican dollars tho' may have effected a radical change in his opinion. I witness the tone of the President's message with feelings of the deepest humiliation. he seems alike indifferent whether the cause of truth, justice, or human liberty ~~was~~ be promoted, so that the single object of concilitating or pleasing the powers of Europe ~~was~~ is effected; and what is most deeply to be deplored is, that the power of the Executive has grown so gigantic, that little is to be hoped were from the representatives of the people themselves. The bold and decided stand taken by yourself, and some of your colleagues has doubtless created in the mind of the President, some apprehensions of being caught in bad company should he adopt the same opinion. Regarding as he does, Mr Calhoun,[2] as the author of original as well as all subsequent sin, it may reasonably be supposed, that he would throw down his army, if not desert to the enemy, should he find himself fighting by his side in the same cause.

Two of our men who were prisoners at Matamoras escaped and arrived here a few days since; they say that there were Six Thousand troops in Matamoras, in high spirit and confident of success. They will doubtless commence operations shortly, if the release of Santa Anna, does not turn there attention home, and thereby retard their movement. Active preparations are being made to give them a becoming reception. Our army consisting of about 1200 men is well organized & disciplined. The efficient organization of the militia is in successful progress—We will doubtless be able to bring 4 or 5000 men into the field. The command of the army will be offered to Gen Hamilton. Gen Green left a few days ago bearing him a letter from the President tendering him the appointment. It is unecessary at this day to say any thing in regard to a country, with descriptions of which the papers of the Union have been teeming for the last year. Suffice to say that little unmerited praise can be bestowed upon this "land of the sun."

Write to me fully, if you please, and direct to Brazoria Texas, care of T Toby & Co of New Orleans.

Yrs truly
Henry Percy Brewster

Dr Archer requests me to present his respects to you, & hopes to see you in less than 6 months, and in the mean time would be happy to hear from you.

HPB

A report has just reached that our rangers on the frontier had a skirmish with a company of Indians in which they were rather worsted.[3] The Indians have concentrated to the number of some hundred upon ~~Indians~~ Robertson's Colony.

✦✦✦

ALS. Tx, TLP. Henry Percy Brewster (1816–1884) practiced law in South Carolina before coming to Texas in 1836, where he became Sam Houston's private secretary. Brewster was acting secretary of war and navy in David Burnet's administration. In 1836, he opened a legal practice in Brazoria. He later became a district attorney and state attorney general. Percy moved to Washington, DC in 1855, but returned to Texas at the onset of the Civil War, during which he served on the staff of

Albert Sidney Johnston and John Bell Hood. After the war he resumed law practice in San Antonio. Waddy Thompson (1798–1868), of South Carolina, was a representative in the Twenty-Fourth through Twenty-Sixth Congresses, from 1835 to 1841. He was US minister to Mexico from February 10, 1842, to March 9, 1844.

1. On April 27, 1836, Thompson proposed that Congress call on the president to provide the House with information about Texas, including "the character of the war now waged there," "massacres said to have been lately perpetrated," and "Indian hostilities." *Cong. Globe*, 24th Cong., 1st Sess., April 27, 1836, pp. 402, 404.

2. John C. Calhoun (1782–1850), of South Carolina, bitter personal and political enemy of Andrew Jackson and an advocate of Texas annexation. Calhoun was a member of the US House of Representatives in the Twelfth through Fourteenth Congresses (1811–1817), proponent of secret annexation in James Monroe's administration (1817–1825), vice president during the presidencies of John Quincy Adams and Andrew Jackson (1825–1832), member of the US Senate (1832–1843), secretary of state (1844–1845), and again member of the US Senate (1845–1850).

3. This is probably a reference to an engagement on January 7, 1837, between Rangers led by George B. Erath (1813–1891) and Indians at Elm Creek, in present-day Milam County, in which two Rangers were killed.

P. W. Humphrys to William H. Wharton

Schooner Invincible New York
Jany. 24th 1837

Sir:

I have not the pleasure of a personal acquaintance with you, but the character which has been given me of you, as a man of strict justice and integrity, as well as being the representitive of our infant government. I presume to write to you upon a subject which if possible I take a deeper interest than yourself, it is with regard to the refitment of the Invincible. I can but hope that you are unaquainted with our situation, for had it been represented to you some steps I feel assured would have been taken for our relief. Capt. Brown is nearly if not equally as unpleasantly situated as ourselves who are aboard vessell.

<Illegible name> knows our many difficulties, and so harassed is he already with the difficulties of the vessell that it would be but too ungenerous further to mortify him with a relation of greviences I am well aware he is inable to relieve.

When we first arrived and whilst the mechanics were overhauling and repairing the vessell, we took boarding on shore (which by the by is still unpaid) which repairs when finished for the purpose of lessening expenses we returned aboard to live, which we have done upon the generosity of a friend who has furnished us with provisions barely upon the vague promises of Messrs Sayre and Williams, none of which promises have been complied with, and now Mr Williams tells us through Mr Treat that he had no money and unless a sufficient quantity of the scrip now in the hands of Mr Treat can be sold to equip the vessell entirely, that none of it must be disposed of.

I will state to you concisely our present situation on board. Our provisions are short many essential articles we are entirely in want of. the grocer is reluctant to furnish us farther we are in debt to our cook who complains most bitterly our wood is barely sufficient to cook dinner, our clothes are at the washerwomans and there they will have to remain untill we get money to pay for the washing. It is hardly necessary to speak farther to you on this unpleasant subject, for indeed Sir we have not even sufficient to buy a glass of grog which only costs three cents in New York, cash.

Our situation as you may perceive for I have told it to you without the least exaggeration is truly deplorable, and I sincerly hope it will not continue so longer than untill we can hear from you.

The officers have requested me as the first Lieut. and in which I am compelled by the circumstances reluctantly to join, to say that unless our situation is relieved within the week we shall leave the vessell and make the best of our way to Texas and there seek other employment however mortifying it may be to ourselves and unpleasant to others.

Capt. Brown informs us that he has written upon the subject of the vessell very frequently and not being able to obtain any decisive answer upon the subject and consequently can give us no satisfaction upon the subject.

I beg you will send me an immediate answer to this that we may if possible alleviate our necessities as soon as can be.

Very Respectfully I have the honour to be Your Obt Servt
P. W. Humphrys

✦✦✦

ALS. Tx, TLP. P. W. Humphrys, an officer on the *Invincible*, was later chief clerk to Acting Navy Secretary William M. Shepherd. He is variously referred to as Humphries or Humphreys and as Peter or Perry by different sources.

Reverend George Montgomery West to Reverend John Fenton

Philadelphia Jan 20th. 1837.

Dear Sir

As you are about to proceed to Washington, I beg to direct your prompt and serious attention to the accompanying Pamphlet respecting Texas and more particularly to the "Address" of the Honble. W. H. Wharton[1] commissioner from Texas now in that City. It contains so many sublime beautiful and just delineations that it deserves general approbation.

I feel interested on the subject of Texas and have had the honor to be the first who advocated from the pulpit the cause of the widows and orphans of the ever to be remembered departed Heroes who fell in the noble struggle for liberty.

My brother in law, Mr. Edward Gardner[2] was among the gallant band who fell with the brave Fanning. I have had an application from the Philadelphia Committee to exert myself more extensively in behalf of a fund for the relief of the Widows and Orphans. I feel quite disposed to do so under suitable conditions and with the sanction of the Texian Commissioner.

As you are fully aware of the interest which I have in consequence of my past public course of action not only in this country but also in the United Kingdom of Great Brittain and Ireland, and particularly with English Noblemen it occurs to me that this fund might become progressively important and that pecuniary means might also be obtained for the establishment of Schools in Texas and ultimately for a seat of Learning similar to that which you are aware we have already established in this Country by British money.

Indeed it seems to me that Texas will have an equitable and sympathetic claim in the event of her independence being acknowledged as numbers of British subjects will doubtless become settlers in that part of the world and means of education ought to be provided for them and their descendants.

Upon the whole if the principles of the reform church which I have the honor to represent in this Country meet the approval of the Honble Mr. Wharton together with what I have already stated and should he do me the honor to notify the same to me before my departure from this place, I shall turn towards it my most serious attention.

You will of course wait on Mr. Wharton and please write with as little delay as possible and now my dear Sir I commend you to God and the word of his grace. May he protect and bless you with many years of useful life to your family the church and your,

Sincere Friend
G. M. West
Bishop of the Primitive Episcopal Church

✦✦✦

ALS. Tx, TLP. George Montgomery West (1790–1855), a native of Ireland, was a "Wesleyan Methodist" minister when he visited the United States and met Rev. Philander Chase, bishop of Ohio in the Protestant Episcopal Church of the United States. Chase ordained West as a deacon and a presbyter and sent him to Britain to raise funds for Kenyon Episcopal College in Ohio. West raised funds and returned to the United States in 1830 but quarreled with Chase because he thought Chase had consecrated him as his successor. West went on to establish what he called the Primitive Episcopal Church. Fenton, not otherwise identified.

1. "Address of the Honorable Wm. H. Wharton, delivered in New York on Tuesday, April 26, 1836; Also, "Address of the Hon. Stephen F. Austin, delivered in Louisville, Kentucky, on the 7th March, 1836" (New York: William H. Colyer, 1836), in *Magazine of History*, Extra Number 88, vol. 22., no. 4 (New York: William Abbatt, 1922), 211–268.

2. Edward Gardner (d. 1836) [listed as Garner in Texas military records] was in Capt. Ira J. Westover's company.

Levi Woodbury to William H. Wharton

Treasury Department
Jany 26th 1837.

Sir:

I have the honor to acknowledge the receipt of your communication of the 24th Instant covering a letter addressed to yourself by General T. J. Green of the Texas Army in reference to the recent seizure at New Orleans of the Texian "Schooner Terrible" under the presumption of her being a Piractical Vessel.[1]

In reply to your communication I have to acquaint you that the Department has been happy to transmit copies of both letters to the Collector of New Orleans, and requesting that officer to make report of his proceedings together with the grounds upon which they were predicated. Upon the receipt of his answer, it will afford me pleasure to give due consideration and prompt direction in the case.

I have the honor to be Very Respectfully Your Obedt. Servant
Levi Woodbury
Secy of the Treasury

P.S. In the mean time he will himself proceed to a final disposal of the subject if, in conference with the District attorney, he finds any clear legal course he can pursue.

L.W.

✦✦✦

ALS. Tx, TLP. Levi Woodbury (1789–1851), of New Hampshire, served in the US Senate as a Jacksonian in the Nineteenth through Twenty-First Congresses, 1825–1831; was secretary of the navy, 1831–1834; secretary of the treasury, 1834–1845; and associate justice of the US Supreme Court, 1845–1851.

1. Texas commissioned the one-gun schooner *Terrible* as a privateer in November 1835. Under Captain John M. Allen, the *Terrible* prized several vessels off the coast of Mexico, to the alarm of New Orleans shipping interests, who called on the US government for protection. The USS *Boston* captured the *Terrible* and sent the vessel to New Orleans for adjudication.

Robert James Walker to William H. Wharton

Washington City Jany 27. 1837.

Dear Sir

Mr Samuel Grice[1] the bearer of this letter is a very highly respectable and intelligent citizen of Philadelphia. Mr Grice thinks he may visit Texas this spring & you would oblige me by giving him letters of introduction to some of your friends in that country.

Yours truly
R J Walker

✦✦✦

ALS. Tx, TLP.

1. Samuel Grice was a Philadelphia shipbuilder.

James M. Wolfe to William H. Wharton

New York Jany. 28th 1837

Dear Wharton

I arrived here after having encountered much cold and fatigue. Many friends have called on me and place themselves at our service.

Many indeed many I say ask why is Hunt sent to Washington to interfere that you who have stood foremost as the champion in Texas sustai[nin]g the country by your great intellectual endowments & extensive influences among the members of Congress and the heads of Department should have such a Coadjutor is an astonishing fact that leaves many in doubt. You have many friends here who duly appreciate your labors and your untiring efforts in the cause of our struggling country and they say you are the only man to obtain recognition. Believe me I am proud to think I have been associated with you under such circumstances. I think from prospects I can get Brown off which I am now trying believe me I am even here industrious, so soon as you write to me I will return. Treat desires to be rem[embe]red to you and

Preston. Today I will dine with Swartwout. You will find enclosed a letter highly important to Texas.

Accept the assurances of my high regards &c Yours,

J. M. Wolfe

P.S. Excuse this scrawl as many are talking to me.

✦✦✦

ALS. Tx, TLP.

Arthur Henrie to William H. Wharton

Peach Point Texas January 28th 1837

Dear Sir,

My youngest son Daniel L. Henrie[1] sailed in the sloop of war Vincennes as midshipsman in the fall of 1833. I have had no inteligence from him to be relied on since. Will [you] be so good as to call on the Secretary of the navy, and learn all the particulars about him, and inform me by the first oportunity. You can more easly conceive my feelings on this subject than I can express them. Your attention will be received as an act of kindness that will lay me under your lasting obligations.

With Esteem your Sincere friend

Arthur Henrie

✦✦✦

ALS. Tx, TLP. Arthur Henrie was collector of dues on lands at Nacogdoches. He later opened an agency for Texas trade in New Orleans.

1. Daniel L. Henrie, not otherwise identified.

William W. Gwathmey to William H. Wharton

Richmond Janry 28th 1837

Dear Sir

I received your letter of the 29th Decbr only 10 days ago, and should have answered it long since but I hoped before this to have seen you in Washington. But now I find it is impossible to meet you there for Dr A[rcher] has written to Mr Saunders,[1] and in his letter he wishes me to return immediately and as I have been so little at home, I can hardly make up my mind to leave, but you know that it would be too childish and so different from what I have determined to do were I to linger here that I have made up my mind to start the Monday next, and if I can be of any service to you in your absence from home it will give me great pleasure, I assure you, to render you any service whatever, but you know me I hope well enough to call on me without all this.

Santa Anna I hear this morning, is in Norfolk and intends sailing for Veracruz in a few days, and that he has effected nothing in Washington, but I will hope that Congress will recognize us this session. I received a letter from Dr Stone a few days Since. He was in New England on the 10th of this month and expects to be here in 3 or 4 weeks. He is trying to get the stocks taken, for a bank in Texas, with 5,000,000 of money for its capital. I am afraid it will fail for I think the Capital is too great, and it is one of the Drs schemes, and like most of his, I am afraid it is rather on a too large a Scale. He is the president, and that is all that I know about it.

When you start home, I beg of you to come and stay at least one or two days here. Papa[2] says you must come and see him before you return. He is anxious to see you, and is as much interested as any of us.

Remember me particularly to Mrs. Wharton, Miss Anne[3] and Waller and Say to Mrs W. that I delivered her message to Dr A's

Daughter,[4] but did not receive any answers, and I wish she would persuade some of our beauties to go out with her. The Town is full of them.

Remember me to my friend Coln Bee and believe me as ever your friend

Wm. W. Gwathmey

I wish you would write either to Dr A or myself occasionally just to let us know how things are going on. I sent your letters to the care of N & J Dick, New [Or]lls[5] Wm W G.

✦✦✦

ALS. Tx, TLP. William Watts Gwathmey (1817–1898) went to Texas as a young man and remained for four years. He returned to the United States and became a tobacco and cotton dealer in Alabama and later a cotton commission merchant in Norfolk, Virginia.

1. Saunders, not otherwise identified.
2. Temple Gwathmey (1783–1848), a Virginia planter.
3. Anne Wharton, daughter of William H. and Sarah G. Wharton.
4. Mary E. Archer (1815–1842).
5. Nathaniel and James Dick were New Orleans cotton merchants.

George B. McKinstry to William H. Wharton

Brazoria 28 January 1837

Sir

Permit me to ask the favor of you, to forward the enclosed letter to Col. Bee, he gave me two drafts on Messrs Gasquet Parish of New Orleans,[1] which have been protested, and am anxious he should receive the enclosed as early as possible.

Yours Most Respectfully
Geo. B. McKinstry

✦✦✦

ALS. Tx, TLP. George B. McKinstry (1801–1837), a native of Ireland, arrived in Texas in 1829 and became a coastal trader based in Brazoria. He was involved in the

Anahuac disturbances and participated in the Convention of 1832. Stephen F. Austin died at McKinstry's house in Columbia, Texas.

1. The merchant firm of William A. Gasquet and Daniel Parish was based in New Orleans and New York.

James Pinckney Henderson to William H. Wharton

Columbia Texas
Jan 29th 1837

Dr Coln

We have received your dispatches of the 22nd, 28th & 31st of Decr[1] all of which are satisfactory as to manner but not so as to matter. We are all surprized here to see the coldness of the Administration at Washington. We hope however that things will change in appearance as soon as Genl Santa Anna arrives. There is something very strange indeed hanging over the matter. The report of Mr Morfit does not appear to warrant the Message of President Jackson. We will however find no fault until we hear all

I have no official communication to make as nothing of importance has transpired since our last dispatches. All things remain quiet. The militia are all now being organized and turn out extremely well so far as we have any report; they are satisfied that they will not be call[ed] upon until it becomes absolutely necessary. We have from Matamoras information stating that the Mexican soldiers there are very much dissatisfied and that the number of men under Genl Bravo are greatly less than report had named them to be—that they could not invade us again unless they could raise more men and obtain a large amount of money. I cannot be convinced that they will ever invade Texas again. Reports have reached us that some of the States in the interior are about revolting with the intention of a separation. Genl Johnson[2] & Coln Grayson have arrived. The army appears to be well satisfied and anxious to meet the Mexicans. Genl Johnson will leave in a few days for Army. His Excellency D G Burnet and Coln Hill[3] are candidates in this County for Senator. Preperations are now rapidly making at the Cty of Houston for the meeting of Congress. I have been assured by several that it is a beautiful situation for a Town.

Genl Rusk has not yet arrived at this place when we heard from him last he was unwell at Nacogdoches. The Cabinet will not leave this place until we remove to Houston. You complain of not hearing from Texas. I have written several letters to you and presume others have done so. I will continue to write by every vessel but you must expect some miscarriages.

I have ordered the Laws passed by Congress to be printed in pamphlet form and as soon as they are finished I will send you a copy of them. The Telegraph is sent to you regularly it contains however but little news. I heard from your house on yesterday all was well. Your brother John A. has declined visiting the US. for the present and so has Judge Colinsworth.

Present my respects to Mrs Wharton and Genl Hunt and accept for yourself my best wishes and the assurance of my high regard &c.

J. Pinckney Henderson

✦✦✦

ALS. Tx, TLP.

1. These are respectively Wharton's dispatches numbered 1, 2, and 3, published in *DCRT,* 1: 157–158, 158–160, and 166–168.

2. Albert Sidney Johnston.

3. William Green Hill (1801–1860), from Nashville, Tennessee, came to Texas in 1830 and fought in several engagements during the Texas Revolution. He was elected senator from Brazoria to the First Texas Congress.

James Treat to William H. Wharton

Exp mail

New York January, 30th 1837.
Monday 2 P.M.

My dear Sir:

On Saturday Evening 6'clk I received your valued favour of 27th and am much obliged for the information it contained, for which accept my sincere thanks.

I have kept the remarks in relation to St. Anna's views Entirely to myself, and friend S[wartwout] as I well knew the importance of so doing. The public mind must be left to remain where it is, as regards St. Anna for the present. If the truth was known, it would certainly operate against the recognition when the question comes up. You see I was right about his inability to enter into any treaty, unless entirely provisional or conditional. I am most happy to find that the Texan question for recognition remains on its own merits and is not at all connected with the affairs & present Negotiating with Mexico. Thus, I hope you will, go ahead. I have seen [the] arrival of Gen Hunt, and presume he will hurry on to Washington, to participate with you in your Labours & Honors. It was doubted in N. Orleans on the 21st inst. whether his appointment was bona fide. It must be of course or he would not thus have been announced. Perhaps he has only come to make another commission (2 instead of 1), in relation to any treaty, that may, succeed your recognition, & not as a co minister. I am very anxious to learn that Judge Ellis[1] has arrived at Washington, and also to learn the position of things in mexico, cause of his departure, if in anger &c &c all about it. Letters from V. Cruz, 3d Inst. brought per Boston sloop ~~from~~ at Pensacola, but they do not account for the departure of Judge Ellis, & on the contrary, say that nothing has transpired in relation to the motives of his sudden departure, so I suppose he has his Secret still with him. I had a letter from Williams yesterday. He says nothing about the Invincible but authorizes me to give Capt Brown $320, if I can dispose of a Script or Section of Land at 50¢ cash, of which, I have notified Capt Brown this morning. This is only a temporary relief for Capt B & officers say for momentary wants. Still it is something. Col. Wolfe is here, and now with Capt Brown, examining into the state of the negotiations as regards the dispatch of the Invincible, and I had expected they would have returned to my office, that I could (If Col W. did not) communicate the results. It is now so late, I shall not see them probably before post. I have shewn your Letter to Swartwout & he desires his special remembrance to you & good wishes.

Col. W. as well as myself, in cooperation will do all that can be done to get off the Invincible Thro' the aid of Mr Williams script, but as I do not know the result of Col W's examination to day with Brown & the other parties intended & having claims on her, cannot say more at present. I wish you would send me a paper containing the Documents accompanying the President's Message sent to the House on Texas & Mexo. on Thursday last. It may not be published fully here.

I wrote Mr Weaver a day or two since with all the news. You may see the letter.

My health is better now, and if it improves I hope Soon to See you in Washington, but dont omit to write on that ac[count] until I inform you of my day of departure, which I will do. Remember me to Mr. Weaver & also to all the friends of the good cause whom I may know.

I am in great haste & very Truly Yours,

J. Treat

2 1/2 P.M. I have letters on the way from Texas not yet arrived. They are or will be up to 15th from Galveston Bay. Ann Eliza. to Sail from V Cruz 8th next daily expected Laura.

✦✦✦

ALS. Tx, TLP.

1. Powhatan Ellis (1790–1863) had been a judge on the Mississippi Supreme Court (1817–1825), a US senator from Mississippi (1825–1832), and a federal judge for Mississippi (1832–1836). President Jackson appointed him US chargé d'affaires to Mexico in 1836, with instructions to press the claims of US citizens against that government. Unable to resolve the claims, Ellis closed the legation and returned to the United States in December 1836. President Van Buren reappointed Ellis to the post, which he retained until he was replaced by President Tyler in 1842.

Monroe Edwards to William H. Wharton

New Orleans Jany 31st 1837

Dr. Sir

In the fall of 1832 when I spoke of laying of a town on what is called Edwards Point on Galveston Bay Col. B. R. Milam[1] & Yourself assured me you would take an interest. The matter has been suspended until the present time when on the suggestion of several Gentlemen from Alabama who have bot an interest, I have concluded to lay of a town. An excitement has been gotten up in favor of the place & many are of the opinion that its advantages a[re] superior to those of Galveston. 10 feet can be carried up to the place on the lower side of Red Fish Barr & some of the knowing ones here are inclined to think that its superiority over Galveston is undoubted, besides a report is current here that Galveston overflows which has lowered it very much in the estimation of the public. The Gent[leme]n who have started the matter some of whom you know are Judge A. S. Lipscomb,[2] Messrs Poe,[3] Gaines[4] Whitehead[5] & Ware[6] all men of wealth & influence. I made a reservation of one fourth considering myself bound to Thorne[7] Major Whiting[8] & Yourself. The stock is at present divided in to forty shairs estimated at $2,000 each. The first price was $100 a shair & if you wish to take an interest you can have one or two shairs at that rate. Arrangements will be made immediately to put up a large warehouse & other necessary buildings to commence a town. The success of it is considered certain, be good enough to let me know your determination on the subject as soon as convenient & you will do me a favor.

We have nothing very important from Texas or Mexico except the news brought by Mr. Robinson[9] from Tampico he says that the whole Mexican army are dispearsed & that Texas has nothing to fear, things remain tranquil in Texas.

Genl. M. Hunt passed through this place a short time since on his way to Washington City he was formally announced here as the Minster from Texas to the U.S. & the annunciation for some days created some speculation, by some it was supposed that Houston gave him the appointment to superceed you, others conjectured that he is to be associated with you, but the most of us here are of the opinion, that the appointment was confered on him mearly as an honorary compliment, be the motive what it may, it has done Texas no credit here, & the honorable Gent[lema]n himself has created any thing but a favorable impression here.

We are all in a state of suspense here in relation to the affairs of Texas at Washington & hope in a fiew day to be released from our suspense by hearing some thing definate on the subject of our affairs.

Some volunteers are going down occasionally to Texas & if we should need them there is no doubt but can get any number.

I remain Respectfully Yr obt Svt
M. Edwards

✦✦✦

ALS. Tx, TLP. Monroe Edwards (ca. 1808–1847) was an infamous slave trader and forger who settled on Galveston Bay in the 1820s. He engaged with a partner to smuggle slaves into Texas from Cuba. When his effort to cheat his partner by forging documents was exposed, Edwards fled. He was later arrested in New York for a different elaborate forgery scheme for which he was sentenced to the state penitentiary at Sing Sing, where he was killed, perhaps beaten to death by guards after a failed escape attempt.

1. Benjamin Rush Milam (1788–1835), originally from Kentucky, was an Indian trader on the Colorado River in 1818. He obtained an empresario grant in Texas but was not able to attract enough settlers due to Mexican restrictions on immigration. In 1835, Milam joined Texas revolutionary forces and was killed by a sniper in San Antonio in December.

2. Abner Smith Lipscomb (1789–1856) studied law with John C. Calhoun and opened a practice in Alabama. From 1823 to 1835, he was chief justice of the Alabama Supreme Court. In 1839, he came to Texas, where he served as secretary of state in the Lamar administration in 1840. He was later a member of the Convention of 1845 and an associate justice of the Texas Supreme Court.

3. George Washington Poe (ca. 1800–1844) had been an officer and acting adjutant general in the Texas army. He settled in Houston and speculated in land.

4. This is most likely William Baxter Pendleton Gaines (1808–1891), an Alabama merchant who moved to Texas in 1835. He was a wealthy businessman based in Nacogdoches and Galveston.

5. Whitehead, not otherwise identified.

6. Nathan Ware was a Louisiana sugar planter who invested in Texas land.

7. Frost Thorn [vice Thorne] (1793–1854), of New York, had obtained an empresario grant from Mexico. He acquired substantial land holdings in Texas over a period of years.

8. Samuel Whiting (d. 1862?), originally from Hartford, Connecticut, attended the San Felipe Convention of 1833 and the Consultation of 1835. He provided the Texas army with supplies in 1836. He later became a newspaper publisher.

9. Robinson, not otherwise identified.

Joel R. Poinsett to William H. Wharton

Charleston
2d. Feb. 1837

My dear Sir

I should have answered your letter earlier; but I had left Columbia before it reached that place and have since been on my plantation near Georgetown S.C. I was governed in what I said of Texas by a sense of justice and a hope, while I vindicated her rights, I might render a mutual service to both countries by giving my opinion of the true course of policy to be pursued towards our young neighbour. I have read with great interest the papers you have sent me, and regret the first package came too late to be distributed among the members of the Legislature. I hope my fears may be utterly groundless. I wished to awaken my friends to the danger of their position. Wisdom says be not too confident. I earnestly hope you may be right.

I have requested my friend Mr. Mason[1] formerly my Secretary of Legation to call upon you & to render you any service in his power during your residence in Washington.

With respect & regard I am Dear Sir Yours truly
J.R. Poinsett

✦✦✦

ALS. Tx, TLP.

1. John Mason Jr. (1797–1859), the grandson of George Mason of Gunston Hall.

Fleming T. Wells to William H. Wharton

New York Feby. 3d 1837

Dr Sir

I am instructed by Capt. Brown to inform you that eleven scrip have been disposed of in discharge of the debts of the Invincible—that four more will be today for the same—that provisions to the amt. of $1600 can be purchased by placing six scrips as security, that we have strong hopes with this and [with what] you can give and with what we can do here, we shall get away in a short time. Mr Wolfe has been with us for several days and we feel ourselves chiefly indebted to him for the progress we have thus far made in our business.

Capt Brown begs you to accept his warmest thanks for the interest you have manifested in our behalf and the exertions you are making for our relief.

Also in reference to Mr. Wolfe, to remind you how high he estimates his exertions and zeal in our affairs and hopes you will prevail upon him to return with~~out~~ all dispatch to assist in getting us off.

For myself I must say the exertions of Mr Wolfe contrasts <u>well</u> with those of others from whom we had a just right to expect more. And for yourself individually please accept the assurances of our sincere regard.

I am with much respect, Your Most Obt. Svt.
F. T. Wells.

✦✦✦

ALS. Tx, TLP.

James Treat to William H. Wharton

New York Feby. 3d 1837.
Friday 12 oclk.

My dear Sir:

Altho' without any thing from you, or our friend W[illiams] for some time, and notwithstanding I replied to your last, Some days since, <u>yet</u>, I now fulfil my promise to advise you of arrival of the Vera Cruz Packet, at the port late last evening, altho' She brings nothing <u>Specially new</u>.

You will see the news, <u>generally</u>, and more fully in the <u>Courier & Inquirer</u>, than in any other paper—I furnished Mr. Hoskins with the <u>data</u>, and it was, <u>expressd</u> so <u>as to</u> bear on the <u>public mind</u>, at <u>Washington</u>: tho' the <u>facts</u> may be <u>relied upon</u>. A letter rec. by <u>me</u> from Veracruz, dated Jany 10th. says, <u>as follows</u>: "our chargé d'Affaires, not being able to get on to his satisfaction in his diplomatic relations with the Mexican Govmt., demanded his passports, which he finally obtained, and embarkd in the U.S. ship Boston for Pensacola on the 3d. inst. bearing with him the archives of the Legation. It is rumored that a resolution is before the Mexican Congress to declare <u>war</u> immediately with the U. States, and I really am apprehensive that the heads of Govmt. are silly enough to pass such an act; or, at least, a non-Intercourse act with the U.S. The two Californias have separated from Mexico, and sworn to remain an independent Govmt. unless Mexico should consent to re-establish the federal Govmt. They charge the U.S. Squadron in the Pacific with being the indirect cause of bringing about the separation of the Californias, which every one must know, has not a shadow of foundation—the Public prints assert it. A Pronunciamento has just taken place at Queretaro (city, & seat of Govmt. of the former State of same name adjoining Zacatecas) in consequence it is asserted of the Mexican Govmt. wishing to, reduce the value of the copper circulating medium to the prejudice of the Holders. Rumors are afloat that Gen Bustamante, is to be declared Dictator of the Republic. The new constitution, was solemnized and proclaimed, at this Place on the 8th Inst. but I am unable to send you a copy, or give you any of its features at this time. It is said to be of a character sui generis." I have a letter from city of Mexico dated 20th & 27th December from which I translate as follows:

Under the first named date. it says: "an Express arrived from the army of the North, has brought the third resignation of Gen Bravo, with a protestation, that he absolutely declines continuing the command of the army. Here, all are convinced of the improbability of sending forward said Expedition (against Texas) as the Govmt. is in want of every description of resources, and in addition, sickness and desertion, have considerably reduced its numbers &c. &c."

Under date of 27: the writer says "Mr. Ellis has presented to the Govmt his claims, and asked for his Passports. This step indicates clearly that there may (will) be, a rupture between the two nations, &c. &c."

The above Extracts, which, comes from respectable Sources will give you an Idea of the position of things in Mexico when taken in Connection with what you will find in the C[ourier] & Enquirer.

The U. States sloop Natchez arrived at Vera Cruz 8 Jany and took the first authentic news of the release of Gen St. Anna. They were satisfied, that he was coming to Washington. The Govmt paper refers to him in respectful & complimentary terms; and the Censor at Vera Cruz expresses great satisfaction at his Release. There has been no outlawry declared against him, nor a word said about it, even in any of the newspapers. That was a N. Orleans forgery. The papers, one and all, are entirely silent as regards Mr. Ellis. His name even is not mentioned anywhere that I have seen, and in announcing the departure of the Boston. They do not even say He embarkd in her. This is really rather Singular: on the other hand, the papers, are full of Gorostiza & his mission, Pamphlet, &c. The official organ declares that he has fulfilld his mission to the satisfaction of the Govmt sustained the honor & dignity of the nation &c: his final letter to the State Dept. is, first published to create an impression and then commented on &c. Then is announced the publication of the Pamphlet issued by Gorostiza in Phil. &c. &c.[1]

The Concord sloop of war, was off Tampico 7th Jany.—Dates from Matamoros to 8 Jany by the Tampico, at New Orleans and dates from Tampico to 12 Ulto.

Dr Bonita[2] also at N. Orleans—nothing new. The conspiracy which was to have be very serious & probably Successful (had it not been previously disclosed) had blown over. Prisoners discharged. Olarte,[3] the chief who had declared for the Federation near Papantla, had had some skirmishing and sustained himself—a Mexican vessel had arrived from Havana, where she was permitted to Load & unload but prohibited from the use of her flag—until Spain had given her orders—Some arrests had taken place in Mexico, and the suspicious parties ordered to remote & different points, merely on suspicion. So much for what it maybe worth to you—Please shew this to Mr. W. and say I had no time to write him today. I hope to see you both, on Monday or Tuesday—I ought to have left here today, but arrival of Packet has detained me.

Col. Wolfe, was to have left this morning—presume he did—would leave Phila. tomorrow with Williams, if ready, for Washington. I should [have] been happy to have joined them but fear I cannot. Can you Secure a place at Gadsby's. for me & a friend, say on Monday or Tuesday next? Or are they empty (not crowded) so as to render this unnecessary? If needful please secure two Rooms or two beds in one room.

P.S. has [Powhatan] Ellis arrived? What does he say? How will his report effect the recognition? St Anna is off I suppose—It was very lucky for him to have met Ellis at Norfolk (if he did as I suppose) so as to obtain the latest news from his country—Col Wolfe's letters will inform you about the Invincible; if not will report on arrival. My sheet is full & I must close.

Yours very truly & in Haste
J. Treat

✦✦✦

ALS. Tx, TLP.

1. Manuel Eduardo de Gorostiza, the Mexican minister in Washington, objected strenuously when US troops crossed the Sabine and occupied Nacogdoches, arguing that Texan claims about Indian depredations were manufactured. When it became clear that the Jackson administration would not remove the troops quickly, Gorostiza, on October 15, 1836, demanded his passports. Before he left he protested US action in "A Pamphlet Printed and Secretly Circulated by M. E. Gorostiza, Late Envoy Extraordinary from Mexico; Previous to his Departure from the United States and by him Entitled 'Correspondence between the Legation Extraordinary of Mexico and the Department of State of the United States, respecting the Passage of the Sabine by the Troops under the Command of General Gaines" (Washington, DC: Peter Force, 1837). *The Washington Globe*, February 14, 1837, published an account from the official government paper in Mexico, the *Diario del Gobierno de la Republica Mexicana*, December 27, 1836, which praised Gorostiza for the "propriety, dignity and energy with which he conducted his diplomatic mission near the treacherous, infamous, and dissembling Government of North America."

2. Bonita, not otherwise identified.

3. Mariano Olarte (d. 1838), a Totonac Indian, led a rebellion against the Mexican government near Papantla, north of Vera Cruz. The Papantla Rebellion sought a return to the Federalist Constitution of 1824. Olarte was killed by government forces in 1838.

Branch T. Archer, Stephen F. Austin, and William H. Wharton made James Wolfe secretary of the Texas Legation soon after their arrival in Washington, DC. For unknown reasons, President Houston replaced him with Fairfax Catlett in December 1836. The letter below explains little but is suggestive.

James M. Wolfe to William H. Wharton

Philadelphia Feb. 3 thd. 1837

Dear Sir

I arrived here last evg. from N. York on my way to Washington city and would have answered your favor there but for this late hour at which it was handed me.

Your letter teems with abuses which every man will say is underserving after the services rendered Texas and did I believe that many persons who now have influence in that Country would ever be the permanent Citizens, it would be my duty to notice their unwarrantable attacks on my character. I have written to Judge Lipscomb, Messrs Dobson & Williams of Mobile[1] to shew in the whole state of Alabama what I got of Col. Darrington[2] whether it was seven hundred dollars to vest in lands as soon as the land offices were opened and dare the world to say more however as I have a copy of my individual receipt to Darrington, it is but fair that it should be published at a proper time. I fear my dear friend altho you stand high in the United States and in Texas whether your character is not impugned by the scapegoats of Texas who are ever que vivo to decry any and every one who looks upon them with contempt, thank God my standing is too good to be sullied by forgers and thieves and jurors who never knew practically what dishonesty was, I well knew how the thing was managed in my absence tho have my word for it I am glad the appointment has been conferred upon another it was not any solicitation no never would or should an appointment be conferred upon me in the unsettled state of things in Texas as my friend in N. Orleans writes me and as they say in N York scarcely has an officer rested in the United States before another arrives to clog him. Let Texas be recognized is all I ask then we will have men of character to estimate your labours and consider of mine agreeably to the merit they claim.

I have made arrangements to get the Invincible off and Brown will probably write to you. Col. Hockley was in my room and left for N York I gave him letters there Sam. Williams is here and has recov[ere]d. Treat was to have met me here to day to proceed to W[ashington, D.C.]. if he arrives tonight we will start immediately, all your friends here and in N. York desire to be rem[embere]d. to you. Be pleased to remember me to Mrs. W. and Mister Waller & receive the assurance of my high regard.

Yr friend
Wolfe

✦✦✦

ALS. Tx, TLP.

1. George Dobson (d. 1855) and Nathaniel Felton Williams (1800–1884), a younger brother of Samuel May Williams, were partners in a Mobile, Alabama, merchant house. The firm went bankrupt in 1837, and Williams moved to Texas, where he established a sugar plantation. He later moved to New Orleans and then to Baltimore.

2. Col. John Darrington (1786–1855), an army officer before resigning to become a planter in Alabama.

James Treat to William H. Wharton

Xpr mail

New York Feby 4, 1837.
Saturday 2 P.M.

My dear Sir,

I had this pleasure yesterday, at length. I had not then received my papers—among them, I find the Enclosed Slip, published in the city of Mexico 28th Decr. 1836; Tenor of which you will perceive. I thought this might be important, as going to shew, that St. Anna really had friends & adherents there, and thus increase confidence in his Success & fulfilment of his Engagements &c &c.– I therefore translated it for the Courier, with comments and thought it would produce a good effect in Washington. But I see by the Courier this morng that it was crowded out, by the Mexican correspondence contained in the Globe of yesterday—I therefore hand you the original Enclosed, which you can make such use of, as may in your opinion be advantageous. Please shew it to Mr. Weaver, and let him use it if he wishes, and can do, so, without any prejudice to your views & objects respecting Texas.

I have nothing from you or Weaver for some time.

I could not get away today, arrival of this Packet from V.C. and departure of another tomorrow for same place, has detained me, I think I will leave on Monday next (day after tomorrow). I am very anxious to get to Washington, where my instructions would long since have led me, could I have got away, & my health been better—I write this tho overwhelmed with other numerous letters, for Mexico &c I have letters from Texas 25 Decr & 1 Jany. Say some dozn or more pages, which I shall not have time to read until this Evening—The two letters of instructions from Forsyth to Ellis published in the Globe, and the present aspect of things must aid your cause & increase the probability of admission &c. I have recd the Washingtonian & Gazette Extra Feby 1st. I thank the Sender.

Yours &c very truly,
J. Treat

P.S. 1/4 to 3 P.M. I have just heard from a Passenger in the Ann Eliza left V. Cruz 11 Inst. That: The feeling in favour of St. Anna at the city Vera Cruz & throughout the State of Vera Cruz, is decidedly in favour of St. Anna & that should he arrive there he will be recd with open arms &c. I place great reliance on this statement. The informer is a long resident in V. Cruz & probably knows the feeling there.

Yours &c
Treat

+++

ALS. Tx, TLP.

Charles L. Wingfield to William H. Wharton

Norfolk 5 Feb. 1837.

Dr Sir,

I had the pleasure of meeting with you last spring, when you promised to pass thro' Norfolk & spend a few days with me. I take it for granted that the interesting & important events which occurred in Texas at & about that time, prevented you from coming this way. I congratulate you on getting thro' so signally successful. And hope you will be able to make it a great flourishing & happy country. Cannot you now or before you leave the country come & spend some days with me here.

Having a large family exclusively of sons I feel anxious to look out for a new and flourishing country for them & should be glad to have your advice on that interesting subject. My son Charles, who is now in Mississippi wrote me a few days ago saying he was determined to go to Texas in a short time. Will you do me the favor to advise me what point he had better direct his attention to? Please inform me when you expect to return to Texas & what will be your route. And if agreeable I will give him an introduction to you.

Wishing you good health & a happy termination of your conference with this Govt.

I have the honor to subscribe myself Your friend & relation

Cha. L. Wingfield

P.S. My friend Col. Povale[1] will hand you this. C. L. W.

✦✦✦

ALS. Tx, TLP. Charles L. Wingfield, not otherwise identified.

1. F. R. Povall [vice Povale], not otherwise identified.

James M. Wolfe to [William H. Wharton and Samuel May Williams]

Washington City, Feb 6th 1837

Honl Sirs,

I have the honor to inform you that during my stay in the City of New York last week I found one of the Texian Vessels, Invincible, under an attachment for the sum of two thousand dollars or thereabout and Sundry bills against it for repairs amounting to ten thousand dollars, in or near it. The Commander Captain Brown and crew ~~without~~ almost pennyless. Captain Brown called upon me knowing that I was acting as the private secy. of Mr. Wharton solicited of me subsidy for the discharge of said Vessel and for his relief. I visited many of the claimants and persuaded them to take scrip for four or five thousand dolls. in discharge of their debts, holding myself responsible for the amt. provided it should not prevail the balance has to be paid in cash or its equivalent. Believing that it would greatly redound to the credit of my adopted Country, I hastened to ask of my friends assistance for its relief.

The Situation in which my adopted country Texas is now placed and her want of credit in N. York authorizes me to say that no obligations of a governmental nature could or can now be used, as I am informed, that can or will release her, and if my poor services as they have ever been unceasing in the cause of Texas may < . . . > a Continuance especially in this Case my friends and myself will divide our means in setting that vessel afloat. You will perceive no other means but money or its equivalent will be taken and it is to be sold under an attachment as I believe the 19th or 20th inst.

I have the honor to be yrs &c.
J. M Wolfe

✦✦✦

ALS. Tx, TLP.

Jeremiah Brown to William H. Wharton

New York, Feb. 6. 1837

Respected Sir,

I again take the liberty of addressing you in relation to my own affairs. I have been enabled, through the assistance of your Secretary, (Col. Wolfe) (who is entitled to much credit,) to pay off the largest half of the debt due from the Invincible—a balance is however still wanting, of about $5000—2000 of this can be paid in Govt Scrip, the balance Cash, and I am ready for sea, this includes advance for officers, seamen and every thing.

I have this morning had an interview with Col. Hockley, who is here for the purpose of purchasing two Steam Vessels and two Brigs—what his means are, I know not, but I should suppose that it would be for the interest of the Govt to fit out the Invincible, (as most of her debts are paid) instead of purchasing new vessels. And beleiving that a line from you to him, would have the desired effect, I write you for the purpose of obtaining the favor.

As attempts have been successfully made in my adopted country to supplant me in my command, and that too without affording me an opportunity of justifying myself, it is but natural that I should call on old and tried friends to assist me in warding off the blow which has been aimed at me by those who have not one-sixteenth part of the claim on the Country for services rendered that I have—By the public journals I perceive that Capt. Taylor, (at the Balise) has been appointed Port Captain. What services has he ever rendered the Country? None!! He has never been on her shores—he has never been in any way identified with her interests. Notwithstanding, he is appointed first in command while I am not even confirmed by the Government as a Master Commandant. This is not right.[1]

Can you not, Sir, without injury to yourself, address the Government in my behalf? The facts in relation to my unpleasant situation, have, in this, been placed before you, and you are competent to judge of my claims.

I shall this day commence putting on board my provisions for a four months cruise, and shall be obliged to wait for pecuniary assistance before I can put to sea. To Col. Wolfe I am under great obligations for his assistance, and am anxiously awaiting a letter from him in relation to further efforts promised by him.

Please address me by return mail, and you will confer a special favor on

Yr Obt. Srt.
Jeremiah Brown

Can you not forward me a copy of the Navy Laws of the U. States, by doing so you will confer a special favor. They can be obtained on application at the Navy Dept.

✦✦✦

ALS. Tx, TLP.

1. Despite Brown's protestations, Thurston M. Taylor was named commandant of the Navy Yard at Galveston, and when the *Invincible* reached Galveston in March 1837, Brown was replaced in command of the vessel by Henry L. Thompson. Before the year was out the navy charged Thompson with profanity, drunkenness, embezzlement, and tyranny toward his crew. He died in November 1837 before trial on those charges.

Thomas Toby and Brother to William H. Wharton

New Orleans February 6. 1837

Sir

We are in reciept of your favor 27 ulto. and notice all you say on the subject of the Terrible—The facts are correct as stated by Genl Green & we feel satisfied our district atty will stop the proceedings against her. We had & bonded her some days since to enable her to sail again for New [Orleans] and now we have received Instructions to purchase her for the use of the Govt—We are gratified to learn that Santa Anna had made a favourable impression in Washington & that he depart[ed] in a national vessel for Vera Cruz—Our latest account from Mexico says that great rejoicing took place in the City Mexico and in fact throughout the Country on hearing of Santa Anna having been liberated, but the papers say he left Texas unsh<. . .> & had not committed himself in any way. Tornel[1] when in command at Vera Cruz had refused to obey Bravo as he co[nsiders] S.A. his Commander in Chief. He will no doubt have the whole army again with him—If so all will go well & we feel pretty well satisfied he will act up to his agreement—

We regret much Sam Williams sickness & also to hear that the Invincible is still in N. York—This captive vessel is now too small, and we must have in our navy such vessels in size as can cope with the Mexicans. Their Navy last account, was in Vera Cruz—Some prepartations have been made for an invasion, but it will not go into effect—It is at the moment out of our power to render any assistance to the officers of the Invincible—We have sent into Mississippi a large amt of Scrip, which we hope to dispose of there. If so it will place us in funds & we shall make you a remittance, which we regret we cannot do at this time—Enclosed we hand you a slip from this days paper.

I am Vy Respectfully Your Obedt Sevts
Thomas Toby & Bro

✦✦✦

ALS. Tx, TLP.

1. José Maria Tornel y Mendívil (1795–1853) was a consistent supporter of Santa Anna. He was several times minister of war and the navy.

John S. Wormly to William H. Wharton

Cumberland [Maryland] February 6 1837

Dear Sir,

Your intimate knowledge of the country, as will your official character as representative of Texas at Washington, must be my apology for applying to you for information respecting that country, as I intend to emigrate thither in the early part of spring. I am a man of family and wish to receive information upon which I can rely and hence my application to you as a source the most authentic and intelligent.

I am anxious to know in the first place, whether a citizen of the United States can acquire an immediate interest in the lands of Texas without renouncing his allegiance to the United States, in short, what are the preparatory steps necessary to be taken to aquire lands in Texas. Secondly, in what region or district can the most eligible lands be bought, and at what prices? Whether the authorities of Texas have established any place as yet, as their permanent seat of government, and what is the name of such place? Are the lands in the vicinity thereof as fertile and good as elsewhere in Texas, and what are the facilities of trade &c? Any further information which you think may be valuable to me, I would like to receive. I should like to receive your opinion on the present prospects of Texas, whether there is any doubt of her recognition by Congress, and of her ability to protect herself against Mexico &c. &c. You will please also inform me of what officers I shall first apply in order to obtain lands. Should I be enabled under the laws of the Texan government to hold a portion of its territory, my intention is to make large invesments in land, and to contribute forthwith to the cause of Texas not only my funds but perhaps my bodily services also. I have little or no doubt of the triumph of Texas, and that speedily, but your opinion and views nevertheless would be gratifying to me, and I shall feel myself under great obligations to you, if you will write me an answer to this letter as soon after its reception as your official and other duties will permit you.

I am Sir, with great respect Yours &c.
John S. Wormly

✦✦✦

ALS. Tx, TLP. Wormly not otherwise identified

John M. Allen to William H. Wharton and Memucan Hunt

Washington City Feby 10th 1837

Gentlemen

I was instructed by president Burnett of the Republic of Texas to proceed to Baltimore in the United States to Build a Brig of war for the use of the Texian Service and have in compliance with my orders endeavored to build it forthwith, but owing to the want of credit on the part of the Texian Republic in Said City as well as in the United States generally—and the facts that two of the vessels of Texas have been for Some say four months time and one is yet under attachment for debt in N. York—will prevent me from doing any thing until that vessel in N. York is released, and then I think it probable that I can proceede to build—Col. Wolfe has informed me he will be able he thinks to release the Invincible—tho, without his assistance that vessel will be Sold and myself prevented from building another—I will thank you to notify me whether the Govt. of Texas has in anywise through you as Her minister &c changed her orders given me which you have read &c

your obedt Svt
J. M. Allen
Texas Navy

✦✦✦✦

ALS. Tx, TLP.

David Abel Russell to William H. Wharton, with Enclosure

House of Reps. D.C. February 10th 1837.

Sir

I have recd. the enclosed letter from a friend desiring information relating to his son who is now in Texas. Allow me to submit the same to your consideration [and] ask from you the information Sought, if within your power.

As soon as your other avocations will permit I shall solicit your answer with a return of the enclosed

I Have the Honor to be with great Respect your Obt. Servt.

D. Russell

✦✦✦

ALS. Tx, TLP. David Abel Russell (1780–1861) represented New York as an anti-Jacksonian and Whig in the Twenty-Fourth through Twenty-Sixth Congresses, 1835–1841.

Enclosure: John White to David Abel Russell

Ellington Chautaqua County (N York)
[January 2, 1837]

Dear Sir

it is near a Quarter of a Century since you and I became acquainted, but it is some time since we have either seen or communicated with each other. I Removed to this County about three months ago: and take the liberty of addressing you on a Subject in which I have great Anxiety—in the Year 1819 my son Walter C. White left N York and went South since which time I have had no sattisfactory information about him untill last fall I heard he was in New York, that his place of Residence was Texas. I lately saw an extract from a Texas paper wherein the name of Walter C. White was associated with a Mr Wharton as Two Senators from the district of Columbia, Brazoria &c in the Texican Congress <.....> for stat<.....> the above partie[s] <......>

Washington, will you be so condecending as to see Mr Wharton and find out whether the said Walter C. White might be my son or one of the same name.[1] Should it turn out to be my son, inquire his occupation and Situation in life wither single or married; I also wish you to inform me how letters may be forwarded to Texas and by the Safest Route; My dear friend be so good as to answer to this at as Early an Hour as your Convenience may permit; I wish you to direct your answer to this line to James A. White Silver Creek, Chautaqua County NY, Will you be so good as to send me occasionally a Washington paper as I wish to hear from my frends; direct your papers to me Town of Ellington Chautaqua Co.

I remain With Respect Your Humble Servant

John White

ALS. Tx, TLP. Damaged, with some words missing. John White, not otherwise identified.

1 Walter C. White (d. 1837) arrived in Texas in 1821. He was a trader and subscribed $10,000 in bonds for Texas. It is not clear whether he was John White's son.

Edward Hall to William H. Wharton

New Orleans Feby 10th 1837

Dear Sir

On reading the proceedings of Congress I was struck with the abominable, Blind ignorance, of the Young mens Anti Slave Society of Philadelphia whose petition was presented by Jno Q. Adams on the 30 Last month, the following is an Act Supplementary to an Act for the punishment of Crimes and Misdemeanors published in the Texas Telegraph on the 11 Jany.

Sectn. 1st. Be it enacted by the Senate & House of Representatives of the Republic of Texas in Congress assembled. That if any person or persons shall introduce any African Negro or Negroes contrary to the true interest & meaning of the 9th sec of the general provisions of the Constitution, declaring the introduction of African negroes into this republic, to be piracy except such as are from the U States of

America, and had been held as slaves therein, he on this shall be considered guilty of Piracy, and upon conviction thereof, before any Court have Cognisance of the same, Shall Suffer Death without the Benefit of Clergy.

Sec. 2nd. Be it further enacted, That if any person or persons shall introduce into the republic of Texas, any Africans or any Slave or Slaves, from the U States of America, except such Slave or Slaves as were previously introduced and held in Slavery in that republic in conformity with the Laws of that Government, he or they shall be deemed guilty of Piracy, and upon Conviction thereof, before any Court having Cognisance of the same, Shall Suffer Death

Signed Ira Ingram
Speaker of the Hous of Repres.
Richard Ellis
Prest of the Senate
approvd 21st Decr. 1836
Sam Houston[1]

We have recd the Telegraphs of the 21 & 27 January nothing very important in them. Prest. Houston has just returned from a Visit to the Army, which he reports to be in fine spirits and condition, and all young men, eager for a fight. We are on tiptoe for the result of Santa Annas Mission.

The Legislature of this state have a resolution before them to Instruct the Senators & Representatives in Congress to Vote for Mr Walkers resolution to recognise the Independence of Texas[2]—Texas stocks are looking up.

We hope to have something from ~~you~~ Congress soon of a cheering nature. You will perceive I have written upon the Gallop, to be in time for the Express Mail.

Your Ob St.
E. Hall

Mr. Crallé,[3]

I send you the above for the purpose of giving the lie to the abominable charges, which our particular friends, the abolitionists have so kindly alleged against us. I also refer you to an Editorial in the Texas

Telegraph herewith sent, in relation to Governor McDuffie's late extraordinary message.

Wm. H. Wharton

P.S. of course you will omit the names &c.

✦✦✦

ALS, with postscript by Wharton. TX, TLP. Edward Hall was the inspector of military arms and supplies purchased in New Orleans for Texas.

1. The act is in Gammel, 1: 1257–1258. Ira Ingram (1788–1837) moved to Texas from New Orleans in 1826. He was a member of the Convention of 1832 and the Convention of 1833. He served in the Texas army during the revolution. He represented Matagorda in the First Texas Congress, in which he was elected speaker, but he resigned from Congress when it became known that he had been in prison for forgery in New York.

2. Robert J. Walker introduced a resolution to recognize Texas independence on January 11, 1837. *Cong. Globe,* 24th Cong., 2d Sess., p. 83.

3. Richard Kenner Crallé (1800–1864), editor of the *United States' Telegraph.*

Wilhelm Christoph Frederick Bernbeck to William H. Wharton

Chambersburgh 11 Febr. 1837.

Sir,

As your Honor perhaps will be apprized of, on my leaving Texas in September last on furlough, I have been authorized by his Excellency David G. Burnet, the then President of the Republik, for the purpose of recruiting men for the service of Texas, under the existing law of which in the mean time expressly written copies were given to me, which were signed by the President himself and your Honor's respected brother John A. Wharton, then Secretary of War.

Besides that a letter was handed to me by the President, upon my humble request, directed to Mr. Tom Toby & Broth. agents for the Republik at New Orleans, in which orders were given to them to defray the Passage of all such men as I might raise from the western Countries down to New Orleans.

After delivering this letter on my arrival at New Orleans I received the following note:

"New Orleans 30 Sept 1836.
Mr. Wm. Bernbeck is authorized to raise men for the army of Texas. We will pay the passage of such men as he may raise from the western Country to this place on their arrival here in Government Security <.......>.

Messrs Th. Toby & Bro Agents
for the Republik Texas in the U.S."

Relying on the faith of the this Document I published <.......> German papers in this country <.......> German Countrymen <.......> Society to the Republik of Texas "free of expences" under the conditions to do military services etc., thereby holding out to them a view of erecting a german Settlement in Texas after the time for military service had passed over.

As, during a residence of 4 years in these United States my particular connections amongst my german countrymen never had become very extensive, I as yet addressed myself exclusive to them only, being of opinion that from this quarter I shall get as many volunteers as I shall want.

My call has been responded by a most general applause—a great deal of interest has been shown and manifested by the germans to aid our cause — large numbers have made their applications to join me. I think I dare say that not much less than the number of a Battailon is ready to follow me under the promised condition that I procure their passage. That this number will much increase yet by publishing now a general invitation, as I intend to do shortly before our departure from Pittsburgh through the means of the handbills and inglish papers, there is not much doubt.

Such, Sir, were my prospects in fulfilling my engagement with the government of Texas to recruit for the Army, when, on the point to make the last preparation for our departure, by producing my credintials, I had the misfortune to learn, that the firm Thos Toby and Br. had stopped payment and that, consequently, no Steamboat could be chartered upon their letter of credit. To judge of my difficult situation in which this news has placed me, I can leave to you, Sir, without any further assertion. The mom[ent,] however, that the failure of that house was affirmed to <.....> (beginning of last month), I addressed myself to <..............> Houston comumenting him my <..........> for means in some <.......> to enable me to take my men to Texas, but the great distance from here to Texas, what unavoidably must cause a long delay; the possibilities that even the correspondence might get lost on the road, have created some doubts of my hopes which I first intertained from this procedure, and will now make me feel uneasy.

Having received the other day a file of Texian papers, I perceive that your Honor have been authorized by Congress to negotiate a loan for the government of Texas, and whilst I fervently hope that you already may have been successful in this negociation I have taken the liberty of making your Honor acquainted with our situation as above discribed and humbly to request your aid and assistance. If it is in your power I solicit the more that you will do so, as I am afraid that I, by a much longer delay of our departure, shall loose many of my since gotten volunteers. A yet more urging reason for me to wish for a speedy departure, is because a crisis seems to approach when soldiers may much be wanted [in] Texas.

Much of an advantage would it prove to be to Texas if allso an agent could be appointed in Philadelphia, who would forward volunteers from there by sea to Texas. I could send at least myself one hundred of them by that route, who are unable to come to Pittsburgh, for to join me, by paying their own expenses. If another Agent should be appointed already in New Orleans, your Honor will please direct him to send me his note; if not you, perhaps, will appoint one if it is in your power, and send me news of it however the case may stand.

I am in hope that your Honor soon will favor me by an answer, and shall remain respectfully

Yours

<.......>

✦✦✦

ALS. Tx, TLP. Damaged, with words missing.

James Pinckney Henderson to William H. Wharton and Memucan Hunt

Department of State
Columbia Texas
Feb 11th 1837

Sirs

I am instructed by the President to direct you to enter into such negotiations with Genl Santa Anna or any of the authorized agents of Mexico as may in your opinon or judgement best advance the interest of Texas and bring about a termination of the present war between the two countries, as regards the terms of the intended treaty you are to be the sole judges. In great haste

Verry Respectfully
J Pinckney Henderson
Secy of State

✦✦✦

ALS. Tx, TLP. Published in *DCRT*, 1: 184.

Samuel May Williams to William H. Wharton

Phila. 11th February 1837

My dear Sir,

I was truly mortified yesterday, on making, an accidental application at the post office to find that your letter of the 4th from Baltimore had been lying there some days. Had the letter not Contained any thing relative to your monied inconveniences, I should have felt less sensitive on the subject, for the delay in hearing from me might be attributed to indifference. A feeling thank God that does not exist in my breast toward you, when an opportunity is presented me whereby I can serve you.

I had remained perfectly tranquil on the subject, up to yesterday, for I believed that between you and Henry [H. Williams] matters would be arranged. He mentioned to me, that he had requested you to draw, and offered to me as an excuse for so doing that he had a very heavy amount to pay during the close of last and beginning of this month. I knew it would be somewhat vexatious to you, to pass a draft, yet hoped you could by the aid of some friend do so, sooner than suffer inconvenience. I have written to Henry and requested him to remit you some money, and trust no further difficulties will be presented.

My project for the sale of 80 Sections of Land here although it moves on slowly, I am pleased to say I think is going on securely, and will be in a few days completed.

I have nothing from New York, beyond what I have communicated to Mr Wolfe relative to Col. Hockley's movement. On the subject of the Invincible I am without any thing further than you have already heard from Treat.

Please to let me hear from you and direct to me [at the] U.S. Hotel and I shall surely get it. Desiring to be presented to Mrs W

I remain Sincerely & truly yr friend & Obt St

Samuel M. Williams

✦✦✦

ALS. Tx, TLP.

Alphonse Joseph Yves Pageot to Memucan Hunt and William H. Wharton

Washington February 11th 1837

Gentlemen

I have received the letter you did me the honor to adress to me, in the 8th instant,[1] with several documents, in relation to Texas, accompanied with the request that "I should ascertain from my Government, as promptly as practicable, whether a Diplomatic Agent from Texas, would be received by it for the purpose of negotiating a Treaty of Amity & Commerce."

The functions I have the honor to fill near this Government do not permit me to enter officially any communication that does not emanate from its constituted authorities, or to interfere in any question which is not connected with the interests that arise from the existing relations between France & the United States. I am therefore compelled, by a sense of duty, to abstain from transmitting to my Government the request expressed in your letter of the 8th instant.

I am, Gentlemen, with great consideration Your's

A Pageot

✦✦✦

ALS. Tx, TLP. Alphonse Joseph Pageot was the French chargé to the United States, 1835–1837 and 1839–1840, and minister, 1842–1848. Pageot was married to Mary Ann Lewis, daughter of Andrew Jackson's friend Major William B. Lewis.

1. Wharton and Hunt to Pageot, February 8, 1837, *DCRT,* 1: 198.

James J. Mackall to William H. Wharton

New Orleans 11th. Febry 1837—

Sir,

I am anxious to receive information relative to the claim of John G MacKall's[1] which has been layed before the Committee on Claims [by] Mr. Daniel Jenifer,[2] a member from the State of Maryland. I will thank you to write me word speedily as possible specifying precisely the situation of the above business. I must also ask you to direct your letter to the care of Mr. A. Somerville,[3] Columbia Texas.

Your compliance with my request will confer a great favor on, Your obt. Servant

James J. Mackall

✦✦✦

ALS. Tx, TLP. James J. Mackall received a land bounty for Texas service (he is not otherwise identified). *Abstract of Valid Land Claims Compiled from the Records of the General Land Office and Court of Claims of the State of Texas* (Austin: John Marshall, 1859), 380.

1. This Mackall claim was a petition by the legal heirs of John G. Mackall, of Calvert County, Maryland, for property destroyed by British forces during the War of 1812. The claim was eventually denied for lack of evidence. *Senate Reports of Committees of the Senate*, 32d Cong., 1st Sess., Report No. 475, December 1, 1851.

2. Daniel Jenifer (1791–1855), of Maryland, an anti-Jacksonian in the Twenty-Second Congress, 1831–1833, and a Whig in the Twenty-Fourth through Twenty-Sixth Congresses, 1835–1841. He was also US minister to Austria, 1841–1845.

3. Alexander Somervell [vice Somerville] (1796–1854), originally from Maryland, served in the Texas army at San Jacinto. He was briefly secretary of war in the Burnet administration and was a member of the Texas Senate, 1836–1838. In retaliation for Mexican raids on Texas, President Houston ordered Somervell to undertake an expedition against Mexico in 1842. Somervell disbanded his force after attacking Laredo and Guerrero, but three hundred men continued and were taken prisoner by Mexican forces.

Joseph Eggleston Segar to William H. Wharton

Richmond Feby 12th 18387

Gentlemen,

As you will see from the proceedings of the Virginia Legislature, I have offered a resolution proposing the immediate recognition of the Independence of Texas. I intended to call up this resolution tomorrow—but finding much opposition to the measure I shall defer it a few days, in order to operate, as we say here, out of doors, & thus to produce a more favourable state of feeling & opinion on the subject.[1]

In the mean time, I will be pleased & aided much in this matter by your transmitting me, without delay, all the information within your reach. I would like to have one of the pamphlets containing Colo. Wharton's & Genl. Austin's speeches, made at N. York & Cincinnati[2]—

I am anxious also to be informed, in an authentic form, whether Genl. Jackson sustains the movement made in this matter by Mr Walker, of Mississippi, and whether our Senators &c wish any action on this subject by the Legislature. The argument used here against the measure I propose, is that our representatives in Congress are on the spot & knowing best what ought to be done, do not require any instruction. Please inform me particularly on these points—with any other information your view of the subject may suggest as being valuable.

Very Resply I am Your Obt. Servt.

Jos: Segar

✦✦✦

ALS. Tx, TLP.

1. *Speech of Joseph Segar, Esq., on the Motion of Mr. Chapman of Monroe to Instruct the Senators and Request the Representatives in Congress from the State of Virginia to Vote for the Immediate Recognition of the Independence of Texas, Delivered in the House of Delegates of Virginia, Feb. 23, 1837* (Richmond: Shepherd & Colin, 1837).

2. The pamphlet Segar refers to contains prints of speeches made in New York and Louisville.

James Tongue to William H. Wharton

Washington February 14th 1837

Dear Sir,

Inclosed is a letter addressed to the delegation from my county (Anne Arundel). I hope and believe the resolution I have requested them to make will be done. It will afford me great pleasure to serve your cause in [any] way—after reading the letter you will please to seal it and drop it in the post office. If I should conclude to send one of my sons to Texas I will either let him accompany you or call on you for letters of introduction to your friends in texas—

For my standing in society I refer you to Mr. Kent of Senat or Mr. [Daniel] Jenifer, Mr. McKim, Mr. Howard in Congress—and Mr. Maxcy Solicitor of the Treasury.[1]

Your most obt svt
James Tongue

✦✦✦

ALS. Tx, TLP. James Tongue (1779–1843) was a Maryland physician.

1. Joseph Kent (1779–1837), of Maryland, a Republican in the Twelfth through Thirteenth Congresses (1811–1814) and the Sixteenth through Nineteenth Congresses (1819–1826), governor of Maryland (1826–1829), and an anti-Jacksonian and Whig in the Twenty-Third through Twenty-Fifth Congresses (1833–1838). Isaac McKim (1775–1838), a Republican and Jacksonian Democrat representing Maryland in the Seventeenth and Eighteenth Congresses (1821–1824) and the Twenty-Third through Twenty-Fifth Congresses (1833–1838). Virgil Maxcy (1784–1844) was solicitor of the Treasury, 1830–1837, and US chargé to Belgium, 1837–1842. Maxcy was killed in the gun explosion on the *Princeton* in 1844.

Henry Howell Williams to William H. Wharton

Baltimore February 14th 1837

Dear Sir,

Your Esteemed favour of yesterday is at hand. Your Draft on me for 500$ five Hundred Dollars at 30 Days from 15th Inst favour of Fairfax Catlett Esq will be duly honored and I [am] much pleased that you found it convenient to pass a draft on me, for notwithstanding I am at the moment a little pressed It will be very convenient to pay the money 30 days hence.

I am much gratified that you continue Sanguine that the Independance of Texas will be acknowledged before Congress rises. With my best respects to Mrs Wharton

I remain Very Truly your Obt Servant
Henry H. Williams

✦✦✦

ALS. Tx, TLP.

R. S. Wharton to William H. Wharton

Washington City
Febry 14 1837.

My Dr Sir

Permit me to introduce to your acquaintance my worthy friend Mr Harrison[1] who will deliver this.

My object is to place Mr. Harrison before you in as favorable point of view as his acknowledged merits and talents will justify. But I will not trouble you with an elaborate effort in view of that and I shall content myself with merely observing that he is a kind-hearted honorable man. In these respects I vouch for him.

I have deemed it my duty to say thus much on behalf of my friend Harrison, inasmuch as it is well deserved, and as I have suggested him to you to be employed in doing writing of a confidential nature.

Mr Harrison is a particular friend of Dr J. O. Wharton and the Mason family.[2] He has resided in their section for years and in a word may be classed as being one of them—You may entrust business in his hands of the most confidential nature with the utmost safety, whilst his talents and qualifications will guarantee your entire satisfaction.

With profound respect I am, sir, affectionately Yours

R. S. Wharton

✦✦✦

ALS. Tx, TLP. R. S. Wharton, not otherwise identified.

1. Harrison, not otherwise identified.

2. John O. Wharton (ca. 1804–1875) was the son of Tennessee Senator Jesse Wharton (1782–1833), who raised William Harris Wharton and his brother John Austin Wharton following the deaths of their parents. John O. Wharton married Elizabeth Ann Mason (1803–1857), a member of the prominent Virginia family.

John Austin Wharton to William Harris Wharton

Liberty Bedford Co: Va. Feb. 14 1837.

Dear Cousin:

You have, no doubt, received a letter which I wrote to you some two, or three weeks ago. I should have written agreeably to promise, but I had nothing of interest or importance to communicate. I sent you by mail, some ten days or more since, the Lynchburg Virginian, the paper in which I had "Phocion"[1] republished, and a few comments of my own. As I anticipated, I had too little information and ability to do justice to the subject, and I discover from the public prints, that I was mistaken in supposing that the expedition under Gen: Bravo had been abandoned. The result of any attempt, however, which Mexico can make, on the independence of Texas, cannot be doubtful. The Spanish-American wants perseverance and stile & is deficient in energy & courage. Texas, it seems, is better prepared for the combat than she has ever been before. If accounts be true, her army has grown to be formidable for numbers as well as courage, and she possesses the advantages of a government completely organized and in successful operation. Among reflecting men, there can be now but one opinion as to the issue of the contest—Since I heard from you, Santa Anna has been at Washington, but I suppose he effected but little in your favor. What is likely to be the fate of Mr. Walker's movement in favor of the recognition of Texan Independence? Will not a measure, so much in accordance with the former usages of the government, and the wishes of a large portion of the American people, be adopted without a serious opposition? The only question involved in the case, is a question of delicacy. The United States once possessed the country, and have been supposed, for some time past, to be desirous of regaining it – and if it were at all a doubtful matter whether Texas would be able to maintain her present position, I should be in favor of acting in perfect conformity with the most approved notions of delicacy. But I regard the battle as "lost and won," and so, I think must every intelligent man. Under all the circumstances of the case, the course for us to pursue appears to be a plain one. Recognition will violate no principle of national law—and I presume no stipulation of our Treaty with Mexico—I cannot therefore believe that congress will adjourn, without adopting such measures as will prove perfectly satisfactory to you.

I wish you would write to me as soon [as] convenient, in reply to a letter I wrote you some little time since.

I hardly know what to say in relation to my bill with Doct: Roane[2] —and I certainly should never mention the subject to you again if you were certain you paid it—but I do not like the idea of Uncle Jesse's[3] Estate losing anything by me. If I can find out who is his representative, I shall feel myself in conscience bound to refund—

I should like much to hear something from your brother and sister. Please let me hear from you shortly– My respects to your Lady, and accept for yourself the assurances of my unabated esteem and affection.

Jno: A. Wharton

✦✦✦

ALS. Tx, TLP. John Austin Wharton (1803–1888) was an attorney, judge, banker, school superintendent, mayor of Liberty, Virginia, and rector of St. John's Episcopal Church.

1. A letter from "Phocion" urging Congress to recognize Texas independence was published in several newspapers about this time. See, for example, the *Daily National Intelligencer,* December 24, 1836. Phocion, the Athenian statesman and military leader, was known for his austerity and honesty.

2. Roane, not otherwise identified.
3. Jesse Wharton.

Thomas Walker Gilmer to William H. Wharton

Charlottesville
Feb. 16, 1837.

Dear Sir

On my return from Richmond to day, I had the honor of receiving yours of the 14th instant. The letters of introduction which you were so kind as to forward, have not yet arrived, & a previous letter enclosed by my friend Col. Preston, was sent to Richmond, from which place I hope to receive it before I set out for Texas. I am under great obligations to you for the information & facilities so promptly furnished, in the prosecution of my arrangements for a visit to your country. I expect to leave home on Thursday next, the 23rd inst. & shall from Guyandotte descend the Ohio & Mississippi to New Orleans, whence I wish to obtain a passage to the Texan coast, & shall adopt the suggestions you have so kindly made. I hope we shall meet in Texas, and I regret very much that I have not had an opportunity of forming your personal acquaintance and of welcoming you to all the hospitalities of my own home. May I ask the favor of you to return my acknowledgments to your colleague for the letters which I am happy to learn were forwarded by him with yours. I hope they will arrive before I leave home, though our mails are at this season very irregular. I shall go to Texas with the most favorable impressions of the country, and an enthusiastic admiration of the unsurpassed gallantry of its citizens in the cause of independence & liberty. Since I have thought seriously of visiting it, I have been surprised at the deep & pervading interest which is felt in Virginia for its future destinies. A great number of persons have declared to me their purpose of emigrating thither, if the report which I have promised them shall answer our expectations. I wish to form an accurate opinion of the climate, soil &c. &c.

which I shall communicate to the public of the United States on my return. I am glad to perceive that the danger of an invasion from Mexico is no longer to be seriously apprehended. If it were, I could venture to assure you that many a stout arm and intrepid heart would leave Virginia & join your ranks– I should have been very much pleased if we could have had a personal interview before I leave Virginia, but I hope we shall soon meet in Texas—I hope to be there by the 18th or 20th of March.[1]

accept the assurance of my sincere esteem yours
Thomas W. Gilmer

✦✦✦

ALS. Tx, TLP. Thomas Walker Gilmer (1802–1844) practiced law in Charlottesville, Virginia. He was a member of the Virginia House of Delegates, 1829–1836 and 1839–1840, and governor of Virginia, 1840–1841. He was also a member of Congress, 1841–1844. In February 1844, President Tyler appointed Gilmer secretary of the navy. He was killed in the explosion on the *Princeton* on February 15.

1. Gilmer traveled to Texas in 1837–1838 as an agent for a group of Virginians who were interested in land acquisitions. Once in Texas he was appointed by the government as a commissioner with Albert T. Burnley to negotiate a loan for Texas. He was unable to accomplish the assignment, but Texas awarded him $5000 in Texas bonds.

Thomas Jefferson Green to William H. Wharton

Charlestonn S.C. Feby 16th 1837.

Dear Sir:

I arrived here last night from Mobile where I was unexpectedly detained by our agent Mr. David White, in getting my drafts upon him settled.

Since my arrival here I have opened a negociation with Genl. James Hamilton, for funds to put our bank into operation– Genl. H. who has a larger control in the money market than any other individual in this country thinks most favourable of the scheme. We have not yet entered into specifications, but our prospects are bright—I shall leave here in two days for Washington city which place I calculate to reach by the last of this month—Genl. H. will probaly follow me soon after—

I wish you immediately upon the rect. of this letter, if you know where Samuel M. Williams, is to write him to meet me in Washington on the 1st of next month—he is one of our commissioners and it will be highly necessary that I should there meet him.

Not only yourself, but Texas, nationally is mainly interested in the negociation for it will be the only present means of geting money into the country. Please remember me most affectionately to your Lady & Waller.

Your friend & hml Servt.
Thos. J. Green

✦✦✦

ALS. Tx, TLP.

Edwin Gilliam Booth to William H. Wharton

Feby. 17th 1837—

Dear Sir,

May I solicit your indulgence for the trespass committed on your kindness in obtruding on your notice—a subject for your attention which I can only rely on those feelings of philanthropy—which are sometimes possessed to a sufficient extent to prompt the performance of a disinterested favour—During the last summer—Several gentleman & myself at the Virginia Springs—purchased of Col D. C. Barrett[1] of Texas—a fraction of a league of land about 3500 acres—lying on the Colorado River, six miles above Mina or Bastrop in Milams Colony—being a part of the premium lands—selected by R. M. Williamson as agent of B R Milam, as Empressario for the Mexican government. As the land is said to be very fertile—and of considerable prospective value—I am induced to solicit, from you any information you may possess—concerning the section of country in which it is situated the validity of Milam claims—or the parties above alluded to—the routine by which a title may be secured to a non resident of Texas—and whether it would be safe to settle it in any limited period—I also purchased of said Barrett—a 12 acre [tract] in Mina, concerning the prospects of which I would be pleased to hear—Barrett exhibited a regular and complete concatenation of conveyances embracing a very full—unconditional deed from Williamson as Milams Agent—to him for valuable consideration—I have been informed that Williamson says, Barrett has not fully complied with the conditions under which he made the deed to the land—and that he Williamson will contend for the land—I am unable to see however how a full and unconditional deed drawn and recorded by E. M. Pease (whose standing I would be glad to know) can be affected by a failure to comply with the conditions under which it was made—Williamsons recourse I think in that view—would clearly be against Barrett and not the land—Should you be able to date a reply to this as early as the 10th of March you will please direct it to Salubrity P[ost] Office—Gadsden County Florida after that period, my address will be Darvills P[ost] Office Dinwiddie Cty Virginia. The favour of your attention will be enhanced by its conferment on an entire stranger.

Very Respectfully
Edwin G. Booth

PS. You will oblige me by referring me to some lawyer about Mina in case I should be compelled to employ one. It is said—Williamson intends to contend for land (notwithstanding the unconditional deed given to Barrett) on the ground that Barrett has not paid for the land.

✦✦✦

ALS. Tx, TLP. Edwin Gilliam Booth (1810–1886) was an attorney in Nottaway County, Virginia.

1. Don Carlos Barrett (1788–1838) practiced law in Pennsylvania before coming to Texas, where he opened a legal practice with Elisha M. Pease. He was a delegate to the Consultation of 1835 and was the main author of the document supporting the Mexican Constitution of 1824. He subsequently chaired the committee to draft a plan for the provisional government and was elected to the Provisional General Council. In April 1836, Barrett went to Blue Sulphur Springs, Virginia, for health reasons, where he met Booth. He returned to Texas in 1837.

George Washington Hockley to [William H. Wharton]

New York
18th Feby. 1837

My Dear Sir

Your letter dated 14th is just arrived, having been delivered by mistake to Mr. G. W. Holley,[1] and now sent by him. The draft you mention was drawn by Col. Bee, for a part of the expences of the escort of Genl. Santa Anna, and shall be paid as soon as we can make arrangements, through Mr Yates or otherwise, — of the time you can form as just an opinion as myself. Certainly nothing will raise our credit until our Independence is recognized, but this amount can be paid sooner than it would be collected by a Suit, which is to be avoided on many accounts. Will you assure Mr Allen that it will be paid?

Tis unaccountably strange that Dunham[2] did not send the money by [John] Fisher—he had it with him, and that is one cause of its scarcity with me.

My Dear Sir you are altogether in error as regards me. The abrupt departure I thought you understood as caused by my expectation to overtake Genl. S[anta] A[nna] at Balto. I called on you, however, without the formality of leaving my card. The coldness & formality complained of exist entirely in "misconception" — dismiss such ideas. I never profess what I do not feel, and had those feelings been aught but cordial and friendly, to you, it would have been perfectly apparent.

I write you in a hurry, this is our last day before the <.....> of the Invincible, and I hasten to endeavour to get the money or make some arrangement. Col. Wolfe not arrived. Make my respectful compliments to Mrs Wharton, and believe me, truly this in great haste

Your friend & Mo Ob Servt
Geo. W. Hockley

✦✦✦

ALS. Tx, TLP.

1. G. W. Holley, not otherwise identified.

2. Dunham, not otherwise identified.

J. Pinckney Henderson to [William H. Wharton]

Columbia Texas
Feb 18th 1837

Dr Sir

I have received your letters [to] genl Austin in which you complain of not he[aring] from Texas and allow me to compliment you upon your faculty of scolding. As they were [not] addressed to me I will take no part of it to <......> but try in future to merit none.

We have but little local news to give you. All things move on well at home. The pe[ople] are satisfied with their Government and find themselves able to protect it against <......>.

Recent intelligence from Coln Sagene[1] at Sant Antonio informs us that the Mexicans at Matamoras intend invading Texas so[on]. A spie captured by him alledges that they intend to come into the country with about 700 cavalry and take possession of Bexar a[nd] Goliad with a view of treating with us. This is not much to be relied on. I do not believe they will again invade us. All the militia in this region are enrolled and ready < . . . > when called upon, they turn out well. We [have] had no recent intelligence from th[ere] and consequently know not how Congress has disposed of our case. You perhaps have heard of the unpleasant difficulty which took place between Genls Johnston and Huston when the former took command of the army. Genl Huston being displeased at the appointment of Genl Johnston and have challenged him the day he took command. They fought and on the 5th fire Genl J—received a severe wound in his thigh. Genl J—is a perfect novice at such business but stood it bravely. Harmony is completely restored in the army and between the two Genls and Genl J is fast recovering from the wound which was in the flesh alone. The army is well supplied—increasing daily and are in good cheer and anxious for the fight. We feel perfectly secure against Mexico if the Indians were checked one would fear nothing.

In about three weeks the Cabinet will remove to the Cty. of

Houston which is improving rapidly. I have resigned the office of Atto. Genl. and accepted the appointment of Secy of State, Genl Rusk having declined from his own and his families indisposition.

Coln W G Hill has been elected to the senate from this District.

Tell friend Hunt I will write him soon again. I hope next [to] hear from you that the U.S. have recognized our independence and perhaps more. Wh[at day] and hour did Genl Santa Anna leave? Whe[re] did he sail for? and had he heard of Busta[mante's] return to Mexico from France? I will write soon again.

Yours with Great esteem &c
J. Pinckney Henderson

✦✦✦

ALS. Tx, TLP. Damaged, with missing text.

1. Juan Nepomuceno Seguín (1806–1890), a native of San Antonio, was an officer in the Texas army during the revolution. His unit fought at San Jacinto, and Seguín became the military commander, and later mayor, of San Antonio. He also served two terms in the Texas Senate. In 1842, Seguín went to Mexico. He fought against the United States in the Mexican-American War, but returned to the United States after the conflict.

Samuel Swartwout to William Harris Wharton

N York 18 Feb 1837

My dear friend,

Thomas E. Davis[1] & myself have this day released the Invincible from her difficulties and if Col Wolfe comes prepared to pay for the shipment of her crew, we may sail in 48 hours for Texas.

The amount we paid was about 2400 Dolls. I have only time to tell you this before the mail closes. She would have been sold by the Sheriff but for our exertions—Present my respectful compliments to Mrs Wharton Genl. Hunt & Mr. Treat.

Yrs etc
S. Swartwout

✦✦✦

ALS. Tx, TLP.

1. Thomas E. Davis was a New York real estate speculator and developer.

J. Pinckney Henderson to William H. Wharton

Columbia Texas
Department of State
Feb 19th. 1837

Sir,

Your despatches No 1, 2, 3 and 4 have been received, also your despatch of the 15th of January not numbered, but which I take to be the next in No.[1] and I am instru[cted] by his Excellency the President to inform you that he is well ple[ased] with the prospect of your success in your mission and the abili[ty] which you display in conducting the negotiations.

From recent information received by the Executive in relation to hostilities committed on the frontier settlem[ents] of Texas by Caddoe & Kickapoo Indians, it again becomes my duty to instruct you Gentlemen to loose no time and spare no labor in again representing to the Government of the Unite[d] States the necessity of its again occupying the station it formerly held near Nacogdoches in Texas with a sufficient number of Soldiers to keep those Indians from committing such outrages [in] future.

The information above alluded to as recently given to [his] [E]xcellency the President of this Republic is that a party of Kic[kapoos in] conjunction with some of the Caddo tribe amounting i[n all to bet]ween eighty and one hundred warriors made an attack a few weeks [s]ince upon our upper settlements on the eastern waters of the Brazos River and murdered several families; that the attack was made with[o]ut any thing to provoke it on the part of the citizens of this Republic and threatens to extend through the settlements in that Region a[s fa]r as the line between this Republic and that of the United States without [this] Government being able to check it owing to the necessity of its holding [all the] the soldiers of the Government in readiness to meet the Mexicans [i]n the west in the event of another invasion from that quarter.

These Indians now occupy that region of country east of the Naches and bordering on the line of the United States and have emigrated from the limits of the United States to that region without the consent of this [Go]vernment or the Government of Mexico and taken possession of the grounds [they] now occupy. It is rumoured and accredited here that a general [com]bination of the different tribes of Indians in the north and East has [been] formed and encouraged by the Mexican authorities to commen[ce] general war in that region upon the whites and as those Savages have [no] idea of the boundary between Texas and the U. States or their seperate [p]olitical existence they will not confine their aggression to our citizens alone, [5]00 soldiers stationed near Nacogdoches alone can prevent the continua[tion of] such depredations.

You mention in your despatch No. 4 that complaint had been made [to the] Government of the United States by some officers of the Brig Pocket.[2] You can assure that Government that this Government will at any [tim]e cheerfully hear the claimants and give all such as are entitled to it, speedy Justice as soon as their claims are properly laid before it.

I have the honor to be Gentlemen your &c &c
J Pinckney Henderson
Secy of State

✦✦✦

ALS. Tx, TLP. Document edges damaged. Published in *DCRT,* 1: 194–195. Missing text taken from *DCRT.*

1. Wharton's dispatches of December 22, 1836, No. 1, *DCRT,* 1: 157–158; December 28, 1836, No. 2, *DCRT,* 1: 158–160; December 31, 1836, No. 3, *DCRT,* 1: 166–168; January 6, 1837, No. 4, *DCRT,* 1: 168–172; January 15, 1837, [No. 5], *DCRT,* 1: 174–177.

2. The American merchant vessel *Pocket* sailed from New Orleans in March 1836 with a cargo that included military supplies for Mexico. Several Mexican naval officers were among the passengers. Captain Jeremiah Brown, on the *Invincible,* prized the *Pocket* near the Rio Grande on April 3, 1836, and escorted the ship to Galveston. When the *Invincible* went on to New Orleans, the aroused merchant community of the city had Brown and the crew arrested for piracy. William Bryan and the Toby brothers, Texas supporters in New Orleans, eased the situation by purchasing the

Pocket for $35,000. Subsequently, however, Captain Brown was charged in a civil suit by the *Pocket's* insurance carrier, which required further financial intervention by Bryan and the Tobys. In 1838, Texas and the United States signed a treaty in which Texas agreed to pay claims worth $11,750 for the *Pocket* and another prize case, the *Durango* (*Treaties*, 4: 125–131).

Robert Mayo to William H. Wharton

Washington, Feby. 22d. 1837.

Dear Sir,

Having expressed, in several conversations with you, my determination to become a Citizen of Texas, which determination, I also communicated to my friend Doctr Archer when here last winter, I now avail myself of your friendly permission to show you the accompanying letters from eminent citizens of Virginia, & other distinguished individuals in the Departments here, who have been acquainted with me for several years, that you may have it in your power to advert to these testimonials (if you would think proper) in confirmation of any favorable impression my short acquaintance may have made with you, in addressing a letter you have so kindly offered to do, in my behalf, to the President of Texas. I have had the favor of personal acquaintance, with General Houston, in Washington, a few years ago, as I have informed you, & flatter myself he is as favorably predisposed from that acquaintance as I could desire, to receive tidings through you, of my wish to become a Citizen of Texas, if some situation could be assigned me in the government so as to prevent me from falling into embarrassments as a new emigrant without much of pecuniary resources.

Your kind offices, Sir, in this endeared hope of my future life, will ever be cherished with the warmest gratitude.

I have the honor to be, Sir, With high consideration,
Your Obedt Servt
Robert Mayo.

✦✦✦

ALS. Tx, TLP. Robert Mayo (1784–1864), a Virginia physician, edited the *Jackson Republican* in 1826, which supported Jackson for the presidency, and became a clerk in the War Department. However, when he did not receive the position of Librarian of Congress, he turned against Jackson. In 1839, Mayo published *Political Sketches of Eight Years in Washington*, in which he accused Jackson and Sam Houston of a conspiracy to "dismember the Mexican dominions." (Baltimore: Fielding Lucas, 1839), 16.

James Hamilton to William H. Wharton

Charleston Feby 22d 1837.

Dear Sir—

When your polite favor ~~of~~ reached this City I was absent from home and since my return multiplied engagements have prevented my more early acknowledgedments of the kindness which dictated your Letters—

I assure you, you owe me no obligations for the course which I took in the Senate of S. Carolina on the subject of Texas. It was altogether consistent with my own views of justice & policy, and altho I had to differ with an old & approved friend & political associate in the person of our late Governor I never approached any politic[al] question as a Southern man with a more undoubting conviction that our true interest is to stand by Texas as her close ally either in the issue of Independence or annexation.

I greatly regret to see the miserable lukewarmness & procrastination attending the bace discussion whether you shall or shall not be recognized by our government during the present session. Sectional and political views have now entered into the consideration of this subject which much frustrate for a time the wishes of your friends & your object, until one of two events occurs—Either a pacification between Texas & Mexico resulting from Santa Anna's reestablish[ment of] his power; or another San Jacinto which must be decisive of your struggle.

Genl Thos J. Green has just left me on his way to Washington—As it can be no secret to you I feel myself at liberty altho' his dispatches were confidential to state that I deeply regret that the circumstances of my family and my domestic engagements absolutely on inseparable moral grounds forbid my leaving home for any length of time during the present year which of course precluded the possibility of my accepting the Command of the Army of Texas which the Congress of your Republic has tendered in a manner so eminently complimentary & gratifying to myself.[1]

Pray say to Genl Green that in conformity with my promise that I have written fully to Mr Biddle[2] and that I shall on his account write him (Genl G) directing to any place which he may advise me.

I remain with great Consideration & esteem very respectfully & faithfully Your obt servt

J. Hamilton

P.S. Be so kind as to make my respect to Col. Wolfe if he is still in Washington and present to him my best acknowledgment for his kind Letter.

✦✦✦

ALS. Tx, TLP.

1. On December 22, 1836, Texas offered Hamilton command of its army (*Secret Journals*, 315). Hamilton's domestic arrangements included care and support of his own eleven children plus guardianship of eight children of a deceased cousin.

2. Nicholas Biddle (1786–1844), president of the Bank of the United States.

Barnard Elliott Bee Sr. to William H. Wharton

Pendleton [South Carolina] Feby 22d / 37

My dear Sir,

Your letter of the express mail did not reach me till yesterday. Do say to Mr Chilton[1] I can have no draft. The money has been remitted from Charleston to meet the Lexington draft of $500! As to the $1500 in Washington I wrote to Mr Yates today he must attend to the whole —but as this will depend upon our recognition (for I suppose he cannot get money until that event) I shall have my portion $500 placed in the Bank, and Col Hockley will his. This will leave Pattons[2] unprovided, but I will immediately write to Col Hockley so that he may share it—You shall be put to no inconvenience—I shall leave this for Texas by the 15th March—as I perceive Congress meet on the 1st April so that if you wish me to attend to anything for you, write to me.

I fear we will not be recognized this session! I cannot account for this without Genl Santa Anna requested it! It has occurred to me that he thought he would be able to smooth his way at home upon all points, if the recognition was postponed! The pride of his People seemed to be the chief difficulty he apprehended. ~~and if he could get them to consent to the disposal of Texas to the U.S.~~ He appeared to me to think if he could at once dispose of Texas to the U.S. without any allusion to it as a revolted Colony, he would be happy, and that this would be more possible without than with a recognition of Independence! But I am by no means certain he took this view with Gen'l Jackson, tho' I repeat, I do not know him how else to account for the delay, if all parties appeared to me to be in favor, of acknowledgement—annexation was another thing—and the question of purchase, will involve the same question.

Peace, I consider as established, and if we could be only wise at home, I would just as soon be Independent, as annexed—I found my family quite well—I wish I could persuade Mrs. Bee[3] to pass the Spring with Mrs. Wharton. Remember me to her & your Son.

I am Sincerely Yours
Barnard Bee

+++

ALS. Tx, TLP.

1. Chilton, not otherwise identified.

2. William Hester Patton [vice Pattons] (1808–1842) arrived in Texas from Kentucky in 1832. He was a soldier in the revolution and served at San Jacinto. Patton was one of the commissioners appointed to escort Santa Anna to Washington. He was murdered by bandits at his home south of San Antonio.

3. Ann Wragg Fayssoux Bee (1789–1858).

James Tongue to William H. Wharton

Prospect Hill Farm
Anne Arundel County
Maryland Feby 23d.
1837

Dear Sir,

I take the liberty to address a few lines to you—perhaps one of my sons can make it convenient to go out with you, provided it would be agreeable to you—we would prefer to get every information—to sell our comfortable homes is a very serious consideration, but so it is my mind has been running on Texas some time; and I am under the impression it will be better for my children. I know that to break up in an old settled and comfortable situation in life and settle in a new country is very trying to ladies who have been accustomed to all care, comforts and many of the luxuries of life. To myself it is a matter of little consequence except I believe I shall get clear of a rheumatic affection that I have been afflicted with for years. If we should conclude to go there will be several respectable families and it would be desireable to us to settle near as possible to good society. Now if convenient I will thank you to inform me what grants of land are given to actual settlers? and where those grants will be located? If we settle near to each other can we purchase land and at what price per acre? We would prefer to be near the sea coast, or near, indeed immediately on some navigable river where we could ship our produce immediately to the atlantic cities, and where we could receive in return such articles as our families would require. I have been a regular bred physician and practiced many years, for the last ten years have been scaling vessels, and ship Timber of white oak and yellow pine and I believe I am perfect master of that business—If Texas should build a navy I think if proper inducements were offered to me by the government, I could be instrumental in establishing a navy yard, and geting good carpenters—tho' I must confess at my time of life I would prefer to be making cotton on a good, healthy farm on or near to some good society and where the productions would amply reward farming operations—provided I sell out my lands in Maryland I shall be obliged to sell on a credit.

After I saw you I heard the Texian government wanted to have some naval vessels built in Baltimore—if such is the fact and any assistance I can render I will do it cheerfully without fee or reward as I am personally acquainted with all the principal shipswrights in Baltimore—I should be pleased to hear from you on the subject of this letter as soon as it meets your convenience.

Yours with much respect
James Tongue

Governor Kent of the U.S. Senate, Honbl Mr McKim, Mr Jenefer and Mr Howard of congress can inform you of my standing in society.

✦✦✦

ALS. Tx, TLP.

James M. Wolfe to William H. Wharton

New York Feb. 25th 1837

Dear Wharton

I have sent the Invincible to sea with orders to repair to Galveston bay and directed Captain Brown to report himself to the Secretary of the navy. You will now see who is the friend of Texas. The Invincible started today. Mrs Brown[1] is on her way to Virginia and will call to see you at Washington[;] brother[2] has made preparations to receive you and Mrs W and to entertain you during your stay here. I have been visited daily by our friends here who desire to be rem[embere]d to you

yr friend J. M. Wolfe

✦✦✦

ALS, Tx, TLP.

1. Mrs. Brown, not otherwise identified.

2. Wolfe had two brothers in New York: Joel and Udolpho. They were very successful liquor importers.

Samuel May Williams to [William H. Wharton]

Phila 25th February 1837

My Dear Sir,

I duly recd your esteemed favor of 21st. and in accordance shall endeavor to arrange business here, so as to be with you on the 1st. and to meet Genl Green, to whom please present me if he is with you when this reaches you.

I am sorry that the question of our recognition stands so badly in Congress. Yet for me I will neither despair nor complain, if we are true to ourselves we can in my opinion get on without it, at any rate as a Texian I am willing to try—and hope never to be found wanting when I can serve the cause of my Country. You may rely upon me for what I am worth in any capacity or in any situation and at all times.

I have no news to give you—I shall have some few of the Citizens of this City interested in Texas lands, and hope to get more– for I want of matter, I do not extend—

yours truly
Samuel M Williams

✦✦✦

ALS. Tx, TLP.

John Richardson to William H. Wharton

Liberty Va 26 Feby 1837

Dear Sir,

Indisposition has detained me here until now and my pecuniary concerns will do the same until the middle of April. In the meantime the attention of several of my neighbours of respectability and independence has been turned to Texas and I have frequently been asked

What quantity (if any) of land is granted by the new Government to <u>actual</u> <u>settlers</u> and what are the general provisions of the law in regard to them? The scarcity of printed information upon the subject will I trust be an apology for my requesting a reply from you at your leisure together with any thing else that you may consider useful to those who have an idea of emigration. I have little doubt but several families leave here for Texas during the present year should the political aspects of the country remain as at present.

Have the surveys commenced?

With great respect Your mo obt servt
John Richardson

+++

ALS. Tx, TLP. John Richardson, not otherwise identified.

Carey Allen Harris to William H. Wharton

Washington, 27th Feby 1837

Dear General

Permit me to introduce to you my friend Dr. Reynolds,[1] U.S.A. who wishes to see you in Regard to some matters in Texas. If you can communicate any facts or can forward his views in any way, I will esteem it a favor to myself if you will do so.

Yours Truly
C. A. Harris

+++

ALS. Tx, TLP. Carey Allen Harris (1805–1842), of Tennessee, formerly chief clerk of the War Department, was commissioner of Indian Affairs, 1836–1838.

1. Reynolds, not otherwise identified.

Jeremiah Brown to William H. Wharton and Memucan Hunt

New York Feb 27 1837

Messrs Wharton & Hunt

My Brother will pressent you this. He escorts my wife to Charlotte Ct House VA where she will remain untill I return & having left her without means & destitute of funds I would ask a favour in the way of loaning me say as you can spare $150 or $200 you would imprint a kindness Lasting please pay the same to my broth. Thomas.[1]

& I Remain cincerly yours

J Brown

N B Mr Wolf promised me the above sum but I am obliged to sail before seeing him

(Poscript) This day the Invincible sails in complete Repair partly Maned & Provisions for the same with the advice & consent of Messrs Wolf & Swartout.

✦✦✦

ALS. Tx, TLP.

1. Jeremiah's brother, not otherwise identified.

Wharton was frustrated in Washington. He complained frequently about the failure of his government to stay in touch with him, grumbling on one occasion about "how embarrassing it is to be asked fifty times a day what news from Texas and to be compelled to reply I have no despatches" (Wharton to Austin, December 31, 1836, DCRT, *1: 166–168). Of course, the illness and death of Secretary of State Austin on December 27, 1836, and the appointment of Henderson as his replacement slowed communication from Texas, but Wharton had a point when he objected, for example, that he had not received any instructions regarding negotiations with Santa Anna, who was about to arrive in Washington (Wharton to Austin, January 15–17, 1837,* DCRT, *1: 174–177). On February 12, 1837, Wharton informed his government that he wished to return to Texas when the Twenty-Fourth US Congress adjourned on March 3, 1837 (Wharton to Rusk, February 12, 1837,* DCRT, *1: 184–186).*

J. Pinckney Henderson to William H. Wharton

Department of State
Columbia Texas
February 28th 1837

Sir

Your communication No. 6 February 2d. has been received by his Excellency the President but the other you refer to as having been sent by Mr [William H.] Patton has not reached him.[1]

You request permission to return home as soon as the Congress of the United States adjorns. I am ~~instructed~~ directed by his Excellency to say to you that he regrets that such is your request and desire, but that you may have leave to return after the period refered to and further I am ~~instructed~~ directed by his Excellency to instruct you to hand over to the Honbl Memucan Hunt before you take your departure all official papers in your hands connected with your Mission as he will be instructed at the Same time to remain as resident Minister in your stead.

I am with high consideration Your Humble Servant
J Pinckney Henderson
Secy of State

✦✦✦

LS. Tx, TLP. Published in *DCRT*, 1: 200.

1. Wharton to Houston, February 2, 1837, No. 2, *DCRT*, 1: 179–181; Wharton to Austin, January 15, 1837, No. 5, *DCRT*, 1: 174–177.

J. Pinckney Henderson to Memucan Hunt

Department of State
Columbia Texas
February 28th. 1837

Sir

The Honbl Wm. H Wharton having asked and obtained leave to return home after the Congress of the United States shall have adjorned,[1]

I am directed by his Excellency the President to instruct you to remain at the City of Washington as resident minister after his departure. You will receive from that Honbl Gentelman all of the official documents in his hands in any way connected with his and your mission which he has been instructed to deliver to you.

It is desirable that frequent and easy communication should be established between the Citizens of the United States and those of Texas by means of regular mails in the Territory of the two Governments which shall regularly meet at proper points on the dividing line and this Govermment having established regular weekly mail lines to Gaine's Ferry on the Sabine River and also to Ballous Ferry on the same River you are therefore instructed to use all the necessary exertions to induce the Government of the United States to extend their mail route to each of those points so as to accomplish this desireable object

You will from time to time and frequently communicate to this Department the progress of your mission

I am with the highest Consideration Yours &c
J Pinckney Henderson
Secretary of State

P.S. If the post offices refered to cannot be established immediately on the banks of the said Sabine River you may have it arranged so as to have them at the nearest possible point.

Respectfully
J Pinckney Henderson
Secy of State

✦✦✦

LS, with postscript in Henderson's hand. Tx, TLP.

1. Wharton to Rusk, February 12, 1837, No. 8, *DCRT*, 1: 184–186.

J. Pinckney Henderson to Memucan Hunt

Columbia Texas
Feb 28th 1837

Dr Genl

Since your departure I have written you several letters but time has not allo[wed] an answer. Herein enclosed you will receive instructions from the State Department, Coln Wharton having asked and obtained leave from the President to return home.

All things move on smoothly here but we are necessarily somewhat at a loss to know t[he] precise understanding entered into between Genl Jackson and Genl Santa Anna which I presume they found it necessary to conceal. We all believe that our difficulties will [be] speedily and favourably settled.

Since you left here I have resigned my o[ffice] of Atto Genl and accepted the appointment [of] Secretary of State. Coln P W Grayson has been appointed Atto Genl to fill the vacancy occasioned by my appointment to the office of Secy of State. If this change has not been noticed please have have it done in the City papers as some confusion is brought about by private letters com[ing] here addressed to me as Atto Genl & Genl Austin as Secy of State between which we cannot discriminate. In a few weeks we will move to the City of Houston.

All matters in the army are now quiet, the difficulty between Genls Johnston & Huston having been settled on the most amicable terms. Genl Johnston is still in command.

Nothing is feared now except from the Indians. They continue to commit depredations upon the North Eastern frontier which you will continue to engage in the most solemn manner in pursuance of your formal instructions.

If you can get capital as we spoke of before you left here do so. I can invest it to great advantage. Land is rising slowly but great bargains can always be had.

Genl Sam Houston asks to be remembered in the spirit of great kindness to you he is a good friend of yours and I have, you know spared no pains to impress him and all others with your merits.

Your Friend
J. Pinckney Henderson

+++

ALS. Tx, TLP. Damaged.

Toby and Brother to William H. Wharton

New Orleans Feby 28 1837

Sir

Your favor 18 & 19 inst reached us yesterday, they do really contain Good news & Rea has given the purport of your letter in his paper this morning.[1] Texas is independant & can maintain it, all that is wanted [is] money & if necessary 10.000 men could be to the field in two months notice. The army at last date was about 1200 strong in Camp. We have since dispatched 400 & 100 men ready to leave. These are men from the west, where some of our recruiting officers have been all winter. We consider it useless to send more soldiers, as we feel confident they will not again attempt an invasion. A letter from Campeachy 14 inst says that Mr. (Santa Annas Bro in Law) had been removed from his station at Campeachy & another appointment in his stead an enemy of S.A & that he had instructions to receive him. Also that the Mexican fleet had been sent to sea to intercept him in case he attempts to land.

We are anxiously looking for an arrival from Mexico, which will give us the news of Santa Annas arrival then we feel confident the soldiers will again follow him.

We have dates to 15 inst from Velasco; all is quiet there.

Vy Respectfully Your obedt. Servt
Thomas Toby & Brother

+++

ALS. Tx, TLP.

1. Putnam P. Rea was the editor of the New Orleans *Commercial Bulletin.*

Joseph Eggleston Segar to William H. Wharton and Memucan Hunt, with Enclosure

Richmond, Feby 28th, 1837

Gentlemen,

You have probably percieved from the Richmond papers, that I introduced on Thursday last a resolution, proposing the recognition of Texan Independence. By the nonattendance of friends—together with the fact that many members of the House using altogether the right of the Legislature to instruct their Senators—the proposition was defeated. You are perfectly at liberty to state, upon my authority, if you choose, that a large majority of the Legislature of both branches are favorable to immediate recognition. The general objection however, that we had not time to discuss such matters—& that the subject belonged more properly to the Congress of the U. States & that body was better informed upon this subject than we could be.

Lest the indisposition of the Legislature to act upon this subject might be construed into an argument against immediate Recognition & might lessen the zeal of our Representatives, I this morning offered another Resolution, which was almost unanimously accepted—thru only voting in the negative—that removes all difficulty on this point. Thinking it material I herein enclose a certified copy of the Resolution.

Wishing success to the cause of Texas, I remain Gentlemen,

Very Resplly Your Obt Sert

Jos. Segar

✦✦✦

ALS. Tx, TLP.

Enclosure: Resolution of the House of Delegates of Virginia

Resolved by the House of Delegates of Virginia that in laying on the table the resolution submitted some days since proposing to instruct our Senators and to request our Representatives in Congress to vote for the immediate recognition of Texan Independence it was not designed by this house to express an opinion as to the propriety of said measure or to make any impression on the minds of our Senators and Representatives that the general assembly is opposed to the recognition of Texas,—but that it was the wish and the design of this assembly to have this subject entirely to the Congress of the United States to adopt that measure whensoever they in their wisdom and better information may deem it proper and expedient so to do.

Richmond Feby 28th 1837

I George W. Munford Clerk of the House of Delegates of Virginia do hereby certify that the foregoing is a true copy of a Resolution adopted on this day by the house of Delegates by a vote of ninety seven to three. Given under my hand the day & year aforesaid.

George W. Mumford,[1] C[lerk] H[ouse] D[elegates]

✦✦✦

ALS. Tx, TLP.

1. George W. Mumford, not otherwise identified.

G. M. Stone to William H. Wharton

Richmond Va March 2nd 1837

Dear Sir,

I have this moment arrived here & find a letter from Dr Archer to me, directing me to forward to you on his act. $2,000 by ~~or before~~ the 1st of March—since that period has already past, I feel it my duty to give you this note of explanation & assure you that as soon as I have an opportunity to see our friends all shall be arranged to your satisfaction. In the mean time I should be very glad to hear from [you] at this place especially if you have any news concerning Texas which you might be willing to communicate to me.

I am happy to remain yours with The highest respect,
G. M. Stone

+++

ALS. Tx, TLP.

In March 1837, the United States recognized the independence of Texas. Robert J. Walker, of Mississippi, had introduced a resolution in the United States Senate for the recognition of Texas on January 11, 1837, arguing that there was "no longer any reasonable prospect" that Mexico could reconquer the territory. The vote on the resolution was postponed, but on March 1, 1837, it passed by a vote of 23 to 19. On February 28, 1837, Waddy Thompson, of South Carolina, had offered a resolution in the House of Representatives providing for the outfit and salary of a minister to Texas whenever the president received "satisfactory evidence that Texas is an independent power." The bill passed by a vote of 121 to 76. Jackson approved the measure on March 3, 1847, and nominated Alcée La Branche, of Louisiana, as chargé d'affaires to Texas.

Upon the bills' passage, Wharton informed Henderson that "President Jackson has closed his political career by admitting our country into the great family of nations" (Wharton and Hunt to Henderson, March 5, 1837, DCRT, 1: 201). The president marked the occasion by inviting Wharton and Hunt to the executive mansion for a glass of wine.

Wharton and Hunt, in a gesture of appreciation to Texas stalwarts William C. Preston and Robert John Walker, informed the two men that Texas would like to place their busts in the Texas capitol. The gesture prompted Preston to express his thanks and elicited even greater effusion from Senator Walker.

Robert J. Walker to Memucan Hunt and William H. Wharton

Washington City March 4. 1837

Gentlemen

I have received your communication of this date, requesting on behalf of the independent republic of Texas, permission to have my bust taken to be placed in the capitol of your nation. In my own name and for my poor services I could never accept your proposition. It was as a representative of the wishes of the people of Mississippi, that I moved and advocated, in consonance with my own feelings and judgment, the recognition of your independence. My humble name must soon be forgotten as connected with this or any other transaction, but may it long be remembered, that it was a representative of the state of Mississippi who in the hour of your deepest gloom and danger predicted your success, when not a voice in either house of congress had been raised in your behalf, and who afterwards moved the resolution adopted by the American senate, recognizing the independence of Texas. For my state, then, and not for myself, in her name, and as one of her representatives I accept your offer.

Let me join you in congratulations upon the glorious event of the recognition of your National independence, an event with which your names must ever be proudly associated as the future Franklins of Texas, for I know that without your zealous aid and cooperation, Texas must yet have remained unrecognized. I marked with many a rising hope and ebbing fear your trembling solicitude, and beheld the overflowing joy with which your bosoms throbbed, when my country first inscribed the name of Texas, upon the roll of independent nations. It is done, and you have more than witnessed the birth of a new republic, the only one worthy [of] the name, except our own confederacy. Your star is now beaming in all the brightness of new born liberty. The history of your struggle, is a history of a series of actions of commingled valour and clemency, worthy your glorious parentage, unrivalled in moral sublimity, and which exalt & dignify the character of man. You are the child of our free institutions, the first born of our race who will carry onward and onward still, our language, laws, and liberty throughout our own America. Go on patriotic Americans, go on my countrymen, for such I must call you, go on noble and glorious people, and may the great disposer of the destiny of nations so order the course of events, that the single luminary, which now shines from your country's standard, may break forth a constellation of lights, burning and beaming with our own kindred stars in perpetual brightness from the banner of the American Union.

with the deepest regard and consideration I am yours most truly

R. J. Walker

✦✦✦

ALS. Tx, TLP.

William Campbell Preston to Memucan Hunt

[March 1837]
Washington City

Gentlemen

Alltho' entirely persuaded that your personal kindness has placed much too favorable an estimate upon the importance of my official exertions in the cause of justice—liberty and patriotism involved in the Texas question—Yet I cannot recieve but with great sensibility, what you are pleased to say in you note of 4th Inst.

If I could for a moment believe that my zealous devotion to the recognition of the just claims of your Government had any efficient agency in accomplishing it. I should feel abundantly compensated for the labours and privations of public life and would enjoy an ever accumulating fund of self gratulation in the long and bright cause of freedom and prosperity which opens to your Young Republic. For whether it be destined to add other states to our own constellation or to shine on alone, its ~~destiny~~ progress cannot but be propitious to the great cause of liberty and philanthropy.

But the results which your country is to effect–are in the necessary course of things—in the established order of Providence—propagating and extending our Languages, Laws and Lliberty—and altho' its progress may be subjected to some slight vicissitudes (as all events which require human agency are)—yet the ultimate event is certain and inevitable—beyond the control of politicians or statesman, and vastly beyond the influences of any exertions of mine.

I yield therefore more to your wishes than my own sense of propriety when I comply with the request in your note and feel a deeper sense of your kindness because the compliment prompted by it, is undeserved.

With sentiments of the highest respect and esteem
I am Gentlemen Your obt. Sevt
Wm. C Preston

✦✦✦

ALS. Tx, TLP.

G. M. Stone to William H. Wharton

6 March 1837, Richmond

Dear Sir,

I have the pleasure to acknowledge yours of yesterday which has just been sent to me by Maj Saunders, I enquired this morning for it at the P.O. but did not receive it.

I wrote to you consequently informing you of the failure in my expectations of a letter from you—which you will receive perhaps tomorrow.

Maj Saunders has concluded to remit you a draft on Baltimore (which I enclose in this) as being most likely to oblige you as you mention the desires of immediately settling this act:

For my part I am Sorry to be so situated as to cause some delay in the receipt of the other half—but shall set out for Texas in a few days & on arriving at Natchez shall remit it to your merchant named in your letter, from that place—if it be possible. If not shall deposite it their to your order. Any letter sent here to the care of Mr Saunders will be forwarded to me, therefore if required you may communicate with me at any time, or you may write to Natchez—

I am delighted with the news of our recognition & am pleased to Congratulate you on your happy success in that negociation.

We know your difficulties & indeed so strong did they appear to me on the morning of the 3rd Inst. that in writing to Dr Archer assured him that we could not expect that favor during this session it being the last day and as far as we could learn no more action was likely to take place on that subject.

I shall be much gratified to correcte that error.

I am Your obt servant
G. M. Stone

✦✦✦

ALS. Tx, TLP.

G. M. Stone to William H. Wharton

6 March 1837. Richmond, Virginia

Dear Sir

I feel it necessary to make another effort to affect a mutual correspondence between us on the subject which Dr Archer has requested me to settle with you—

On arriving here on the 2nd Inst I informed you by letter that I have just received a request from Dr Archer to forward \$2000 to you, on his credit, & that it should be done immediately. On seeing Maj Saunders a gentlemen of this City I received your letter of the 12 Ult: requesting prompt attention to that request, I then again attempted to inform you by letter, as before, that you would oblige Maj Saunders & myself to accept drafts on Natchez & Orleans for the amount, but that it would be forwarded at least <u>\$1000</u> to you at Washington directly if you found it inconvenient to accept the drafts, ~~at least \$1000~~. The part that I shall pay is now in Greensborough Ala where I deposited it after collection not expecting to want it here & having to pass through that village on my return to Texas when I could get it again. We are expecting you here from report when I should be very happy to meet you & many others express a desire to meet & become acquainted with you & Mrs Wharton, ladies too are among this number. If you do come all matters will be arranged to your satisfaction, but if you do not be pleased to let me know your decision on this subject that I may attend to it promptly as I am nearly ready to return to Texas & am anxious to get out as soon as convenient. I expected a letter from you this morning but was disappointed.

You would please to inform Genl Green that I would be happy to hear the particulars of his success in the bank agency & at what minimum stock would best be sold &c. I think from appearances that I shall meet with no difficulty in disposing of the shares at this place entrusted to my care. People here appear to appreciate the institution properly & indeed Maj Saunders thinks that it will rise in value daily & recommends some delay in selling on that account, but I shall be governed much by the advice of Genl Green. I may leave this place for a few days tomorrow but I shall leave an agent to receive & act on any communication with which you may favour me. I congratulate you on your success in serving Texas & the cause of liberty generally, in securing a recognition of our Republic, under the circumstances of prejudice & fanaticism against which you had to contend. The world of philanthropists will appreciate the importance of the act in the cause of freedom & in the defeat of this rage & folly of crusading priestcraft.

Yrs with the highest respect
G. M. Stone

excuse haste.

✦✦✦

ALS. Tx, TLP.

Samuel Rhoads Fisher to William H. Wharton

Navy Department
Columbia March 7th 1837

Dear Sir,

I have the honor to receive yours of 6th ulto: on 28th of same month, and reply to it at the first opportunity.

With respect to the Capture and subsequent condemnation of the

Brig Pocket & Cargo I have nothing officially—But being in Galveston some days after the Brig Pocket was brought in, I went on board at the request of Secretary Potter,[1] to assist in the examination of the various papers on board of her—many of which were in the Spanish language. It is impossible for me to State in detail, or with minute accuracy all that occurred, but I have no hesitation in saying that my conviction, from the gross misconduct of the Capt. (Howes)[2] was and still remains to be that he was a great Scoundrel– his prevarication– equivocation, and downright lies, and affected ignorance of what a "Register" or "crew list" was satisfied me. There were Commissions for Mexican officers on board, and a survey, or surveys of the Island and Harbour of Galveston—a plan of fortification, and a long letter to Gen: Santa Anna from a man (I think of the name of Hogan)[3] recommending a particular mode for fighting the Americans. Daniel Somers,[4] one of the mates, also told me there was gun powder on board, but as they had not broken bulk I did not see it. There were several gentlemen present among others I think Judge Dinsmore,[5] and I think I am safe in saying we all felt fully justified in considering vessel and Cargo, as lawful prize, from the facts and evidence which appeared before us. I have subsequently understood from Capt. J. D. Boylan,[6] who then was lying in Brazos St. Iago, that he saw the Invincible when she captured the "Pocket" and that the pocket had the private signal of the commercial House of "Rubios",[7] agents for the Mexican Govt. flying at her foretop-gallant mast head, that he is familiar with said Signal, and knew it was theirs. The agents in New Orleans (Bryan)[8] I have always understood had paid the Capt. of the Pocket, for his Brig, and demurrage, and had his receipt. I will also mention that there was a man on board a Mexican whose name I do not remember, who had with him a commission, or appointment from the Mexican Government as Capt. of the "port of Galveston" (precocious anticipation!!!)—These are facts, and about the leading ones with which I am acquainted. It has often been said that the world knows more about one's affairs than the Individual, and so I presume it is in our present political relations. At Washington you appear to know less than we do here, for "out of Doors" say that we are speedily to be annexed, and scarcely talk of rcognition; and very properly, for if the former be true would not the latter act only as a clog?

It gives me pleasure to perceive the active Services of Major Catlett are in operation, and congratulate you upon having the assistance of a gentleman in whose qualifications I have reason to have so much confidence.

We remain much as usual, and our characteristic apathy or confidence is apparent everywhere.

I have the honor to remain with high consideration
Your friend & Obedient Servt
S. Rhoads Fisher
Secretary of the Navy

✦✦✦

ALS. Tx, TLP.

1. Robert Potter (ca. 1800–1842), Texas secretary of the navy from March 17, 1836, to October 22, 1836. Potter, a North Carolinian, was a US Navy midshipman, 1815–1821. He was admitted to the North Carolina bar, served in the state legislature in 1826 and 1828, and was a Jacksonian in the US House of Representatives, 1829–1831. Potter was reelected to the North Carolina House of Commons, but was expelled in 1835. He then came to Texas. He signed the Texas Declaration of Independence, served on the committee to draft the Texas Constitution, and was at the Battle of San Jacinto. Potter served in the Texas Senate from 1840 until he was murdered in 1842.

2. Elijah Howes, of Indian Fields, Massachusetts, not otherwise identified.

3. Hogan, not otherwise identified.

4. Daniel Somers, not otherwise identified.

5. Silas Dinsmore (ca. 1796–1846), chief justice of Matagorda County.

6. James D. Boylan was captain of the Texas vessel *Viper* and later of the *Brutus*.

7. Cayetano Rubio (1791–1876), with his brothers Juan and Francisco, ran a mercantile firm with varied commercial and financial interests.

8. William Bryan was appointed Texas agent in New Orleans in December 1836. He provided considerable financial support to Texas. He was replaced by Toby and Brother as agent, but later became Texas consul in New Orleans from 1839 until annexation.

John O. Wharton to [William H. Wharton]

Philadelphia March 8th 1837

My dear Sir

Mr J. T. Mason[1] who arrived here last night tells me you were kind enough to express much solicitude about my present situation as well as your determination to pay me an early visit. I feel that I could not do less than return you my hearty thanks for the one, & present the receipts for the other.

I am happy to say I am rapidly recovering from the operation to which I submitted some 10 days ago, in truth I am as nearly well as to be able to sit up without pain and with very little fatigue and am induced to hope I shall be able to leave this for Baltimore in a few days, with brighter hopes of the entire restoration of my health than I have had for months.

I congratulate you most cordially upon the favourable result of your labors during the winter in behalf of your adoptive Country, as well as upon the bright & brilliant prospect before her– May she become all your ardent fond fancy could desire & may you reap the reward which your distinguished success in her behalf so richly entitle you to, is the sincere prayer of your friend & Relation.

J.O. Wharton

P.S. Where is Genl. Green? I would write to him if I knew where my letter would find him—present me kindly & affectionately to your good Lady. Will you & she not come & spend a month with us now?

✦✦✦

ALS. Tx, TLP.

1. John Thomson Mason (1787–1850) was born in Virginia, but in 1812 moved to Kentucky, where he was appointed US marshal. He was superintendent of Indian Affairs in Michigan from 1830 to 1831, but resigned to become the agent of the Galveston Bay and Texas Land Company. Mason purchased and donated the ship *Liberty* to Texas and advanced funds for the purchase of the *Brutus*. He traveled frequently between New York and Texas and died of cholera in Galveston. He was a cousin of John O. Wharton's wife, Elizabeth Mason.

George Washington Hockley to [William H. Wharton]

Philadelphia
8th March 1837

My Dear Sir,

In consequence of an injury received a short time ago I have been unable to use my right hand—which has prevented me from congratulating you upon the successful termination of your labors in the cause of our adopted country. To your unremitted exertions, and able management I chiefly attribute the recognition of our Independence by the United States. We are now on the list of Nations, and of no contemptible rank—for we can safely challenge the world to show more forbearance, chivalry, magnanimity and mercy to the foe. Please present my compliments to Mrs Wharton and to Col. Wolfe also, and to the latter be good enough to make the apology with which this letter commences for not writing to him.

believe me, very sincerely and truly–
Your friend and Mo Ob. Servant
George Washington Hockley

Tomorrow I leave for New York and shall be pleased to hear from yourself and Col. Wolfe at that place. I send from Five to Eight hundred men from this place to Texas in about a month– armed and equipped– for two years service — if you have any articles of furniture, &c &c you wish sent out the vessel can take them. Excuse this my hand is still painful.

✦✦✦

ALS. Tx, TLP.

John Campbell to Memucan Hunt and William H. Wharton

9th March 1837

Gentlemen

I have the pleasure to acknowledge the reciet of your note of yesterday and am gratified in having had an opportunity of rendering a service however small to your infant Republic in organizing its financial system upon its first entrance into political life.

The manuscript volume of documents illustrative of the Treasury System of the U.S. with a historical sketch of the same from the commencement of our revolution to the present time which I have prepar'd and compil'd for my own private use I present to you with great pleasure under a hope it may be found useful to your government in its first movement as an independent power.

The Documents are principally from the pens of distinguish'd men who were placed at the head of the Treasury Department at an early period of our government and whose production will never fail to instruct and interest those whose duty or inclination may lead them to examine this subject.

Among them you will find the productions of Alexander Hamilton and Albert Gallatin[1] whose names alone are a sufficient guarantee of their great value.

I sincerely hope they may be found useful to your Government and that your young and rising country will in a short time be restor'd to tranquility & peace and become a happy home of political & religious freedom.

I have the honor to be with great respect your Ob St
John Campbell

✦✦✦

ALS. Tx, TLP. John Campbell (ca. 1789-ca. 1866), of Alabama, was Treasurer of the United States from 1829-1839.

1. Alexander Hamilton (1757–1804) had been the first secretary of the Treasury, 1789–1795; Albert Gallatin (1761–1849) was secretary of the Treasury from 1801 to 1814.

John Forsyth to Memucan Hunt and William H. Wharton

Department of State
March 10 1837

The Secretary of State presents his compliments to the Hon. Mr. Hunt and the Hon. Mr. Wharton, and will be happy to see them at the Department at 12 o'clock tomorrow, when he will examine their credentials, and fix a time for introducing them to the President.

✦✦✦

Unsigned note. Tx, TLP.

James Treat to William H. Wharton

New York March 10th 1837. Friday.

My dear Sir,

I arrived on monday night, after a fatiguing journey, found my clerk sick, and any quantity of business on hand, unanswered letters &c. &c. I did not see Williams, passing thro' Phila. tho' I left a note for him, giving him the news from Washington &c: Saw Col. Hockley, who told me, he would be here in a few days. Allen was snugly fixed at Phila., Swartwout & friends all well, and desired to be remembered to yourself and & madam. Also Gen. Hunt. We have no news either from Mexico, or Texas, or N. Orleans, later than you had from thence before I left you. We have all been in doubt about the confirmation of the agent for Texas: whether confirmd or not & whether it is Foote,[1] or Labranche:[2] or whether the confirmation was by the old or new Senate. I think myself Labranche was the man, not confirmed by the old, but the new Senate. Please inform me how it is.—also when he will depart for Texas. Say Labranche: also, when [Powhatan] Ellis will go, & in what way we will open negotiations, &c &c. Above all please inform me, when you leave Washington, & if you come this way to Embark. Should you do this, as I take it for granted you will from what you told when I took leave of you, we can settle our little money affairs, here—for this reason, I do not remit the amt supposing it the same thing to you. Should you change your determination & go from Washington by Land, South, dont fail to let me know in time, to receive my answer before you leave. dont forget this. Has Mr Poinsett arrived? You should make his early acquaintance on his arrival there, as he will doubtless have influence in the cabinet, and especially in relation to Mexican & Texas affairs. I shall write Mr. P. in a day or two & call his attention to these matters.

I left Washington without hearing from Gen Hunt in answer to my note, or seeing him. I hope & trust he will have been able to raise the money for me from Gen Foote, as anticipated, for I want it very much, as money is worth 2 to 3 p% pr month, here now & likely to continue. Give my compts to Gen Hunt, I may write him tomorrow, meantime I hope he will not forget me. We are all anxiety to learn the news of St. Anna's success, which I trust we shall soon hear—I missd Col Wolfe. I hope Texas will now begin to look up—Nothing from Yates. I think there is no prospects of his filling up his Loan, until money becomes easier. Present my Respectful Compts to Mrs. W. & remember me to Major Cattlett.

believe me in great haste & truly Yours—Cordially
J. Treat

don't forget my remembrance to that excellent fellow Mr. Weaver

✦✦✦

ALS. Tx, TLP.

1. Henry Stuart Foote (1804–1880), of Mississippi, an attorney and editor of the Jackson *Mississippian*. He became an advocate of Texas and published *Texans and the Texans, or Advance of the Anglo-Americans to the South-West*, 2 vols. (Philadelphia: Cowperthwait, 1841). Foote, a Democrat, was a US senator from Mississippi in the Thirtieth through Thirty-Second Congresses, 1847–1852, and governor of Mississippi, 1852–1854.

2. Alcée La Branche (1806–1861), of Louisiana, was made the first US chargé d'affaires to Texas by President Jackson, a post he held from March 3, 1837, to April 2, 1840.

James Tongue to William H. Wharton

Prospect Hill Farm
Near Tracey's Landing post office
Anne Arundel County
Maryland
March 10th. 1837

Dear Sir,

I did myself the pleasure to write to you about ten days ago — in which I said one of my sons would probably go in the same vessel with you to Texas—but he prefers to go by the way of the Mississippi to visit some of our relations near Natchez—and from thence go by the way of the Red River or by land via Nat[ch]itoches—I wish to know if not imposing too much trouble on you relative to the grants of land the texian government gives to actual settler, and when it will be located to them. If we determine to settle in texas, there will several families go, which are all respectable and would make valuable citizens to any country new or old—my impressions are we had all rather purchase land where we could settle near to each other, and on navigable water near the sea. Some of us would be first rate Tobacco planters. It is desireable if my son goes to Texas that he should have the advice and opinion of some old resident; who could give him all the necessary information—where it would be the most advisable for us to settle—terms—payments and a great many other things it would be necessary to know. I should be pleased to hear from you on this subject.

Yours with much respect
Jas: Tongue

✦✦✦

ALS. Tx, TLP.

Following recognition of Texas independence, Wharton and Hunt were received by Secretary of State Forsyth on March 12, 1837. They were informed, however, that since their credentials were not in the "usual form," they could not formally be accept-

ed as diplomatic representatives. Wharton returned to Texas. In July, Hunt presented a new commission as minister to the United States, which Forsyth accepted.

John Forsyth to William H. Wharton and Memucan Hunt

Washington, 13th March, 1837.

The Undersigned Secretary of State of the United States, has the honor to return to Messrs Wharton and Hunt the papers which he received from them in an interview at this Department on the 11th instant.

The President regrets that he cannot receive those gentlemen as the diplomatic representatives of Texas without letters credential in the usual form. As these are deemed indispensable, the President hopes they will be obtained with the least possible delay. Meanwhile, however, they can assure their government that all the rights of Texas as an independent power are recognized as fully as if its ministers had been formally received. The President considers the Texan flag as entitled to all the privileges stipulated for the Mexican flag in the treaty between the United States and Mexico, and the United States will claim for their flag all the benefits of that treaty in the Texan forts until some other arrangement shall be made between the two governments.

The Undersigned has been instructed to receive Messrs Wharton and Hunt to discourse on any matters of interest to the respective governments, whenever it may be thought useful. An Exequatur will be issued immediately to the Consul of Texas if it should be desired.

The Undersigned avails himself of the occasion to offer Messrs Wharton and Hunt assurances of his great consideration.

John Forsyth

✦✦✦

LS. Tx, TLP. Published in *IAA*, 12: 4–5.

J. Pinckney Henderson to Memucan Hunt

Columbia Texas
Department of State
March 14th. 1837

Sir

This is nothing connected with your duty as the Representative of the Government at the Court of Washington which requires more constant attention than the subject of Indian hostilities in Texas, to which you have been so frequently instructed to Call the attention of the Government of the United States.

News of new depredations and murders by the Indians reach his Excellency every week. This day news has reached him that the Honbl Mr Robinson a member of Congress and five of another family have within the last ten days been murdered by the Caddo Indians.[1] Those Indians have come over from the Territory of the United States and Settled or rather are now wandering over that of Texas, without any permission from this Government or that of Mexico. Before our separation by the declaration of our Independence, and by the treaty with Mexico that (the Government of the United States) is bound to keep those Indians and all others within its Territory from committing depredations on the Territory of this Republic

These facts you will not delay in laying before the proper authorities at Washington and urge the necessity of that Governments immediately mounting at least five hundred (500) men to range on the frontier between Red River and the Brazos River to prevent depredations in future of a like character.

I am with Great Respect &c &c
J. Pinckney Henderson
Secy of State

+++

ALS. Tx, TLP. Published in *DCRT,* 1: 202–203.

1. In February 1837 a band of thirty to forty Indians raided the Cummins Creek and Rabb's Creek area, in what is now Fayette County. John G. Robinson (also sometimes referred to as Robison or Robertson) was a member of the First Texas Congress. Returning to his home after the congressional session, John Robinson and his broth-

er, Walter, were killed. The same day the Indians killed several members of the James Gotcher family and made captives of one woman and three children.

J. Pinckney Henderson to Memucan Hunt

Columbia Texas
March 16th 1837

Dr Hunt

Consider all things as moving on in a smooth regular channel without any excitement or great variety and you will have our situation in Texas at this time.

I am excedingly anxious to hear from you by the next arrival as we have had nothing from you individually since your arrival in Washington. Vessels are expected every day from N Orleans but none have arrived within the last two weeks, what has been done with our case by Congress we know not but hope we will soon hear of its favourable disposition.

I fear that a negociation with Van [Buren] during the recess of Congress will be unavailing, and unless something is done by way of Treaty with Mexico all will be delayed until next winter.

Our army is increasing fast and is now stronger than it has been at any future period.

Great prudence in your action is now necessary so as not to excite northern jealousy against your mission. I know you will perceive and avoid this policy[.] in a diplomatist it is necessary in any other character it is detestible

Write to me often and disclose fully your private and political disposition and I will attend as far as I have it in my power to favour your inclination

Your Friend
J Pinckney Henderson

P.S. The treaty to which I refer in the instructions which accompany this letter is the Treaty between Mexico and the United States of April 5th 1831 Article 33—which you will refer to.

JPH

✦✦✦

ALS. Tx, TLP.

John Woodward to William H. Wharton and Memucan Hunt

New York 18 March 1837.

Gentlemen,

I some time since sent you my Commission as Consul Genl for recognition, but have not heard from you. Fearing some accident I will thank you to inform me whether it has been received.

Very respectfully Your friend and obt Servant
John Woodward

✦✦✦

ALS. Tx, TLP.

William H. Ellis to William H. Wharton

Canandaigua (New York) March 18, 1837

Dear Sir

Having a strong inclination to emigrate to your country I have thought fit to address you to obtain more particular information than I have thus far been able to obtain.

I wish to ascertain first, what are the terms for Land? What part is considered most healthy? What [is] the price of various bra[n]ches of Mechanical Labour? What Articles would be most likely to bear transportation from this place? and which [is] the most favorable season of the year to emigrate? Together with such information would be likely to interest one under circumstances above stated.

If you would be so kind as to send me an immediate answer to the above you will much oblige your

Most obedient Servant
William H. Ellis

✦✦✦

ALS. Tx, TLP. William H. Ellis (1802–1885) was a carpenter and building contractor in Canandigua.

John Forsyth to William H. Wharton and Memucan Hunt

Department of State
Washington, 21st March, 1837.

The Undersigned Secretary of State of the United States, has the honor to acquaint Messrs Wharton and Hunt that he received and laid before the President their note of the 14th instant communicating intelligence of recent robberies and murders by Indians within the limits of Texas, and suggesting the propriety of a reoccupation of Nacogdoches or some other point west of the Sabine by troops of the United States, with a view to prevent a reoccurrence of similar outrages.[1] The President submitted the letter of Messrs Wharton and Hunt to the Secretary of War, who in his report on the subject states that after an attentive examination of the positions now occupied by the forces of the United States it appeared to him that they were better calculated to effect the object of keeping the Indians in check than if the troops were concentrated at Nacogdoches, but that General Arbuckle[2] would be directed to move some of his [force] to a position within the [undisputed] boundary of the United [States] nearer the place where the aggressions complained of are represented to have been committed, and to use increased vigilance in observing any hostile movements of the Indians in that quarter.

The Undersigned embraces this opportunity to offer to Messrs Wharton and Hunt the assurances of his distinguished consideration.

John Forsyth

✦✦✦

LS. Tx, TLP. Published in *IAA*, 12: 5.

1. Wharton and Hunt to Forsyth, March 14, 1837, in Senate Executive Document 14, 32d Cong., 2d Sess., p. 5.

2. General Matthew Arbuckle (1778–1851) commanded US forces at Fort Gibson on the Arkansas River and Fort Towson on the Red River.

William C. Montross to William H. Wharton

Nunda Valley Livingston Co. New York
March 21st 1837

Sir,

I have a strong inclination for Texas, but find difficulty in getting information from there, that can be relied on—

In a conversation on the subject a few evenings since with our congressman, the Hon. John Young[1]—he told me that he had the honor of your acquaintance, & that he was confident you would take pleasure in giving me any information that I might desire– Accordingly, he advised me to address you on the subject—

The information I wish for, is concerning the inducements to emigrate to your Republic. Lands are offered as an inducement to go there. Are those offers made by responsible persons, & in good faith, & will they be fulfilled? If so, how much land to an emigrant– & where located? What their value—and for what purposes adapted?

Now as for myself—I am a young single man—bred to the law— & should it be desirable to myself or any one else—can go to Texas with recommendations from some of our most distinguished citizens.

If there are any inducements for such a person as myself to remove to the Republic which you have the honor to represent at the seat of our government—please tell me what they are.

As early an answer as may suit your convenience, would much oblige me– & perhaps do your state some service — Many others here are anxious for information on these subjects—

I am Sir, with the greatest respect your humble servt
Wm. C. Montross

✦✦✦

ALS. Tx, TLP. William Montross (1818–1860).

1. John Young (1802–1852), a Whig in the Twenty-Fourth Congress, 1835–1836, and the Twenty-Seventh Congress, 1841–1842. He was also governor of New York, 1847–1849.

Mortimer F. Delano to [William H Wharton]

Waterloo N.Y. 1837 March 22d

Sir

I transmit to your honorable consideration the following draft of a ball I invented by myself it is calculated for the distruction of shipping and fortifications of all kinds. You will observe on the right end a spring which is let in to the end and covered with a cap so that it is inclosed and protected by the cheek, on another side and by the cap on the end. The area that is marked No 1st is hung on a pivit and shuts down in no 2d and when discharged from a cannon is thrown out as you see. The end marked No 3 is calculated to strike first and when it penetrates to spring number 1st it explodes the ball being filled with powder it destroys what ever it hits and thus renders your enemies at your mercy. I have a modle now made and having shown it to several they unanimously concur in the belief of its successful operation. If you should concur in the same opinion and will let me know it, and can give me, any encouragement of a station in your Navy or Army it shall be at your command as well as myself.

Yours respectfully
M. F Delano

We have seen Mr M. F Delanos modle and have full confidence in its successful operation

Isaac Kimbel[1]
James De Bois[2]

✦✦✦

ALS. Tx, TLP. Mortimer F. Delano (ca. 1818–1845) was an attorney in Rochester, New York. Delano included in his letter a pencil diagram of his weapon. His letter is reproduced in the document images.

1. Isaac Kimbel, not otherwise identified.

2. James DeBois, not otherwise identified.

On April 29, 1837, John Forsyth informed Fairfax Catlett that the State Department had learned from the American consul in Mexico City of a proposal in a secret session of the Mexican Congress to sell Texas to Britain. Forsyth gave Catlett an extract of the report, which he sent to Henderson in a dispatch on May 7, 1837 (DCRT, 1: 212–217).

William D. Jones to John Forsyth, Mexico City, Mexico, March 28, 1837

Extract

Consulate of the U S A
Mexico 28th March 1837.

Sir,

General Michilesia presented a project to Congress, in secret Session, on Saturday night last, to dispose of Texas, and as far South, as necessary, to the British Government, at the rate of twenty five cents per acre, in order to pay off the British debt, which is about Sixty Eight millions dollars, first establishing, the boundary line, between the United States and Mexico, in conformity to Treaty stipulations,[1] and it is not doubted, under the present State of feeling of the concurrence, of the Chambers, in the project proposed, the matter is kept quite a secret.

General Bustamente has received the Votes of the Departments for the Presidency, as far as heard from. If elected, it is said, that Santa Maria, now in Spain, or Canedo, in Peru, will be Minister of Foreign Relations, Lobuja of Finance,[2] War Department, no good man found yet, Interior not fixed upon but insignificant.

Government have been in Treaty with Rubio and others for a loan of 480,000 $ monthly for which the entire control of the Marine

Customs, in the Republic, were to be given, notwithstanding there [are] several millions of Custom house paper, still afloat, issued for previous loans,—the negotiation, I am this afternoon informed, has failed—

W. D. Jones

✦✦✦

Copy. Tx, TLP. After Powhatan Ellis closed the legation in Mexico in December 1836, William D. Jones became the de facto US diplomatic representative to Mexico. Jones, of Ohio, was US consul in Mexico City from March 3, 1836, to March 3, 1843.

1. The proposal was made by General José Marino Michelena (1772–1852).

2. Miguel Santa María (1789–1837); Juan de Dios Cañedo (1786–1850) became foreign secretary in 1839, but was preceded in that position by José María Ortiz-Monasterio (1799–?); Joaquín Lebrija was finance minister from April 23 to October 18, 1837.

J. Pinckney Henderson to Memucan Hunt

Department of State
Columbia Texas
Apl. 2nd 1837

Accompanying [this] you will receive a copy of Nathaniel Town [send's][1] Esq. commission as consul for the Port of New Orleans which you are hereby instructed to give full faith and credit to.

It will be necessary for you immediat[ely] to apply to the Government of the U.S. an[d] produce the commission in order to ob[tain[his exequatur as consul in the accustomed manner which you will forward to him as speedily as possible

I am with high regard &c
J Pinckney Henderson
Secy of State

✦✦✦

ALS. Tx, TLP. Document damaged. Published in *DCRT,* 1: 203.

1. Nathaniel Townsend (1804–1864), originally from Oneida, New York, served as Texas consul at New Orleans from April 2, 1837, to September 20, 1838. He later went into business in Austin, but returned to New York during the Civil War.

James Pinckney Henderson to Memucan Hunt

Columbia Texas
Apl 7th 1837

Dr Genl

I just have time whilest Mr. Townsend waits to enclose your ne[w] letters of credence which I hope will [be] satisfactory. They are now directed as <.....> wished before to direct them but as Genl Austin had erred in Coln Whartons <.......> thought I must addopt the same er[ror] and therefore I did it against my judgment. I will write you pro<. . .> soon.

Your Friend &c
J. Pinckney Henderson

✦✦✦

ALS. Tx, TLP. Document damaged.

William L. Lambeth to William H. Wharton

Lynchburg Virginia
April 10th. 1837.

Dear Sir,

Considering you as the proper Representative of Texas, in the U.S., I will make no apology for troubling you with this letter.

The condition of Texas appeals to us all, of the South, particularly; and whether we can render her any effectual Aid, or not, in her struggle, perhaps our good wishes, may avail something.

I wish to acquire some *certain* & *specific* information of the prospects which a company of volunteers would have, upon marching thither, in the month of September, or October, next.

Would there be any *doubt*, about their being received into the Army of Texas, on the same footing as the rest of the Soldiers, *now* there? Would soldiers upon joining the Army *then*, be entitled to land,

& how much? <.......> how much? What pay, & how much [for]officers? Captain, Surgeon, Lieutenant, &c.?

Are you authorized to guarantee the terms of reception on arriving in Texas?

What description of arms & accoutrements would be the best to take to Texas?

Which route from Natches would be the most advisable—by water to New Orleans, & thence to Brazoria? or land march by Natchitoches?

Has Texas any Accredited Agent in Natches, & New Orleans, and who are they?

What direction should be given to letters from the U.S. to Brazoria?

When would a letter reach Dr. B. T. Archer?

You must pardon the trouble I am about to give you, and any information that occurs to you, which would be useful to those person[s] who desire going to Texas, that I have not herein asked for, you please to do me the favor to speak of it.

Accept the <....> of Yr. Obt. Servant,
W. L. Lambeth

✦✦✦

ALS. Tx, TLP. Document damaged. William L. Lambeth graduated from the University of Maryland Medical School in 1820. Anne Royall, in *Mrs. Royall's Southern Tour, or Second Series of the Black Book,* 3 vols. (Washington, DC, 1830) describes Lambeth as "a young, sprightly, intelligent man, refined and polished in his manners, and no quack, by the way" (1: 105).

John Forsyth to Fairfax Catlett, with Enclosure

Department of State,
Washington, 14th April, 1837.

Sir:

An extract from that part of your letter of the 8th instant,[1] together with the enclosure, suggesting the expediency of again advancing the troops of the United States to Nacogdoches or some contiguous point, having been referred to the Secretary of War, I now transmit a copy of the reply of that officer. An extract from that part of your letter which relates to the establishment of a communication by post routes between the United States and Texas, has been referred to the Post Master General.

I have the honor to be, Sir, Your obedient servant,
John Forsyth

✦✦✦

LS. Tx, TLP. Published in *DCRT*, 1: 205–206.

1. Catlett to Forsyth, April 8, 1837, *DCRT*, 1: 204–205.

Enclosure: Joel Roberts Poinsett to John Forsyth

War Department
April 14th 1837

Sir,

I have attentively examined the papers referred to me by you on the 11th containing an Extract from a note addressed to the Department of State by the Secretary of Legation of Texas, together with the newspaper and a copy of the documents by which it was accompanied; Complaining of murders and depredations being committed by a party of Caddoes and Kickapoos upon the inhabitants of the upper settlements of Texas on the Eastern waters of the Brazos river, and Containing further suggestions as to the expediency of again advancing the troops of the United States to Nacogdoches or some other contiguous points.

Immediately on the receipt of the former communication on this subject by the Hon. Mr Wm H Wharton and the Hon Mr Memucan Hunt,[1] measures were taken by this Department to augment the force on the frontier where a hostile feeling among the Indians has appeared, and orders were dispatched to the [officer] Commanding there to use increased vigilance to restrain all hostile manifestations on the part of the Indians, and to maintain our treaty stipulations. These orders will be reiterated and every exertion will be made to increase our force along that frontier, where it is believed military stations can be occupied better than Nacogdoches affords for the purpose of Compelling the Indians to maintain peaceable relations with the whites, by force if it should become necessary to use force for that purpose.

I have the honor to be Your Obt Servt
J. R. Poinsett

✦✦✦

Copy. Tx, TLP. Published in *DCRT,* 1: 206.

1. Wharton and Hunt to Forsyth, March 14, 1837, Senate Document 14, 32d Cong., 2d Sess., 1853, Serial 660, p. 5.

Joseph Eggleston Segar to Texas Legation

Eastville, Va.
May 1st. 1837.

Dear Sir,

Being much inclined to emigrate to Texas, I take the liberty of soliciting at your hands, some information respecting the country & its prospects.

I shall be gratified by information on these points— 1. whether it is likely the Texan congress will adopt the Common Law as the legal system of the Republic. 2. What are the prospects of the Profession in Texas? 3. At what price is it likely the price of public Lands will be put? 4. Are the choice Lands principally taken up by the present grants or not?

Any other information you may think proper to give me, will be most gratefully received. I propose visiting the country in about a month & if I can make satisfactory arrangements, shall resign my seat in the Legislature & emigrate with my family the [en]suing fall. If you can be of any service to me in my proposed visit, particularly by giving me letters of Introduction to leading gentlemen in Texas I shall highly appreciate the service.

Excuse the liberty I have taken, while I remain,

Very Resply, Your Obt. Servt

Joseph Segar

✦✦✦

ALS. Tx, TLP.

Peter Wagener Grayson to Memucan Hunt

Houston May 4 1837

Dr Sir,

General Henderson being somewhat indisposed I have releived him of the trouble of making out the enclosed papers which you will find necessary to your proper acceptance at Washington. He informed me that before leaving Columbia he had made out under a small seal of the Government, what he had then supposed would be a proper letter of credence, but on Consulting the Authority of Wheatons late Treatise of International Law,[1] we have found that a Letter of Credence for a minister pleniopentiary must be signed by the Chief Magistrate of his Country and addressed to the chief Magistrate of the ~~Country~~ Government to which he is accredited.

You will find then in accordance with the authority Referred to, the Letter Signed by the Presidt. & Sealed with the great Seal ~~and also an authorized Copy which you will want to enclose to the Secretary of State,~~ to be delivered when you receive an audience. If you should be able to lay your hand upon Wheaton, in the chapter upon the Rights of Legation, page 174, you will see that the etiquette is, for you to address a letter to the Secretary, notifying him of your arrival, and requesting him to take the orders of the President as to the delivering of your letters &c.

By another Conveyance for greater Certainty, I shall send a Duplicate of the Document enclosed—which you will not want of course if this one <.....> reaches you Safely—

I hope by the time this reaches Washington that you will have arrived there yourself, and in good health out of the poisonous atmosphere of Mississippi, wh[ere] I learn you have been lately, and experienced <.....> indisposition.

<.....> Communicate to you. touching our affairs—Today there will be a bare quorum of the two Houses of Congress—The Presid will deliver his message tomorrow—There are many things which demand the earliest attention of Congress, but God knows if they will have the patience to consider & dispose of them in the proper manner, at this season of the Year, and in this raw place—

In regard to the enemy, there is now every reason to Suppose, that for the present year at least, we may Consider Ourselves Secure—You have seen no doubt in the papers the accounts which have been received of their distracted and hopeless Condition—

The temporary annoyance they have recently given us with their blockading Squadron brought with it no Very Serious Consequences; the happiness is that such a one will not be apt speedily to recur if the Government of the United States remains in the humour which it now discovers, with respect to these piratical rovers.

I am at the present moment writing in the midst of all manner of Confusion & annoyance, and Can not therefore extend myself in a letter, Correspondently to my feelings—

You will be so good therefore as to accept this letter as some earnest of a lengthier Communication as Soon as I have the Convenience of leisure for writing—

In the mean while my Dr Genl. do me the favor to accept assurances of my perfect friendship.

Yrs. P. W. Grayson

PS. I am desired by Genl. Henderson today to say to you that within a short time you may expect further instructions from him—till when, with regard to any Commercial relations with the U. States, you will forbear to say anything special to the Government of the US.

PWG

✦✦✦

ALS. Tx, TLP. Document damaged.

1. Henry Wheaton, *Elements of International Law with a Sketch of the History of the Science* (Philadelphia: Carey, Lea, & Blanchard, 1836). In the available 1836 edition published in London by Fellowes, the etiquette for letters of credence is at pages

266–267. Wheaton (1785–1848) was the reporter for the US Supreme Court, 1816–1827, chargé d'affaires to Denmark, 1827–1835, and to Prussia, 1835–1846.

John Forsyth to Fairfax Catlett

Department of State,
Washington, 8th May, 1837.

Sir:

In compliance with the request in your letter of the 5th instant, I transmit an Exequatur from the President of the United States to Nathaniel Townsend, as Consul of the Republic of Texas for the port of New Orleans. The commission of Mr. Townsend is also returned.

I have the honor to be, Your obedient servant,
John Forsyth

✦✦✦

LS. Tx, TLP.

James Pinckney Henderson to Memucan Hunt

Houston Texas
May 25th 1837

Dr Genl

I have sent you two coppys of the Presidents message.[1] It was written in great haste and in the hustle about the time of our arriving here but I hope it will give our friends in the U.S. satisfactory Information of our desire &c &c.

Please present a copy to the President of the U S and call his attention to what is said on the subject of the Slave trade it will have a good effect in the Yanky land and request for the U.S. to keep a strict lookout in the Gulf to prevent the introduction of Slaves from Cuba.[2] I have lately learned that arrangments have been made in the U.S. for the purpose of purchasing and bringing Negroes from Cuba to this country & that it is their intention to land them in the U.S. near the Sabine in order to evade the law which prohibits their introduction from all other points except the U S. Please continue to call the attention of the Government of the U S to the depredations committed daily by the Caddo Indians on our frontier, every week brings us additional news of their cruelties an murders, but yesterday news was brought us of those Indians having killed five of our citizens on the upper Brazos River. Those Indians have but recently wandered from the U.S. to this country without the consent of this or any other Government. according to the existing treaties the U.S. are bound to keep them quiet. Mr Coffee[3] has a trading house on Red River which you are instructed to complain of to the U.S. Govermt. as he encourages those Indians to commit roberies &c by purchasing the horses &c which they steal from our citizens. Mr. C. is a citizen of the U.S.

Congress has passed a joint resolution requesting the President to send a Minister to England.[4] The President has offered me the appointment. I think I cannot accept. I would be much pleased to go to England in that capacity but at present I think I cannot leave Texas. My friends insist strongly that I should accept and there is I learn but one expectation amongst the people which is that I must go.[5] I have not sought it but so it is I am a great favourite with the community. I have been solicited to run for the next presidency by many and many others have said I must run for the Vice Presidency but I have said to all of them that I am too young by six years, you know the Constitution requires both to be thirty five. Dr. A. Smith[6] is here with me and so is Genl McIntosh.[7] The President is well and often speaks of you.

You must act upon this letter as instructions but you need not put it on your official file as I have mixed private matters in it

Your Friend
J. Pinckney Henderson

✦✦✦

ALS. Tx, TLP.

1. "The President's Message, May 5, 1837," in Amelia W. Williams and Eugene C. Barker, eds., *Writings of Sam Houston, 1813–1863*, vol. 2, *July 16, 1814–March 31, 1842* (Austin: University of Texas Press, 1939), 82–90.

2. Houston condemned the slave trade and noted that thousands of Africans had lately been imported to Cuba with the intention of transferring them to Texas. Since the Texas navy could not be "diverted from our immediate defence," he called on the United States and Britain to use their navies to stop the traffic.

3. Holland Coffee (1807–1846), from Tennessee, established a trading house in

1829 in Fort Smith, Arkansas, where he met Sam Houston. Coffee later started a trading house on the Washita Bend of the Red River. Despite complaints against Coffee, Houston appointed him Indian agent in November 1837, and in September 1838, Coffee concluded a treaty between Texas and several tribes, as well as an Indian treaty in August 1842. He served in the Texas Congress, 1838–1839.

4. "Joint Resolution Requesting the President to Appoint an Agent to the Court of Great Britain," May 15, 1837, Gammel, 1: 1287.

5. Henderson accepted the appointment and was minister to Britain, 1837–1840.

6. Dr. Ashbel Smith (1805–1886) moved to Texas from North Carolina in 1836 at the urging of Henderson. Texas sent him to Europe in 1842 as its representative. He served three terms in the state legislature after Texas became a state. He was a soldier in the US-Mexican War and in the Civil War.

7. George S. McIntosh (?–ca. 1851) was secretary of the Texas Legation to Britain and France, 1837–1839; acting chargé d'affaires, 1839–1841; and chargé d'affaires, 1841–1842.

One thorny diplomatic issue between Texas and the United States involved the boundary between Texas and Arkansas. In 1820, the Arkansas territorial legislature created Miller County along the Red River. When the Republic of Texas, on December 22, 1836, established a land office for Red River County, it included territory already claimed by Arkansas. Texas also allowed residents of the area to elect representatives to the Texas Congress. Arkansas Governor James Sevier Conway complained to US Secretary of State John Forysth, who remonstrated to Secretary of Legation Fairfax Catlett. The nations signed a convention to settle the boundary in 1838 (Treaties, 4: 133–143).

John Forsyth to Fairfax Catlett

Department of State,
Washington, 17th June, 1837

Sir:

I have the honor to inform you that a letter was received at this Department a few days since from the Executive of Arkansas, stating that the Republic of Texas had by an Act of its Legislature proceeded to lay off a series of land districts within its own limits and had further provided for the establishment of a district embracing one entire county and the greater part of another belonging to Arkansas, which Act was said was to be executed at once and a land office under the control of the Texian Republic to be forthwith established in the County of Miller in the State of Arkansas.[1] This information has been received with great surprise, the more especially as provision was made to Congress at its last session for running the boundary line between the two countries.[2] During the unsettled state of this line, the Government of the United States has carefully refrained from extending the limits of its occupation in that quarter, and I have now the honor to request that you will forthwith apprise the Government of Texas that while the question is pending, no encroachment can be permitted upon the territory occupied by the United States.

I have the honor to be, Sir, Your obedient servant,

John Forsyth

✦✦✦

LS. Tx, TLP. Published in *DCRT,* 1:230.

1. "An Act to Establish a General Land Office for the Republic of Texas," Gammel, 1: 1276–1284.

2. 5 US Statutes 172 (1837).

Robert Anderson Irion became Texas secretary of state on June 13, 1837, in place of J. Pinckney Henderson, who had accepted the position of minister to Britain and France.

Robert Anderson Irion to Memucan Hunt

Department of State,
City of Houston, June 26th. 1837.

Sir,

I am instructed by the President, to call your attention to the various subjects embraced in this communication. At the late session of Congress a Resolution was passed authorizing the President to appoint a Commissioner to act with a Similar one, on the part of the United States, to define and make the boundary line between the two Governments:[1] it is desired that you will bring this subject before the authorities at Washington, and urge the appointment of a Commissioner for this purpose, and fix the time for meeting on the Sabine. In negociating on this point you will be governed by the stipulations of the Treaty of limits entered into by Spain and the United States in the year 1819, and the subsequent ones, between the latter power and Mexico ratifying said agreement.[2]

This Treaty enjoins that the line shall commence at the mouth of the Sabine, run up that Stream to 32.° N. Latitude; thence due North to Red River, according to Malisha's Map,[3] on which conditions you will insist. It is not at the present time intended to run this line further than Red River. Owing to the provisions, that the Land Office shall open on the 1st of October next, agreeably to existing laws, it becomes very important, that this line should be defined previously to that time, if practicable for it ought to be the base of the Surveys in that quarter.

Very shortly after notification this Government, can have her Commissioner on the Spot.

Another Subject connected with this is Coffee's Trading House on Red River. He is doubtless within the limits of the Republic, it being West of 100 ° W. Longitude from London.

This trade tends to Keep up and Encourage the depredations of the hostile Indians, on our North Western borders, by affording to them relatively a good market for horses, and other property taken from those inhabitants; thus presenting at all times to the Cupidity of those Wily Savages a strong temptation to murder, robbery and theft, which they are now perpetrating to an extent which renders it necessary to send an expensive expedition against them. You will remonstrate to that Government and endeavor to effect his removal by the authorities thereof.

The Cadoes are an enterprising and daring N. American Tribe, who have obtruded themselves into our territory in flagrant violation of treaty stipulations between Mexico & the United States & seem to be the leaders of these hostile bands.

You will again earnestly solicit the early attention of that Government to this Subject, and offer as a theatre for Military operations, should they attempt their removal from Texas, a free passage for troops as far as the Trinity, and the privileges of Establishing depots, garrisons &c. anywhere East of that River: In which event provisions may be transported in Keel, or Small Steam Boats up the Neches & Trinity for their supply.

Another Subject, and by far the most important of all, on which I have been instructed to communicate is that of annexation. You will renew the application for this purpose and urge as speedy action thereon as possible.

On the success of this measure our permanent prosperity and perhaps Existence as an organized Government mainly depends. The longer it is delayed, the more we will be trammeled by foreign obligations and treaties; which will obviously tend to increase the difficulties in the consummation of that desirable end; and finally place us beyond the reach of that remedy (which we hope is now in our power) that will heal our numerous political afflictions, create stability, confidence and harmony among the people; and lead directly to the most happy results. It is more than useless to deceive ourselves on this subject and it becomes my duty to inform you that the situation of the Country is deplorable. Our resources are exhausted at home, and are without credit abroad; and things generally are verging towards Anarchy, violence and insubordination. Annexation is the remedy and it is expected that you will exert yourself to effect it.

In discussing this Subject you will refer for information to the instructions of the Hon W. H. Wharton, by the late Sec'y of State, S. F. Austin, bearing date the 18th. Nov. 1836. It is ample in its details, and presents a clear view of the Situation of the Republic and the wishes of the people.

Gen. J. T. Mason is authorized by this Government to act in conjunction with you privately, and consult you on all subjects touching our diplomatic relations with that Republic.[4] From his experience and long personal acquaintance with many politicians of the United

States, it is believed that he will be enabled to render important aid in effecting the great and paramount object of annexation. You will confer freely with him on all such matters.

Your communication to the President dated Vicksburg, June 1st. Instant, together with other letters therein named, have been received and referred to the proper Departments.

It is supposed that the Hon. W. H. Wharton was the bearer of important dispatches to this Government, they may be lost, if so, you will forward Copies of the same as early as possible.[5]

Rumor says a Charge d' Affairés and a Commissioner to run the boundary line, have been appointed, of which we have had no official information. Is it true? Since writing the above the despatch No 17 from Mr. Catlett Secretary of Legation dated Washington City May 25th 1837 was received in regard to which I have to observe that the President left yesterday for Nacogdoches on business connected with the Indian Expedition and I do not feel competent to authorize the modifications of the instructions alluded to;[6] but I am confident should there be any objection to our admission as a State that it will be satisfactory to go in as a territory and that this modification will be authorised so soon as the President returns. I am clearly of opinion that the true interests of Texas would be promoted to a greater extent by being annexed to the United States as a Territory than as a Sovereign State. Independently of Treaty Stipulations the liberality, wisdom and justice of the Judiciary of that Country will afford a Strong guarantee for the protection of all rights acquired under laws existing anterior to such admission.

Under every aspect of the case, it is necessary that a speedy decision of the U States Government on this subject should be known. One of the strongest reasons is, that our condition emperiously demands that we must be intimately associated with some strong power to whom, in forming an advantageous treaty, important concessions of privileges will have to be granted.

Our Agent Genl Henderson has gone to Europe whose instructions will depend much upon the course adopted by the U States. The solicitude herein expressed does not originate from any particular apprehensions of the Enemies efforts against us; but is owing to the difficulties consequent upon a small population scattered over an immense territory sustaining a separate Government, without means, credit or even harmony among themselves. Such candor and my duty as the official organ of Government require me to inform you, is our situation. Visionary Schemes of a glorious Republic are less calculated to advance the interests of our Country, than the practical common sense proposition to become a part of a great nation, firmly established, and participate in common with them, Security, prosperity and happiness.

I forward you herewith a Copy of the instructions mentioned as having been misplaced at Washington.[7]

Respectfully Your Obt. Servant
R. A. Irion
Sec'y of State

✦✦✦

LS. Tx, TLP. Published in *DCRT*, 1: 232–234 (with some text extracted). Robert A. Irion (1804–1861) practiced medicine in Vicksburg, Mississippi, until he moved to Texas in 1832. He represented Nacogdoches in the Texas Congress in 1836–1837. President Houston appointed him secretary of state on June 13, 1837.

1. "An Act to Authorize the President to Appoint a Commissioner to Run the Boundary Line between the United States and the Republic of Texas," June 12, 1837, Gammel, 1: 1331–1332.

2. The Adams-Onís "Treaty with Spain: February 22, 1819," *Treaties*, 3: 3–64. The boundary provisions are articles three and four. The United States and Mexico signed agreements reconfirming the treaty of 1819 in 1828 and 1831 (*Treaties*, 3: 599–640).

3. For the 1819 Adams-Onís Treaty, the negotiators relied on "Map of the United States with the Contiguous British & Spanish Possessions," by John Melish [vice Malisha] (1771–1822).

4. Irion to Mason, June 22, 1837, *DCRT*, 1: 230–231; Irion to Hunt, June 26, 1837, *DCRT*, 1: 231.

5. Wharton sailed from New Orleans for Galveston on April 10, 1836, on the Texas vessel *Independence*. On April 17, near the mouth of the Brazos, two Mexican (vice Spanish) ships captured the *Independence* and imprisoned Wharton and the rest of the crew at Matamoras. The Texas government sent a delegation, headed by John A. Wharton, under a flag of truce to negotiate for their release, but learned on arrival that Wharton had escaped.

6. Catlett to Henderson, May 25, 1837, No. 17, *DCRT*, 1: 218–221. Catlett suggested that Texas reconsider Austin's stipulation, in his instructions to Wharton of November 18, 1836, that Texas should enter the union as a state without passing through a territorial stage.

7. This is perhaps a reference to Austin's public instructions to Wharton of November 18, 1836, referred to in Catlett to Henderson, May 25, 1837.

Aaron Ogden Dayton to Memucan Hunt

Dept. of State
July 3rd, 1837

The Acting Secretary of State presents his respects to the Hon. Mr. Hunt, and will be happy to see him at the Department, if convenient, in the course of the day.

✦✦✦

Unsigned note. Tx, TLP. Aaron Ogden Dayton (1796–1858), of New Jersey, chief clerk of the State Department, March 3, 1837–June 9, 1838.

Aaron Ogden Dayton to Memucan Hunt

Department of State
Washington, 3d July, 1837.

Sir,

I have the honor to acknowledge the receipt of your note of the 1st. instant, enclosing a copy of your letter of credence as Envoy Extraordinary and Minister Plenipotentiary of the Republic of Texas to the United States, and requesting the appointment of a time for the delivery of the original. In reply, I have the honor by the President's direction to state, that he will be happy to receive you for that purpose at 12 o'clock on Thursday next, the 6th. instant. If, therefore, you will call at this Department at a quarter before 12 on that day. I will do myself the honor to accompany you to the President's.

I have the honor to be, Sir, Your obedient Servant,
A. O. Dayton
Acting Secr of State

✦✦✦

LS. Tx, TLP. Published in *DCRT,* 1: 236.

Aaron Ogden Dayton to Memucan Hunt

Department of State,
Washington, 10th July, 1837.

Sir:

I will thank you to furnish this Department with a list of the officers of your legation and of your domestics, in order that, pursuant to law, the same may be communicated to the marshal of this District.

I have the honor to be, Your obedient Servant,
A. O. Dayton
Acting Secretary

✦✦✦

LS. Tx, TLP.

Robert Anderson Irion to Memucan Hunt

Department of State
City of Houston, 14th. July 1837.

Sir,

I have the honor hereby to acknowledge the receipt of a communication, dated Washington, 17th June, ulto being dispatch No. 19 from Fairfax Catlett, Esqr Secretary of legation, with a copy of a letter from Mr. Forsyth Secretary of State of the United States, addressed to said legation on the subject of the land District on Red River, recently established by an Act of the Congress of this Republic, in the Territory under the Jurisdiction of the State of Arkansas.[1] It is true that the Citizens of Miller County of that State have elected and sent members to the Congress of this Republic, who have been permitted to participate in the legislation thereof; and a land District established by said act for the purpose of extending to them titles by this Government to lands of that County. In regard to this subject I have to inform you that the President is still absent at Nacogdoches, and I do not feel Authorized to give any positive instructions thereon; but will submit the same promptly to his Consideration when he shall return. It is certainly a matter of much importance to both governments; and this despatch is the first official communication of the fact that has been received of the appointment of a Commissioner on the part of the U. States to run the boundary line.

The President has not made the appointments necessary to carry said land law into operation; and since this remonstrance is made by the U. States I am confident he will not make them so far as said District is concerned, until the question of Boundary is definitively settled. I would moreover remark that this Government has no disposition to adopt any measures, calculated to disturb the friendly relations that now exist between the two countries, nor persevere in a course tending in the remotest degree to lay the foundation for such a result; which assurances you will respectfully make to that Government. If they claim as Citizens, the inhabitants occupying that territory, and deem it improper for them to legislate in this Republic, they certainly have it in there power to restrain them, until it shall be determined whether they owe allegiance to the U. States or to Texas. The Constitution of this Republic, which is the paramount law, where its provisions are specific guarantees to the people of Miller or Red River, County, where said land District is situated, the right of representation in the Congress thereof; of which privilege they cannot be deprived unless by an order of that Government. Despatch No. 18 has not been received.

I have the honor to be, Sir, Your Obt. Servant
R. A. Irion
Sec'y of State

P.S. I addressed you on the 26th ulto, at which period no official information had been received relative to the Charge d'Affaires, or Commissioner to run the boundary line; and the only official intelligence on the Subject of those appointments is the incidental reference to it in the communication of 17th of June.

R. A. I.

✦✦✦

LS. Tx, TLP. Published in *DCRT*, 1: 241–242.

1. Catlett to Henderson, June 17, 1837, No. 19, enclosing Forsyth to Catlett, June 17, 1837, *DCRT*, 1: 229–230 (also above).

John Forsyth to Memucan Hunt

Department of State,
Washington, 24th July, 1837.

Sir,

I have the honor to acknowledge the receipt of your note of the 18th instant.[1] In answer to that part of it which represents that information has been given to the government of Texas of arrangements having been made to introduce African negroes into that country by the way of the United States, I have the honor to state that this government is prepared to use all the means necessary to prevent the execution of such a design. Efficient steps cannot, however, be taken by the United States for that purpose until more detailed information respecting the scheme shall be furnished. It is desirable, therefore, to know what grounds your government has for believing that such a project is in contemplation and the particulars of the information given? Who are to be the actors and participators in the plan? At what point or points, and when, are the negroes to be landed? The Texian government maybe assured that so soon as this information is supplied, the President will lose no time in adopting the most efficient measures to frustrate any attempt to violate the laws of the United States, or to make any portion of their territory the pretext for evading the laws of a neighbouring State against the slave trade.

I embrace this opportunity to offer you renewed assurances of my highest consideration.

John Forsyth

✦✦✦

LS. Tx, TLP. Published in *DCRT*, 1: 248–249.

1. Memucan Hunt to John Forsyth, July 18, 1837, *DCRT*, 1: 249. Hunt informed Forsyth of a scheme to purchase slaves in Cuba, land them on the United States side of the Sabine, and smuggle them into Texas. Hunt said the Texas navy was occupied with protecting the coast and requested that the United States take steps to defeat the plan. In the letter Hunt also complained about Holland Coffee's "reprehensible practice of encouraging the Indians in their predatory incursions" by purchasing stolen livestock and other property from them.

John Forsyth to Memucan Hunt

Department of State,
Washington, 24th July, 1837.

Sir:

I have the honor to inform you that that part of your note of the 18th instant which complains of depredations on the eastern frontier of Texas by Indians from the United States, and of a trading establishment on Red River alleged to be in the practice of abetting them, has been referred to the Secretary of War, to whose Department the subject belongs.[1] More specific information, however, will probably be deemed necessary to enable the officers of the United States to direct their operations with efficiency for the purpose of restraining the Indians and their abettors.

I have the honor to renew to you the assurances of my most distinguished considerations.

John Forsyth

✦✦✦

LS. Tx, TLP. Published in *IAA*, 12: 8–9.

1. Hunt to Forsyth, July 18, 1837, *IAA*, 12: 127–128.

John Forsyth to Memucan Hunt, with Enclosure

Department of State,
Washington, 29th July, 1837.

Sir:

I have the honor to transmit a copy of a letter to this Department from the Department of War, to which a part of your note of the 18th instant was referred, by which you will be reminded of the importance of more particular information on the subject thus referred in order that a proper direction and efficiency may be given to the efforts of this government for the suppression of the acts complained of.

I have the honor to offer you renewed assurances of
my great consideration.
John Forsyth

✦✦✦

LS. Tx, TLP. Published in *IAA*, 12: 10.

Enclosure: Joel Roberts Poinsett to John Forsyth

War Department.
July 26th 1837.

Sir,

I have the honor to acknowledge the receipt of your letter of the 14th instant, communicating an extract from a note of the Minister of Texas, complaining of predatory incursions of the Indians from the United States into that country, and of a trading establishment on the Red river, alleged to be the habit of abetting them.

With respect to the first part of the complaint made by the Minister of Texas, it is too general to admit of its being examined into. If the Minister will specify the time, place and tribe engaged in committing these depredations, measures will be promptly taken to suppress such hostile movements.

With regards to the complaint made against one of the trading. establishments on the Red river, instructions have been given to the proper officer in that quarter of the country to investigate the circumstances connected with this charge, and if it be found that Mr. Coffee has made so improper a use of his license to suspend him immediately and withdraw his privilege to trade with the Indians– There is no law by which the privilege of trading can be restricted to peltries alone, but upon being informed on what part of the frontier depredations have been committed and what tribes are engaged in such unlawful practices, measures will be taken to prevent their plunder being purchased by any one under the control of the Government.

Very respectfully Yr mo obt Servt
J. R. Poinsett

✦✦✦

LS. Tx, TLP. Published in *IAA*, 12: 10.

John Forsyth to Memucan Hunt

Department of State,
Washington, 31st July, 1837.

Sir:

I have the honor to acknowledge the receipt of your note of the 28th instant,[1] and to inform you that it is the intention of the Secretary of War to establish a military post at some eligible point on the Sabine river. Orders will also be given to the commander of the naval forces of the United States in the Gulph of Mexico to cruise off the mouth of that river to prevent the landing of African negroes in the United States. It is hoped that these measures will conduce to the defeat of any project that may have been formed to introduce such negroes into Texas by the way of this country.

I seize this occasion to renew to you the assurances of my high consideration.

John Forsyth

✦✦✦

LS. Tx, TLP. Published in *DCRT*, 1: 251.

1. Hunt to Forsyth, July 28, 1837, *DCRT*, 1: 250, in which Hunt warns of a plot to smuggle slaves from Cuba into Texas.

John Forsyth to Memucan Hunt, with Enclosure

Department of State,
Washington, 5th August, 1837.

Sir

I have the honor to transmit a copy of a letter to this Department from the Department of War, containing an abstract of the answers that have been received at that Department from the officers who were directed to inquire into the alleged depredations upon the inhabitants of Texas by Indians from the United States.

I avail myself of the occasion to renew to you the assurances of my great consideration.

John Forsyth

+++

LS. Tx, TLP.

Enclosure: Joel Roberts Poinsett to John Forsyth

War Department
August 4th. 1837.

Sir:

I have the honor to inform you that answers have been received at this department from the officers on the South Western frontier, charged to inquire into and ascertain the truth of the depredations supposed to have been committed by Indians under the jurisdiction of the United States upon the inhabitants of Texas. They report that murders and robberies have been committed far in the interior of Texas by small straggling parties of Indians, supposed, however to belong to tribes residing within that country. An officer was sent to the Caddoes who have been accused of being concerned in these unlawful acts, but they deny having committed any depredations on the whites, and appear anxious to be on friendly terms with them. The commanding officer says in continuation that it cannot be supposed these people would be so foolish as to commit hostilities against the United States, and they consider the people of Texas, being Americans, as the same people with those of the United States. It is believed, however, that some of the straggling parties which committed depredations in the interior of Texas, were composed of natives of this tribe, and orders have been given to the officers commanding on the frontier to watch with increased vigilance the conduct of the Indians and to prevent their committing any depredations on the inhabitants of Texas. These orders have been reiterated, and will, it is hoped, produce the desired effect.

Very respectfully, Yr mo obt servt,
Signed / J. R. Poinsett

+++

Copy. Tx, TLP.

Robert Anderson Irion to Memucan Hunt

Department of State
City of Houston Augt. 13th. 1837.

Sir

Col Grayson intending shortly to visit Washington City the President has instructed me to inform you that he is fully authorized to confer with you on all matters touching the intercourse and diplomatic relations between the Government of the U States and this Republic; in whom you will find an able coadjutor in effecting the great object of annexation, and to whom I refer you for much useful information, relative to our present political condition at home.

The Col's visit to Washington has caused my communication of this date to be more brief than it would have been, he, being well acquainted with the views of the Government.

Very respectfully Your Obt. Servant
R. A. Irion
Sec'y of State

✦✦✦

LS. Tx, TLP. Published in *DCRT*, 1: 258.

Robert Anderson Irion to Memucan Hunt

Department of State
City of Houston Augt 13th. 1837.

Sir,

I have the honor to inform you that your communication of the 12th. Ultimo marked despatch No. 23 has been received,[1] submitted to the President and duly considered. The able manner with which the various topics connected with our diplomatic relations with the U States have been discussed, and your zealous support of the interests of this Republic, as evinced in that despatch I take great pleasure to state, is highly satisfactory to the Government and gratifying to the Executive.

The policy of this Government with regard to annexation, continues the same. To what extent the instructions heretofore given on this subject may be modified, consistently with the interests of Texas, must in a great degree be left to the judgment and discretion of yourself, and those friendly to our cause who are aiding, or may assist to consummate this paramount measure. In the spirit of those instructions you will make the conditions as favourable for Texas as possible

With respect to the South Western boundary this Republic claims to the Rio Grande; Should the U States, however, object to this extension of our Territory insist only on the former limits of Texas which were fixed by the Government of Mexico at the River Nueces.

Should insuperable objections arise to receiving this Republic as a State negotiate for admission as a Territory. In either case stipulate that the U States shall assume the payment of a definite amount, sufficient to cover our National Debt; and for a general guarantee for the protection of all legal and vested rights, acquired under this, and former governments.

In reply to the remonstrance of the U. States by Mr Forsyth protesting against the act of the Congress of this Republic, establishing a land district including territory claimed and in the occupancy of the State of Arkansas, I addressed you on the 14th. July Ultimo, during the absence of the President, to whom, since his return, both have been submitted.

He approves my communication on that occasion; and in order to prevent any further misunderstanding with that Government on this subject, and as the only means within his power of remedying the evil, he has issued a proclamation convening Congress on the 25th. of September next,[2] in order that they may suspend the operation of the law which requires that Said land office shall be opened on the first Monday of October, until that boundary shall be defined.

Very respectfully Your Obt. Servant
R. A. Irion
Sec'y of State

✦✦✦

LS. Tx, TLP. Published in *DCRT*, 1: 256–257.

1. Memucan Hunt to Robert A. Irion, July 11 [vice 12], 1837, No. 23, *DCRT*, 1: 235–241.

2. The proclamation was issued August 10, 1837. *Telegraph and Texas Register*, August 19, 1837, p. 3.

On June 26, 1837, Texas Secretary of State Robert A. Irion ordered Memucan Hunt to renew the application of Texas for annexation to the United States. "On the success of this measure," he told Hunt, "our permanent prosperity, and perhaps, existence as an organized Government, mainly depends."

Hunt gave John Forsyth a lengthy note on August 4, 1837, proposing annexation. He provided a political history of Mexico and the political instability and tyranny that led Texas to rebel. He described "kindred ties" that bound the nations and pointed to the "immense resources" Texas would add to the United States. And, he suggested, if Texas concluded diplomatic relationships with other powers, they might create insurmountable difficulties in future arrangments with the United States (IAA, *12: 129–140).*

However, Texas would again be disappointed. On August 11, 1837, Hunt wrote Irion that he had "ascertained beyond a doubt" that the secretary of state was "violently opposed to annexation!!" (Hunt to Irion, August 10–11, 1837, DCRT, *1: 252–256). Forsyth's official reply, on August 25, 1837, confirmed his apprehension.*

John Forsyth to Memucan Hunt

Department of State,
Washington, 25th August, 1837.

The Undersigned Secretary of State of the United States, has had the honor to receive the note of His Excellency General Hunt, Envoy Extraordinary and Minister Plenipotentiary of Texas, dated the 4th instant, proposing a negotiation for the purpose of annexing that country to the United States.[1]

That communication has been laid before the President, who has considered it with just sensibility. In giving to the undersigned instructions to present in reply a prompt and decisive indication of the course it has been deemed necessary to adopt, the President indulges the confident expectation that no unfriendly spirit towards the government or the people of Texas will or can be imputed to the United States.

Neither the duties nor the settled policy of the United States permit them to enter into an examination of the accuracy of the historical facts related by General Hunt, nor to allow them, if even admitted to be correct, to control the decision of the question presented by him. The United States were foremost in acknowledging the independence of Mexico and have uniformly desired and endeavoured to cultivate relations of friendship with that power. Having always since the formation of their government been exempt from civil wars, they have learnt the value of internal quiet, and have consequently been anxious yet passive speculators of the feuds with which their neighbour has been afflicted. Although in the controversy between Texas and Mexico circumstances have existed and events have occurred peculiarly calculated to enlist the sympathies of our people, the effort of the government has been to look upon that dispute also, with the same rigid impartiality with which it has regarded all other Mexican commotions.

In determining with respect to the independence of other countries, the United States has never taken the question of right between the contending parties into consideration. They have deemed it a dictate of duty and policy to decide upon the question as one of fact merely. This was the course pursued with respect to Mexico herself. It was adhered to when analogous events rendered it proper to investigate the question of Texian independence. That inquiry was made with due circumspection and the result was not arrived at until its probable consequences had been accurately weighed. The possibility of a collision of interests, arising, among other causes, from the alleged superior aptitude of the climate and soil of Texas for the growth of some of the staples of the United States, was not overlooked. A sense of duty and a reverence for consistency, however, it was considered, left this government no alternative, and it therefore led the way in recognizing Texas. A hope was certainly entertained that this act and the motives that conduced to it, even if no other considerations were to have influence, would point out to the government of Texas the propriety, not only of cherishing intimate and amicable relations with this country, but of abstaining from other connexions abroad which might be detrimental to the United States. Apart from this, however, it was presumed that that government would enter upon the execution of the intentions intimated by its Envoy Extraordinary with respect to connexions with foreign powers, with a full understanding of the just and liberal commercial stipulations existing between the United States and other nations. A pervading principle of those compacts is impartial treatment of the citizens, vessels and productions of the parties and their respective territories. As it was not to be believed that the commercial allies of the United States would swerve from their engagements, no apprehension was felt that the interest of this country would suffer from the arrangements which Texas might enter into with them.

The question of the annexation of a foreign independent state to the United States has never before been presented to this government. Since the adoption of their Constitution, two large additions have been made to the domain originally claimed by the United States. In acquiring them, this government was not actuated by a mere thirst for sway over a border space. Paramount interests of many members of the confederacy and the permanent well being of all, imperatively urged upon this government the necessity of an extension of its jurisdiction over Louisiana and Florida. As peace, however, was our cherished policy, never to be departed from unless honor should be perilled by adhering to it, we patiently endured for a time serious inconveniences and privations, and sought a transfer of those regions by negotiations and not by conquest. The issue of those negotiations was a conditional cession of those countries to the United States. The circumstance, however, of their being colonial possessions of France and Spain and therefore dependent on the metropolitan governments, renders those transactions materially different from that which would be presented by the question of the annexation of Texas. The latter is a state with an independent government, acknowledged as such by the United States, and claiming a territory beyond, though bordering on, the region ceded by France in the treaty of the 30th of April, 1803. Whether the Constitution of the United States contemplated the annexation of such a state, and if so, in what manner that object is to be effected, are questions in the opinion of the President it would be inexpedient under existing circumstances to agitate.

So long as Texas shall remain at war while the United States are at peace with her adversary, the proposition of the Texian Minister Plenipotentiary necessarily involves the question of war with that adversary. The United States are bound to Mexico by a treaty of amity and commerce, which will be scrupulously observed on their part so long as it can be reasonably hoped that Mexico will perform her duties and respect our rights under it. The United States might justly be suspected of a disregard of the friendly purposes of the compact if the overture of General Hunt were to be even reserved for future consideration, as this would imply a disposition on our part to espouse the quarrel of Texas with Mexico—a disposition wholly at variance with the spirit of the treaty, with the uniform policy and obvious welfare of the United States.

The inducements mentioned by General Hunt for the United States to annex Texas to their territory are duly appreciated, but powerful and weighty as certainly they are, they are light when opposed in the scale of reason to treaty obligations and respect for that integrity of character by which the United States have sought to distinguish themselves since the establishment of their right to claim a place in the great family of nations. It is presumed, however, that the motives by which Texas has been governed in making this overture, will have equal force in impelling her to preserve, as an independent power, the most liberal commercial relations with the United States. Such a disposition will be cheerfully met in a corresponding spirit by this government. If the answer which the undersigned has been directed to give to the proposition of General Hunt should unfortunately work such a change in the sentiments of that government as to induce an attempt to extend commercial relations elsewhere upon terms prejudicial to the United

States, this government will be consoled by a consciousness of the rectitude of its intentions and a certainty that although the hazard of transient losses may be incurred by a rigid adherence to just principles, no lasting prosperity can be secured when they are disregarded.

The Undersigned avails him self of the occasion to offer General Hunt renewed assurances of his very distinguished consideration.

John Forsyth

✦✦✦

LS. Tx, TLP. Published in *IAA*, 12: 11–13.

1. Memucan Hunt to John Forsyth, August 4, 1837, *IAA*, 12: 129–140.

From August 25 to December 31, 1837, except for the following note about Thomas Toby's exequatur as Texas consul in New Orleans, there is a gap in the documents in the Legation Papers.

Aaron Vail to Memucan Hunt

Department of State,
Washington, 17th October, 1837.

Sir:

In compliance with the request in your note of the 15th instant, I have the honor to transmit the President's Exequatur to Thomas Toby, Esquire, as Consul of the Republic of Texas for the port of New Orleans, and to inform you that the same was published in the Globe of last evening. The commission of Mr Toby is also now returned.

I avail myself of this opportunity to offer you renewed assurances of my high consideration.

A. Vail
Acting Secretary

LS. Tx, TLP. Aaron Vail (1796-1878) had served as chargé d'affaires to Britain and was appointed chief clerk in the State Department from 1838 to 1840, when he was appointed chargé to Spain.

Robert Anderson Irion to Memucan Hunt

Department of State,
City of Houston, Decr. 31st. 1837.

Sir,

I have the honor of acknowledging the receipt of your despatch No. 27,[1] a copy of the correspondence between the U. States and Mexico in relation to Texas, and a copy of the Journals of the House of Representatives, which I find very interesting.

I regret the presentation of so many petitions against Texas from the North Eastern States—I had anticipated opposition from that quarter, but did not suppose it would be so detirmined and uncompromising in its character.[2]

The policy of those States has generally been characterized by a disinclination to extend the territory of the U. States to the South west, and, judging from recent demonstrations, that feeling will probably continue, if we have to exist separately, until, pursuing the destiny indicated to us by that significant and beautiful emblem of our nationality, the evening star, inviting alluringly westward, Star after Star to our banner, this now small Republic, by inevitable accessions, will embrace the shores of the Pacific, as well as those of the Gul~~ph~~f of Mexico; presenting to them the spectacle of an immense cotton and sugar growing nation in intimate connection with England,—and other commercial and manufacturing countries of Europe; whose relations shall have been permanently adjusted on equitable principles of reciprocal interests; when, they perchance, in reminiscence, recur to their policy of the present times, may have to deplore the loss of that ascendancy in manufacturing and the carrying trade that they now so triumphantly enjoy, and which could be rendered perpetual by a different course of policy.

The first object of the people of Texas, after having emancipated themselves from Mexican tyranny, was, to restore to the U. States the extensive and valuable domain which had once been hers,[3] and enjoy peace, security and happiness on the Soil which they had reclaimed from Savages and the Wilderness, under the laws and institutions which gave them birth.

This feeling, you know, was not prompted by any fear of a reconquest by Mexico. No Texian since the battle of San Jacinto has distrusted, for a moment, our Capability to maintain our independence; and the experience of every day attests the trust of that Conviction.

All the Departments of the Government are now in harmonious operation. The Second Session of the Second Congress adjourned on the 19th inst.

Our financial system is established on a footing calculated to give satisfaction to all classes of creditors and the collection of Taxes is every day absorbing the public debt.

The impost laws have been amended so as to render them more equal in their operation, and less onerous in respect to particular articles.

The land laws have been amended and the General Land Office is to open the first Thursday in February next for the location of land claims.

Connected with the latter Subject is the unsettled boundary line between the U. States and Texas.

Congress was called together in September last in consequence of the remonstrance of Mr Forsyth, against the authorities of this Republic establishing land offices in the Counties of Red River, which are under the Civil Jurisdiction of Arkansas. This matter is one of serious import to Texas at the present time, for it appears that the Citizens of that border are determined to organize under the Authorities of this Republic, which, from the tone of Mr Forsyths communication, I am apprehensive, may occasion unpleasant collisions in that quarter, and perhaps lead to a disagreable Controversy between the two Governments, which would, under existing circumstances, be a most unfortunate event for us, and should, if possible, be prevented.

The remonstrance of the U. States was communicated to the Senate, which body adopted a report authorizing and requesting the President to appoint a commission, in conjunction with one on the part of the United States, to run and mark the line in conformity with the existing treaties between Mexico and that Government on this subject; limiting their operations, however for the present, to the location of the line from the mouth of the Sabine to the hundreth degree of West Longitude from London, on the Red River.[4]

In accordance with this report the President, by and with the Advice and Consent of the Senate, has appointed Shelby Corzine Commissioner on the part of this Government to run said line.[5] The Country through which it will pass is rapidly settling, to whose inhabitants the uncertainty of the boundary is a source of much vexation, and seriously impedes improvement, as well as the administration of justice.

It is hoped, that the United States Government will not further postpone this appointment of a Commissioner, and I am directed by the President to instruct you to sollicit again said appointment. The fixation of this line is the more necessary, inasmuch as the prospect of immediate annexation is so very remote as hardly to be considered in the range of possibilities.

Annexation with respect to ourselves is now a question of more embarassment than heretofore. From indications evinced by members of the late session of the Texian Congress, the people are becoming less anxious for the success of the measure.

The prompt and decided refusal of the Government of the U. States to act in favor of the proposition, has had a tendency to fix the opinions against admission, of those who were wavering on the subject.

So great has been the change in public sentiment that it is probable should the vote be again taken at the next September election, that a majority would vote against it.

Therefore I do not believe that any future Administration will attempt such a negociation.

Under these Circumstances you will perceive at once that the delay recommended by our friends in the U. States will defeat altogether, and forever, the objects of the proposition.

This result of the negociation, however, only postponed our prosperity, for the difficulties of building up and sustaining a Government, though great, will be overcome by the Chivalry and enterprize of our citizens.

Fresh vigor will be imparted to every arm when it [is] distinctly and generally understood throughout the Republic that annexation is impracticable.

The President desires that you will treat this Subject for the future with great delicacy. It is proper for our diplomatic representatives at the present time to observe a modest, prudent, yet firm Course; being always Careful not to afford grounds of offence to the Governments to which they are acredited—To be always ready to cooperate with the known friends of our cause, and act cordially with them in the promotion of measures calculated to advance our interests.

In the present aspect of the question of annexation it seems there is but little for you to do, more than to watch the movements of Congress relative thereto, Should there be any, and render any proper assistance to members of that body who may be advocating the measure.

That Government having refused to negociate with you as the accredited Agent of this for admission, the latter, therefore, conscious, inasmuch as the correspondence has been published, that the matter is now in the hands of the Congress of that Republic alone; and unless it should be brought up for consideration by them it is not contemplated by this Government to renew the application in any form.

Should a resolution be proposed by the U. States Congress authorizing that Government to enter into a negociation for the annexation of Texas, the instructions heretofore given are deemed sufficient for your guidance therein.

You are aware that no treaty can be binding on this Government till ratified by the Senate thereof.

Since my dispatch of the 20th of September our Indian relations have undergone important changes.[6] During the Spring and Summer there was a decided feeling of hostility entertained by most of the tribes within our limits, towards the people of Texas—This feeling they manifested by frequent depredations on our frontiers. Many of those Indians emigrated in violation of the Treaty between the U.

States and Mexico. More recently our Indian Commissioners have concluded Treaties with several tribes; and report that there now exists a disposition among them generally to make a permanent and general peace; and, it is hoped, that, that desirable object may be attained within the next three or four months.[7]

What influence the Mexican emissaries, who are dispersed among the Indians, and the authorities of Matamoras, operating through their friends, the Cherokees, may have, is entirely conjectural; and it is impossible to forsee with any degree of Certainty the Consequences of their exertions.

Since that date Col. Coffee has also visited this City, and made satisfactory explanations to this Government, relative to the influence which his trading Houses on Red River, exercises over the Indians in that quarter.

Owing to those changes in our Indian affairs it is the wish of the President, that you will let this subject rest for the present.

On the 3d of October our Commissioner near the Courts of St. James and St. Cloud, was at Liverpool, who expected to arrive in London on the 8th, two days prior to the assembling of Parliament — we are daily expecting dispatches from him.

Col Grayson has been appointed Navy Agent for the purchase of a Fleet for this Government, which, will prevent his return. Say to him that the aspect of things generally is much more favorable than at the time of his departure, and make to him my best compliments. Unfortunately, I did not receive his letter of the 7th Instant till after the Adjournment of Congress.[8] I think that body would not hesitate to authorize the proposed obligations in the Bonds. They convene again on the second Monday in April next.

The Presidents health is yet feeble, but improving

I have the honor to be, very respectfully, Your Obt. Servant

R. A. Irion

P.S. the copies of our correspondence with Mr Forsyth mentioned as having been sent to me have not been received.

✦✦✦

LS. Tx, TLP. Published in *DCRT*, 1: 277–281.

1. Memucan Hunt to Robert A. Irion, October 21, 1837, No. 27, *DCRT*, 1: 266–267.

2. In his diary, Massachusetts representative John Quincy Adams recorded on September 20, 1837, that he presented twelve petitions against the annexation of Texas and that "many others were presented by other members." He presented additional petitions on September 28 and October 3, noting that he held back "a considerable number for the winter session." Allan Nevins, ed., *The Diary of John Quincy Adams, 1794–1845* (New York: Charles Scribner's Sons, 1951), 484.

3. It was an article of faith among American expansionists that in the Adams-Onís Treaty of 1819 the United States had settled for a western boundary at the Sabine when it had a solid claim to a border along the Rio Grande.

4. "An Act to Authorize the President to Appoint a Commissioner to Run to the Boundary Line between the United States of America, and Republic of Texas," June 12, 1837, Gammel, 1: 1331–1332.

5. *Secret Journals,* December 5, 1837, pp. 92–93.

6. Robert A. Irion to Memucan Hunt, September 20, 1837, *DCRT,* 1: 259–262.

7. Thomas J. Rusk and K. H. Douglas concluded a treaty with the Ioni and Anadarko on August 21, 1837; Col. H. W. Karnes signed a treaty with the Tonkawas at Bexar on November 22, 1837; and a treaty was signed with the Lipan on January 8, 1838. Dorman H. Winfrey and James M. Day, eds., *The Indian Papers of Texas and the Southwest, 1825–1916* (Austin: Texas State Library, 1959), 27, 28–29, 30–32.

7. Peter W. Grayson to Robert A. Irion, December 7, 1837, *DCRT,* 1: 273–274.

John Forsyth to Memucan Hunt

Department of State,
Washington, 19th February, 1838.

Sir:

I have had the honor to receive your note of this date, stating that Sandy Harris, Esquire, had been attached to the Legation of Texas as your private Secretary.[1]

I have the honor to offer you renewed assurances of my high consideration.

John Forsyth

✦✦✦

LS. Tx, TLP.

1. Sandy Harris (1804–1886) was eventually named secretary of legation. He later lived in Philadelphia, where he was a partisan of the Tyler administration.

John Forsyth to Memucan Hunt, with Enclosure

Department of State,
Washington, 21st February, 1838

Sir:

I have the honor to communicate a copy of a Circular from the First Comptroller of the Treasury of the United States,[1] addressed to officers of the Customs, instructing them to give to the vessels and productions of Texas the benefits of the fifth and sixth articles of the treaty between the United States and Mexico.[2] As those articles will go into operation on the fifth of April, next, I have the honor to request that you will forward the enclosed Circular so that it may reach your government before that time.

I embrace this opportunity to offer you renewed assurances of my great consideration.

John Forsyth

✦✦✦

LS. Tx, TLP. Published in *DCRT,* 1: 313.

1. George Wolfe (1777–1840), of Pennsylvania, was First Comptroller from June 18, 1836, to February 23, 1838. He was later collector of customs at Philadelphia from 1838 to 1840.

2. Articles 5 and 6 provide that the nations will pay the same duties on imports (*Treaties,* 3: 603–604).

Enclosure: Circular to Collectors, Naval Officers, and Surveyors

Treasury Department,
First Comptrollers office, February 17, 1838

Sir:

Refering to the circular from this Office, of the 2nd. instant, I have to communicate for your government that, by information received from the Department of State, it appears the fifth and sixth articles of the Treaty with Mexico are held to be obligatory on the Republic of Texas.

It results, therefore, that the vessels and productions of the latter, being placed on an equal footing in carrying on its commercial intercourse with the United States, are to be treated with reciprocal favour, and enjoy the like privileges and exemptions that are extended to the vessels and productions of Mexico.

Accompanying [this, you will] receive, for the use of your office, a set of laws enacted at the first session of the Twenty-fifth Congress.

Special and explanatory instructions having been issued almost simultaneously with their enactment, in respect to such of those laws as were more directly connected with the revenue system, and to which your instant attention was necessary, I have only, at this time, to enjoin their due observance.

I deem it proper, however, to call your pointed attention to the following proclamations of the President of the United States, viz:

1st. Proclamation, dated the 24th. of June, 1837, respecting the dominions and dependencies of the Sultan of Muscat.

2d. Proclamation, dated the 24th of June, 1837, respecting the dominions of the King of Siam.

3d. Proclamation, dated the 14th [of June, 1837, declaring that the] tonnage duty on the vessels of the Kingdom of Greece are thence-forward to cease to be levied in the ports of the United States.

4th. Proclamation, dated the 11th of October, 1837, declaring the fact, that the duties payable by the vessels of the Kingdom of Portugal, prior to the 25th of May, 1832, are from that day to be levied and exacted.

The object of these proclamations appear to be so obvious as to require no particular explanation.

I am, sir, verry respectfully, Your obedient servant,
(Signed) Geo. Wolf
Comptroller

+++

Secretarial copy. Tx, TLP. Document damaged. Published in *DCRT*, 1: 313–314.

Samuel Finley Breese Morse to Memucan Hunt

Washington city March 1st 1838.—

Dear Sir,

Wishing to show some evidence of my interest in the rising character of the new and independent State which you represent, I take this opportunity to offer unconditionally for the acceptance of your Government the perpetual use of my Electro-Magnetic Telegraph in the State of Texas.—

In my arrangements to dispose of my rights as inventor of this Telegraph for other countries, I have made, and shall continue to make, the single exception in favor of Texas.—

Sincerely wishing that your fine country may be as distinguished for its religious, moral, and intellectual character, as it is for that of courage and energy, I remain Dr. Sir With high personal respect and esteem

Yr Excellency's mo. ob. sevt.
Saml: F: B: Morse

✦✦✦

ALS. Tx, TLP. Samuel F. B. Morse (1791– 1872), artist and inventor of the electromagnetic telegraph. On August 9, 1860, Morse wrote Governor Sam Houston withdrawing his offer because the Texas government had never responded to him. Morse to Houston, August 9, 1860, Samuel F. B. Morse Letters, 1839, 1860, Dolph Briscoe Center for American History, University of Texas at Austin.

John Forsyth to Memucan Hunt

Dept of State
March 2d. 1838

The Secretary of State presents his compliments to Gen. Hunt, and will be glad to see him at the Department to morrow at 11 o'clock if convenient.

✦✦✦

Secretarial note. Tx, TLP.

John Forsyth to Memucan Hunt

Department of State.
Washington, 9th March, 1838.

Sir:

I have the honor to acknowledge the receipt of your note of yesterday's date, transmitting a printed copy of the general land law of Texas, passed at the last session of the Congress of that Republic, and calling my attention to a part of the 39th section of the law with a desire that it might tend to stay proceedings under instructions from the Department which you were informed would be given.[1] I have examined that section, which, if it was framed with a view to prevent collisions that might arise from the execution of the law in the disputed territory, seems to me not to be as definite on that subject as could have been wished. Its efficacy for that object will consequently depend upon the manner in which it may be executed, which, I trust, will be with a proper regard to the rights of the United States. In that case, so far as regards the operations of the Texian land office, the authorities in the State of Arkansas may not find it necessary to act under the instructions that have been given them from this Department.

I avail myself of this occasion to offer you renewed assurances of my distinguished consideration.

John Forsyth

✦✦✦

LS. Tx, TLP. Published in *DCRT*, 1: 318.

1. Hunt to Forsyth, March 8, 1838, *DCRT*, 1: 315. Article 39 of "An Act to Reduce into One Act, and to Amend the Several Acts Relating to the Establishment of a General Land Office," December 14, 1837, Gammel, 1: 1417, provided that the operations of the Land Office would not go into effect in Red River County near any part of the territory in dispute between Texas and the United States.

Several states passed resolutions in 1837 opposing or urging the annexation of Texas. In addition to the Tennessee resolution below, Kentucky, South Carolina, Alabama, and Mississippi expressed support for annexation (Herman V. Ames, ed., State Documents on Federal Relations: The States and the United States *[Philadelphia: History Department, University of Pennsylvania, 1911], 224–228).*

Newton Cannon to Richard Cheatham, with Enclosure

Executive Department,
Nashville, T. March 20, 1838.

Sir:

In compliance with the request of the General Assembly, I have the honor to transmit the accompanying Preamble and Resolutions.

Very Respectfully,
N. Cannon.

✦✦✦

Printed document. Tx, TLP. Newton Cannon (1781–1841) was Whig governor of Tennessee, 1835–1839. Richard Cheatham (1799–1845) was a Whig representative from Tennessee in the Twenty-Fifth Congress, 1837–1839.

Enclosure: Resolution of the State of Tennessee

Passed January 20th, 1838

Preamble and Resolution in favor of the annexation of Texas to the United States.[1]

WHEREAS, we have been anxious and attentive observers of the progress of events in Texas, and have not been unmoved spectators of her late gallant and glorious struggle for freedom, and have seen that freedom achieved by those near and dear to us by the ties of kindred and common ancestry; and whereas, we have seen by a vote of the people of that republic, an anxious desire manifested to become citizens of these United States; and whereas, we believe that the gallant and chivalrous bravery of Texians, in their struggle for liberty and free government, is an assurance of their worth, and sufficient evidence of their qualification to entitle them to brotherhood and citizenship with us; and whereas, also, we believe that the annexation of Texas to these United States is a "consummation devoutly to be wished," and an end worthy our best exertions to attain, if it can be done without an infraction of the law of nations, or a departure from the policy or principles of this government:

Now, therefore, Resolved by the General Assembly of the State of Tennessee, That we desire most anxiously that Texas be acquired by these United States; and resolved, that our Senators and Representatives in Congress be informed of our desire to acquire the territory of Texas, and to annex it to the United States, by treaty or purchase, and at such time as they may deem most expedient.

Resolved, That a copy of this Preamble and these Resolutions be forwarded by the Governor of this State to our Senators and Representatives in Congress, with a request that they introduce them to the consideration of both branches of Congress.

JOHN COCKE,[2] Speaker of the House of Representatives.
TERRY H. CAHAL,[3] Speaker of the Senate.

✦✦✦

Printed document. Tx, TLP.

1. *Acts Passed the First Session of the Twenty-Second General Assembly of the State of Tennessee, 1837–8* (Nashville: Nye & Co., 1838), 450.

2. John Cocke (1772–1854), an attorney, served several terms in the Tennessee House of Representatives and Senate.

3. Terry H. Cahal (1802–1851) served two terms in the state senate and as speaker for one term.

Robert Anderson Irion to Memucan Hunt

Department of State,
City of Houston, March [21st 1838]

Sir,

I have the honor to acknowledge the receipt of your despatch of the 8th. inst. which came to hand yesterday.

I sincerely deplore the present aspect of the relations between the United States and Texas, respecting the boundary line. It has become a subject of discussion between the Chargé d'Affaires of the United States at Houston & this Government. This discussion grew out of the protests which the Hon. Chargé considered himself called upon to make, when he ascertained that the Congress of Texas had, by special enactments, organized the disputed territory, and established Land Offices for the location of lands.[1] In reply to his communication I cited some historical facts showing, that Mexico had uniformly regarded that territory as being clearly within her limits, and that the Government of that country had, from time to time, taken steps to organize it, which their unsettled political condition prevented, &, that, therefore, no right which Mexico ever possessed, relative thereto, had been impaired on the score of prescription, and that Texas must be considered as the successor of the country from which she separated, so far as respects the territory in question,—expressing, at the same time, the great anxiety of this government to have the line run, & some of the causes, connected with the defence of the country, which render the consummation of that object so very desirable & important to Texas.[2]

He misapprehended the positions which were taken in my communication, and made the most extraordinary answer that I have yet read in diplomatic correspondence.[3]

By direction of the President I forward you the general power. If the government of the United States insist on a convention to confirm the treaty of limits, and authorise arrangements for running the boundary line, you will enter into the negociations which may be necessary to effect these objects.

This Government has no objection to such a formal recognition of rights, which are as binding upon the respective parties without it,—except the delay which its ratification will occasion. Treaties of limits do not, like those of commerce &c., expire at given periods, but are as permanent as lines designating private possessions, which can not be changed unless by the consent of the parties concerned.

For your government in the negociations relating to the boundary I refer you to instructions heretofore given on that subject. The present boundaries of Texas, as fixed by an act of congress, are as follows: viz. beginning at the mouth of the Sabine river, and running west along the gulf of Mexico, three leagues from land, to the mouth of the Rio Grandé,—thence up the principal stream of said river to its source,—thence due north to the forty second degree of north latitude,—thence along the boundary line as defined in the treaty between the United States and Spain, to the beginning. This Government does not wish to run the line at present farther than the 100dth. degree of west longitude, to a point on Red River, in latitude nearly 33° 30',—leaving a distance of eight or nine degrees to be run at a future time, when it can be done with less hazard & expense.

The region north of Red River, through which the line will pass, [is] inhabited by hostile Indians,—which circumstance would [re]nder it necessary to send a considerable guard to accompany the commissioners and surveyors. It is hoped that the Government of the United States will not insist on running the line beyond the point above indicated on the Red River.

I have received despatches from General Henderson, up to the 22nd. of December last.[4] He had had several conferences with Lord Palmerston who treated him with great courtesy.[5] His application for the immediate recognition of the independence of Texas, by the Government of Great Britain had been considered by the Cabinet, who declined acting decisively thereon at that time.

It is highly important to us that the question of annexation should be disposed of immediately, for it will embarrass our negociations in ~~England~~ Europe, so long as it is pending at Washington. The Canada insurrection has also had an unfavorable influence on our affairs in England. I have stated to General Henderson that I would request you to keep him regularly informed with regard to the debates that may take place, in the United States' Congress, on Preston's resolutions, or any other subjects that relate to annexation, which I hope you find it convenient to do. It is necessary that he should have the earliest possible intelligence on that subject.

There is no prospect of an invasion this spring. Political matters in Mexico are coming to a crisis. The Constitution of –24 will, it seems, be re-established within the next two or three months. Gen. Urea has declared for the constitution in the state of Sonora. Gen. Cos is in Tamaulipas & has joined the Federalists.

The emigration during the last fall and winter was immense. The depressed condition of the enemy, & the rapid increase of our population, have tended greatly to render the people indifferent to annexation.

I have the honor to be, Sir, with great respect, Your ob'dt servant,

R. A. Irion

✦✦✦

LS. Tx, TLP. Published in *DCRT*, 1: 318–320.

1. Alcée La Branche to Robert A. Irion, January 13, 1838, January 15, 1838, and January 16, 1838, *DCRT*, 1: 281, 282, 283–284.

2. Robert A. Irion to Alcée La Branche, February 13, 1838, *DCRT*, 1: 291–297.

3. Alcée La Branche to Robert A. Irion, February 26, 1838, *DCRT*, 1: 298–310.

4. J. Pinckney Henderson to Robert A. Irion, October 14, 1837, No. 1; November 5, 1837, No. 2; and December 22, 1837, No. 3, *DCRT*, 3: 812–820, 821–831, 831–836.

5. Henry John Temple, Lord Palmerston (1784-1865), Britsh Foreign Secretary.

Robert Anderson Irion to Memucan Hunt

March 21st. 1838

Dear Sir,

The accompanying communication will inform [you] on matters relating to Texas.

I conversed with the President on the subject of yr. request to be recalled before his departure for Nacogdoches.[1] He gave me no definite instructions relative thereto.

I do not think he is willing that [you] should leave Washington till the question of annexation is settled, which we hope will take place shortly.

The boundary too has become a very important question. It will be necessary for you to procure, if possible, the appointment of a commissioner on the part of that Government.

The Power which is forwarded invests you with ample authority to act. Should the U. States insist, as it appears they will, on running the line the whole distance I am rather at a loss to advise you what to do.

Congress has made no provision for running it farther than the 100dth. degree of west longitude on Red River.

From that point to the 42nd. north latitude it is a wilderness of savages, and will not be settled for many years to come.

Upon the whole, considering the great importance of having the line defined without delay, if you cannot induce that Government to limit the present operation to the point above indicated, it will be best to consent to run it to the 42nd. degree.

I will write again immediately on the return of the President.

Hastily, yr. friend &c
R.A. Irion

✦✦✦

ALS. Tx, TLP. Published in *DCRT,* 1: 320–321.

1. Hunt indicated his wish to return to Texas "if but for a short time during the approaching session of Congress" in Hunt to Irion, March 9, 1838, No. 32, and Hunt to Irion, March 12, 1838, No 33, *DCRT,* 1: 315–316 and 316–317.

Robert Anderson Irion to Memucan Hunt

Department of State,
City of Houston, May 18, 1838

Sir,

I have the pleasure to acknowledge your Despatch, No. 34.[1] The boundary question was laid before Congress about four weeks ago, and was referred to the committees of the Senate and House of Representatives on foreign relations. The committee on the part of the House have reported and recommend the adoption of a resolution investing the President with power to suspend the operation of the laws of Texas in the disputed territory on Red River, whenever he may deem it advisable. The committee on the part of the Senate have not reported. The subject was called up in the House to-day and a slight debate ensued.

From indications evinced by certain Members I do not think any discretionary power, touching this matter will be given to the President by Congress. Neither do I believe that the said laws will be changed in any respect. There appears to be a fixed determination on the part of the majority of both Houses to persist in the course which has been heretofore pursued. I may be mistaken.

Under this aspect of the case you will perceive that the only way to terminate the controversy is to run the line, [the] preparatory arrangements for which, it is hoped, you have [ere] this agreed upon with the Government of the United States.

You seem to entertain erroneous opinions with regard to the views of this Government in relation to our western boundary line. It is not now the desire of this Government to negotiate respecting territory beyond the limits of Texas as established by the Act of Congress.[2] From the source of the Rio Grande, the western boundary will run to the 42nd degree of north latitude, intersecting at this point the line of the U. States;—thence with the latter line to the 100dth. degree of W. longitude from London, on the Red River,—thence with said line, as agreed upon between the United States & Spain by the treaty of 1819, to the mouth of the Sabine.

With respect to the Bay of St. Francisco, the South Sea, & Pacific Ocean, and the territories bordering thereon, this Government, at the present time has no concern. They have no connection with the negotiation now pending on the subject of Boundary between this Republic and the United States. Should the latter Power,—while our limits remain as they are,—acquire territory in that quarter of the World; it must be by negotiations with Mexico, and not with us. If,—on the other hand, we desire an extension [of territory] in that direction it is a matter between Texas and Mexico, & not with the United States. At a future time this Government may, and probably will, by conquest or negotiation, extend its boundary to the Pacific, but during existing relations, the President can not perceive in what manner speculations concerning the territory referred to have any relevancy to the question now under consideration. Should the Convention of limits not have been concluded before the receipt of this,—if agreeable to the United States, stipulate that it is only to be run at the present time from the 32nd. degree of North Latitude on the Sabine River, to the Red River, which is a distance of about 150 miles. You will not, however, insist on this point.

I herewith transmit a convention of indemnity to American citizens who suffered injuries by the capture of the Pocket, and impressment of the Durango, recently entered into by the Chargé d'Affaires of the United States & this Government, which has been duly ratified by the Senate of this Republic, and I am directed by the President to instruct you to proceed to an exchange of the ratifications thereof, as soon as circumstances will permit. Your Power is deemed sufficiently ample for this purpose.

In regard to the treaty of Amity, Navigation and Commerce, the President prefers that it should be negotiated here.[3] The Chargé of the United States has no power authorizing such a negotiation. Will the United States transfer it to this place?

In the negotiation of this important treaty, the peculiar condition of Texas as contrasted with Mexico should be weighed with great deliberation, in order that its stipulations may establish our commercial relations, with the U. States, on terms of reciprocal interest. The treaty between Mexico & the United States,[4] although framed as it is in the spirit of equality, contains stipulations which would be objection[able] to this Government, owing to the great difference between the extent, position, & organization of the Governments of the United States and Texas. Therefore the President does not desire a hasty conclusion of the treaty.

It is the President's wish in case you are engaged in the negotiation of this treaty, notwithstanding the intimations above made, that you should continue it at Washington, but before its conclusion that you should communicate with this Government on the subject. A short delay can not operate prejudicially to either country, as our intercourse will remain in the mean time as it now exists. It was not contemplated when your general power was made out, that you would conclude such a treaty without special instructions thereon.

The President, in his late address to Congress, recommended the unconditional withdrawal of the proposition of annexation, in the event that the present session of the Congress of the United States should adjourn without acting definitively thereon. Since that time resolutions have been introduced into both Houses, requiring an immediate and unconditional withdrawal, which have been lost principally on the ground that the proposition was made in accordance with a vote of the people, and ought therefore to be withdrawn on the same authority.[5]

The news from the interior of Mexico is favorable to Texas. That country is in commotion, and it is supposed by those who are most intimately acquainted with her political condition, that the constitution of '24 will shortly be reestablished, & Santa Anna placed again at the head of affairs. The ports of Mexico are blockaded by the French.[6]

Present my compliments to Mr. Catlett and inform him that the draft will be paid in a few days.

I have the honor to be, Sir, with great respect, your obedient servant.

R. A. Irion

✦✦✦

LS. Tx, TLP. Document damaged. Published in *DCRT*, 1: 327–329.

1. Memucan Hunt to Robert A. Irion, April 13, 1838, No. 34, *DCRT,* 1: 323–325.

2. In his April 13 dispatch Hunt wrote that in the boundary negotiations with the United States, he would not surrender any claim by the Republic of Texas to territory beyond its original limits as defined by Mexico.

3. No such treaty was ever concluded.

4. Treaty of Amity, Commerce and Navigation, April 5, 1831, *Treaties*, 3: 599–640.

5. On April 17, 1838, the Texas Senate Committee on Foreign Relations recommended that the president be instructed that the proposition for annexation be "unconditionally withdrawn." A joint resolution to withdraw the annexation proposal was defeated on May 2, 1838 (*Telegraph and Texas Register,* April 21, 1838, and May 2, 1838).

6. In April 1838 France began a blockade of the east coast of Mexico in the so-called Pastry War. The French government supported claims made by a French pastry chef in Mexico City that Mexican soldiers had looted his shop in 1828. In addition, Mexico had defaulted on loans received from France. In November 1838, the French

navy bombarded the fort of San Juan de Ulúa and occupied Vera Cruz. During the conflict Santa Anna reestablished himself by taking charge of resistance to the French. The dispute was settled with British mediation in 1839.

Robert Anderson Irion to Memucan Hunt

Department of State,
City of Houston, May 19th. 1838.

Sir,

Should the present session of the Congress of the United States adjourn without having acted definitively on the proposition for the annexation of this Republic to that of the U. States, you are hereby instructed, by the direction of the President, to withdraw immediately thereafter the proposition aforesaid.

I have to honor to be, with great respect yr. obt. Servant
R. A. Irion

✦✦✦

ALS. Tx, TLP. Published in *DCRT*, 1: 329–330.

On June 5, 1838, Memucan Hunt submitted his resignation as Texas minister to the United States.

John Forsyth to Memucan Hunt

Department of State,
Washington, 23d May, 1838.

Sir:

I have the honor to acknowledge the receipt of your note of yesterday's date, announcing your intention to make a visit to your government and stating that during your absence or until the appointment of a successor to yourself, Fairfax Catlett, Esquire, would take charge of the affairs of the Legation of Texas.

You will oblige me by delivering to Mr. La Branche on your arrival at Houston, the accompanying packet of despatches from this department to him. I avail myself of the occasion to renew to you the assurances of my distinguished consideration.

John Forsyth

✦✦✦

LS. Tx, TLP.

John Wesley Crockett to Fairfax Catlett

Ho: Rep:
June 8th. 1838

Sir:

I have just received the letter which I have the honor herein to enclose you. It was enclosed to me by Alfred Benten Esq of Texas who requested me to send it to general Hunt.[1] I send it to you in order that you may forward it to him should you deem it important to do so.

I am sir, very respectfully Your obt. servt

John W. Crockett

✦✦✦

ALS. Tx, TLP. John Wesley Crockett (1807–1852), son of David Crockett (1786–1836), represented Tennessee as a Whig in the Twenty-Fifth and Twenty-Sixth Congresses, 1837–1841.

1. Alfred Benton (1816–1838), originally from Tennessee, took part in the capture of Bexar in December 1835 and the Battle of San Jacinto. The enclosure is not with the letter, and it is not known what it concerned.

Benjamin Stoddert Ewell to Fairfax Catlett

York. Pa June 18th 1838

Sir

I have, for some time past, observed with considerable interest the onward movements of your Government & have entertained a wish to become one of her citizens provided any opportunities offered for the occupation I should wish to pursue.

I am a graduate (in 1832) of the U.S.M.A. & was one of the assistant Professors in the institution for 4 years—3 years in the department of Mathematics & 1 year in that of Nat[ural] & Ex[perimental] Philosophy.

For the last two years I have been engaged in the field duties of a civil Engineer—

The determination of the boundary line between the U.S. & Texas opens a field of employment into which I should like to enter.

I write to you now for the purposes of information. I can refer you to the archives of the War Department for the truth of my assertions & can—if the matter be followed up—procure letters of recommendation from the Superintendant and Professors of the U.S.M.A. I hope I do not ask too much in requesting the above information.

Respectfully &c

Benj. S. Ewell—

✦✦✦

ALS. Tx, TLP. Benjamin Stoddert Ewell (1810–1894) went on to teach mathematics at Hampden-Sydney College (1839–1846), Washington College in Lexington, Virginia (1846–1848), and William and Mary College (1848–1888).

Aaron Ogden Dayton to Fairfax Catlett

Dept of State
June 19' 1838.

Dear Sir,

Mr. Buchanan[1] of the Senate is anxious to ascertain whether a report of the death of Mr Evan Rice Evans, at Houston, on the 27' of October last, be true.[2] Our file of the newspaper published at that place being incomplete, I promised to mention his desire to you, presuming that you might have the numbers of the Telegraph printed about that time, which are not to be found in the Department. If the papers should be in your possession, will you have the kindness either to lend me the file, including the numbers for November 1837, or to look at the obituary head for three or four weeks subsequent to the 27' of October, and inform me whether you find any mention of the death of Mr. Evans. By doing so, you will not only oblige me, but Confer a great favor upon the mother of the young man, who is in great distress at the rumor of the death of her son.

Very respectfully yours Yr obed sev
A. O. Dayton

+++

ALS. Tx, TLP.

1. James Buchanan (1791–1868), later president of the United States, represented Pennsylvania in the House of Representatives in the Seventeenth through Twenty-First Congresses, 1821–1830, and was US senator in the Twenty-Third through Twenty-Ninth Congresses, 1833–1846.

2. Evan Rice Evans (1802–1837) opened a law practice in Washington, Texas, in 1836. He died of yellow fever in 1837.

John Woodward to Fairfax Catlett

Consul genl of the Republic of Texas.

June 23: 1838 New York.

Dear Sir

Enclosed you have an appointment by me of Charles H. Forbes Esquire of this city as Vice Consul for Texas in the City of New York.[1] I also send you a manuscript of my Commission. Be pleased to present both to his Excellency the President of the U. States or the Honbe the Secretary of state and procure his recognition and to transmit it to him as soon as possible addressed to him at No 8 Wall St, New York. I have the honor to be

very respectfully sir your obedient Servant.,
John Woodward

+++

ALS. Tx, TLP.

1. Charles H. Forbes (1814–1844), an attorney.

J[ames] McClelland to Fairfax Catlett

Norfolk Va. June 20th 1838

Sir

I have taken the liberty to Enclose to you a communication for Gen Albert S. Johnston of the Texian Army, which you will please forward to him, should you in a short time have dispatchs to forward to your Government, you will Confer a favor on me by sending the Enclosed with them, as it may in this way reach him in the shortest time

I am Respect[full]y Yr. obt. Svt.
J. McClelland

✦✦✦

ALS. Tx, TLP. This is possibly Dr. James S. McClelland (1810–1877), a naval surgeon. The enclosure is not with the letter.

James Manney to Fairfax Catlett

Beaufort No Ca
June 25th 1838

Sir,

I have requested my friends the Honbl Charles Shepard, & the Honbl Edward Stanly of the House of Representatives to call on you, with my Memorial to the Congress of Texas.[1]

I request the favor of you to transmit my memorial to the President of Texas; by the first dispatches which you may forward—and request him to lay it before Congress at as early a day as practicable.

I have requested the result of my application to be forwarded to you—and I must beg the favor of you to forward it to me, at this place, by mail.

Please to inform me on what Rivers of Texas Steam Boats are running?

From my long and extensive experience in the practice of Medicine, I flatter myself that I could be useful in any community where I may locate.

I am requested to enquire of you if there is employment for land surveyors in Texas? Mr Bryan Heller, a young gentleman of good education and character, son of Isaac Heller Esqr postmaster at this place, is anxious to emmigrate to Texas, should there be a good prospect of getting employment as a Surveyor. His father is our County Surveyor[2] —and B. Heller has acted as Deputy Surveyor for about two years. You will confer a favor by giving an answer to this enquiry, directed to the Post-Master Beaufort, No Ca as soon as convenient.

I am Very respectfully Your Obt. Servt

James Manney

✦✦✦

ALS. Tx, TLP. James Manney (1785–1852). The memorial is not with the letter.

1. Charles Biddle Shephard (1808–1843) represented North Carolina as a Whig in the Twenty-Fifth through Twenty-Sixth Congresses, 1837–1841. Edward Stanly (1810–1872) was a North Carolina Whig in the Twenty-Fifth through Twenty-Seventh Congresses, 1837–1843, and the Thirty-First and Thirty-Second Congresses, 1849–1853.

2. Bryan Heller (1818–1853). Isaac Heller (1795–1847) was a member of the North Carolina House of Commons, 1818–1823, and a member of the state senate, 1840 and 1844.

John Forsyth to Fairfax Catlett

Department of State,
Washington, 28th June, 1838.

Sir:

I have the honor to acknowledge the receipt of your note of the 26th instant, accompanied by a copy of the commission of John Woodward as Consul General of Texas for the port of New York, by the original commission of Charles H. Forbes as Vice Consul of Texas for the same port, and requesting an Exequatur for Mr. Forbes. The Exequatur is accordingly herewith transmitted and the commission of Mr. Forbes is returned.

I avail myself of this occasion to offer you renewed assurances of my high consideration.

John Forsyth

✦✦✦

LS. Tx, TLP.

William H. Wharton to Fairfax Catlett

Eagle Island 30th June 1838

My D Sir.

This will be handed you by our Navy Agent Captain J. G. Tod[1] a gentleman every way worthy of your deepest respect & confidence. He has been an officer in the navy of the U.S. & I have no doubt is better qualified than any one we could select to procure us such a navy or will bring our rascally enemy to terms of peace & reason. I know that I need not solicit for him your kindest & most particular attentions.

I have written to you 3 or 4 times without an answer. Why is this my old Friend? I wrote for a certified copy of my contingent expenses having lost the one you sent. Also in reference to the money due me by Hamer & McKaig.[2] Do press them for the money, send on the certified copy of contingent expenses & write me frequently.

In great haste Truly yr friend
Wm. H. Wharton

✦✦✦

ALS. Tx, TLP.

1. John Grant Todd (1808–1877), born in Lexington, Kentucky, served in the Mexican navy before securing a midshipman appointment in the US Navy. He was discharged from the US Navy in 1836 and came to Texas. In 1838, Todd was appointed Texas naval agent at Baltimore and directed to supervise the construction and outfitting of war vessels for the republic. He was promoted to commander in July 1839 and placed in charge of the Galveston Naval Station. For a time in 1840 he was acting secretary of the navy. Todd left Texas in 1842 and went to Washington, but returned in 1845 bearing the official notice of Texas annexation to the United States. During the War with Mexico Todd reentered US naval service and performed duties refitting vessels. After the war, Todd, with other investors, established the Buffalo Bayou, Brazos, and Colorado Railway in addition to other commercial interests.

2. No information has been found about this debt.

John Forsyth to Fairfax Catlett

Department of State,
Washington, 5th July, 1838.

Sir:

It is stipulated in the Convention between the United States and Texas relative to claims in the cases of the brigs Pocket and Durango, signed at Houston on the 11th of April, last, that the Ratifications are to be exchanged in this City within three months of the signature. That period will expire on the eleventh instant. I am now prepared to make the exchange on the part of the United States and would thank you to inform me if you are ready to act for that purpose on behalf of your Government, and if so, to request you to come to the Department tomorrow at 12 o'clock to make the exchange.

I embrace this opportunity to offer you renewed assurances of my high consideration.

John Forsyth

✦✦✦

LS. Tx, TLP.

When the Second Texas Congress adjourned on May 24, 1838, Representative Anson Jones returned to his home in Brazoria with the intention of retiring from public life. A physician, he planned to resume his medical practice and prepared for his upcoming marriage to Mary Smith McCrory (1819–1907), an eighteen-year-old widow. However, he received an unexpected summons from President Houston. Peter W. Grayson, who had accepted the appointment of minister to the United States, in place of Memucan Hunt, committed suicide on July 9 in Tennessee. Pressed by Houston, Jones reluctantly postponed his wedding plans and made the fatiguing journey to Washington, reaching the city on August 23.

Robert Anderson Irion to Anson Jones

Department of State
City of Houston, July 12th 1838

Sir

It is the wish of the President that [you] will proceed as expeditiously as possible to Washing[ton] City, and assume the duties which will devolve on [you] as Minister Plenipotentiary of this Government to that of the United States of America.

You will on your arrival there take possesion of the archives, documents, papers &c, which belong to the Texian legation.

With regard to the course of policy whi[ch] has been pursued relative to the Diplomatic relation[s] between the two Governments I refer you to instruct[ions] heretofore given, which will be found among the pap[ers] of the said legation.

With respect to the present condi[tion] of Texas, and its policy, both foreign and domest[ic] you are well informed; and the President havin[g] full confidence in your prudence and capacity relies much on the exercise of your discretion in management of the diplomatic affairs of this Government at Washington, being assured that [in] every thing you will act in a manner best calculated [to] advance the true interests of the country. U[nder] these circumstances detailed instructions are not necessary at the present time.

The Convention of Limits h[as] been ratified by this Government, and it is [assu]med by that of the United States also. You will [proceed to] the exchange of its ratifications at the earliest p[ossible] period. The peculiar situation of the inhabit[ants] near our North Eastern Boundary renders [a speedy] action on the subject extremely important and desirable. You will therefore urge the necessity after such exchange shall have taken place of the immediate attention on the part of the U. States to the appointment of the Commissioner contemplated by the said Convention. Concerning the Escort mentioned in the Convention none will be required farther than the number actually necessary to perform the work, for the whole distance contemplated to be marked out at the present time is perhaps not more than One hundred and forty miles, which is through a populated territory.

Anson Jones

Portrait by William H. Huddle (1847-1892). Courtesy of the State Preservation Board, Austin, TX; Accession ID: CHA 1989.107. Photography by Perry Huston, September 28, 1993, post conservation.

It is sincerely hoped that no further impediments will be presented to the definitive and satisfactory adjustments of this question, which has given rise to so much inconvenience to the population referred to, and solicitude to this Government.

I am directed by the President to renew the instructions heretofore given concerning the proposition of annexation.

Should the present session of the U. States congress adjourn without having acted finally upon this subject, you will immediately after such adjournment, formally withdraw the said proposition.

The pendency of this question, as you are well aware, has, and is still embarrassing [ou]r negociations in Europe, which circumstance, [in]asmuch as the Government of the U. States [h]as declined to entertain the proposition, and [the] prospect now exists that the measure can [pro]ceed, renders it expedient that the question so far as the proposition adverted to is concerne[d] should be finally disposed of without further delay.

When you withdraw the propos[al] as above indicated, you will immediately inf[orm] our diplomatic Agent, J. Pinckney Henderson[,] near the Government of Great Britain and [France] thereof, in order that he may be in possession of [that] fact at the earliest possible period. I have inform[ed] him that such notice will be given.

I have the honor to be with great respect Your Obt. Servant.

R. A. Irion

✦✦✦

ALS. Tx, TLP. Document damaged, with missing parts inserted by conjecture. Anson Jones (1798–1858) was born in Great Barrington, Massachusetts, and took a peripatetic path to Texas, living at various times in New York, Harper's Ferry, Virginia, Philadelphia, Venezuela, and New Orleans before establishing a medical practice at Brazoria, Texas, in 1833. Jones served in the army during the Texas Revolution. He served as Texas minister to the United States until President Mirabeau B. Lamar recalled him in May 1839. Upon his return to Texas, Jones was selected to fill William H. Wharton's uncompleted term in the Senate. When Sam Houston again captured the presidency, he appointed Jones secretary of state, a position he held from 1841 to 1844. He was the last president of the Republic of Texas, from December 1844 until statehood was proclaimed on February 19, 1846.

Robert Anderson Irion to Anson Jones

Department of State,
City of Houston, ~~July~~ August [7, 1838]

My Dear Sir,

My communica[tion] of to-day's date will inform in relation to official matters. One thing I will say to you privately. I understand that Mr. Newell, the present Consul for Velasco & Galveston will probably be superseded—such a result this government would regret. He has been and is still, a friend to Tex[as] and is in every way well qu[ali]fied for the place.

I make this suggest[ion] in order that you may apprised of what is going [on] and prevent any unfair arrangement that may have been attempted.

Please present my best compliments to Mr. Catlett.

Truly yr friend
R. A. Irion

✦✦✦

ALS. Tx, TLP.

Robert Anderson Irion to Anson Jones

Department of State
City of Houston, Aug. 7, 1838

Sir,

I have the honor hereby to acknowledge the receipt of Mr. Catlett's communication dated 12th ulto.[1] I am happy to learn that the convention of Indemnity to American citizens for the injuries received on account of the capture of the Pocket, and impressments of the Durango, by officers of this Government, has been ratified by the United States.

You will find by reference to the despatch above referred to, that Mr Catlett has come to the conclusion that a formal withdrawal of the proposition of annexation, is not necessary: — Still it would seem that the matter is questionable. With regard to this subject your instructions are positive; and it is confidently expected that you will act in accordance therewith.

Our north eastern boundary should be defined as speedily as possible; and the President expects that you will use every effort to procure, at the earliest practicable period, the appointment of the commissioners &c, on the part of the United States. According to the convention of limits, the meeting of the commissioners is to take place at New Orleans; and the facilities which Steam Boat navigation now affords, will enable this [Gov]ernment to be prompt in the matter.

It is a subject of gratulation to this Government, that the army of the United States, destined for the protection of their South Western Frontier, has been encreased; for the greatest apprehension that we have with respect to enemies, is that the Indians inhabiting that border, may be induced to pass the line, and assume a formidable and hostile attitude towards the people of Texas.

This measure of the United States Government, its execution devolving as it does on Genl. Gaines, whose experience, discretion, and great energy in military affairs, must tend to quiet the turbulent recklessness of the Indians who have been removed west of the Mississippi.

This Government, as you know, apprehends more danger from them than from the Mexicans. You are also aware that the Cadoes have been influenced to leave the country which they occupied in Red River, and establish themselves permanently in Texas, and are associated now, (and have been for about two years,) with the most hostile of our native Indians.

The President is now absent, at Nacogdoches, and, we learn, is enjoying excellent health. Such rumours as we had prior to your departure, with respect to hostilities in the West continue to arrive; but from the most authentic and recent information the troubles seem to be confined entirely to robbing parties; and are conducted by individuals for the purpose of accumulating property. They seem to have no [Nati]onal character.

Genl. Henderson's first despatch from France, dated 2nd of June ultimo,[2] was received yesterday. He had had an interview with Count Molé, Minister for foreign affairs.[3] Nothing definite or conclusive took place relative to our recognition by that Government. Nothing unfavourable occured.

Make my compliments to Mr Catlett.

I have the honour to be, with great respect, Your obet. svt.

R. A. Irion

P.S. It is expected by this Government that you will afford every assistance to the Com[missione]rs. who are authorized make the loan.[4]

Sam M. Williams has been appointed Navy Agent in the place of Col. Grayson, Decd. to perform all the duties that devolved on him as that agent.

R. A. Irion
Sec. of State

✦✦✦

LS. Tx, TLP. Published in *DCRT,* 1: 342–343.

1. Fairfax Catlett to Robert A. Irion, July 12, 1838, No. 38, *DCRT,* 1: 338–341.

2. J. Pinckney Henderson to Robert A. Irion, June 2, 1838, No. 1, *DCRT*, 3: 1206–1217.

3. Louis Mathieu Molé (1781–1855) was prime minister of France and foreign minister, 1836–1839.

4. The Texas Congress, in 1836, had approved an act authorizing borrowing up to $5 million based on Texas bonds. The effort had been unsuccessful, and on May 16, 1838, Congress reauthorized the measure. Albert T. Burnley (1800–1861), a New Orleans businessman with interests in Texas, and Samuel M. Williams went to Philadelphia where they hoped to negotiate the loan with Nicholas Biddle. Despite their efforts, and the assistance of James Hamilton and Anson Jones, they were unsuccessful. Subsequently, Williams was assigned the task of overseeing the purchase and construction of new warships for the Texas navy.

Aaron Vail to Anson Jones

Department of State,
Washington, 24th. Augt. 1838.

Sir:

Your note of this morning, announcing your arrival in this city, and requesting an audience of the Secretary of State to present your credentials as Minister Plenipotentiary from the Republic of Texas, has just been received at the Department, and I have the honor to inform you, in reply, that the absence of the President and Secretary from the seat of government renders it impracticable at present, to comply with your wish. If, however, previously to their return, you should have occasion informally to address this Government on the business of your mission, your communications will be received, and laid before the Secretary of State without unnecessary delay.

I have the honor to be, with great respect,

Your most obedt. servant,
A. Vail
Acting Secretary of State.

✦✦✦

ALS. Tx, TLP.

Robert Anderson Irion to Anson Jones

Department of State
City of Houston Sept. 7th /38.

Sir.

I had anticipated the pleasure of hearing from you by the late Columbia, her mail however is barren—

Permit me to urge upon you the importance of consummating the arrangements for settling our boundary question with the least possible delay: great solicitude is felt upon this subject, not only by the portion of our citizens within the disputed territory, but by the whole country, and the Government—

Enclosed I send you the note of the Hon John Forsyth, Secretary of State of the United States, to the Hon Memucan Hunt late Minister from this Republic, acknowledgeing advice of the appointment of Fairfax Catlett as Charge of the legation in his absence &c which you will file with the papers of the legation.

Accept the renewed assurance of my consideration and respect
R. A. Irion

✦✦✦

LS. Tx, TLP. Published in *DCRT,* 1: 344.

Stewart Newell to Anson Jones

Galveston September 9th 1838

Sir,

Permit me to trespass upon your time and attention to ask the favour of your influence with the President of the United States and the Hon Secretary of State to grant me the appointment as Consul to Galveston instead of Velasco. I make the request in consequence of having been informed that the Government of the U. States contemplates this Port a separate appointment, when I received my present one, my understanding was clearly on my part that I had charge of Galveston and Velasco and have acted under that impression but should it be then seperated I desire most this Port, and although your acquaintance is but short with me yet I trust you will not refuse my request and more particularly when you shall have received our mutual friend Mr Borden's[1] Letter, who tells me he has written upon the subject and for more certainty of the feelings favourable to my application. I have by request of the Citizens, who signed it, enclosed and forwarded a Petition to the President upon the Subject and have already addressd. the Hon. Secretary of State of the United States upon the subject and enclosed to him Letters from Hon. R. A. Irion and G. Borden Jr Esqr

I have the Honor to be Sir Your Obt Servt.
Stewart Newell

✦✦✦

ALS. Tx, TLP.

1. Gail Borden Jr. (1801–1874) came to Galveston from Mississippi in 1829. He raised stock and worked as a surveyor in Fort Bend County. Borden established the *Telegraph and Texas Register* in 1835, which he published until he sold his interest in the paper in 1837. Borden was collector of customs at Galveston, 1837–1838, and again from 1841–1843. He was also an agent of the Galveston City Company. In the 1850s Borden developed and patented the process for condensing milk and other foods. He left Texas for a time to pursue business opportunities in the United States, but returned after the Civil War.

Ezekiel Hale Barstow to Anson Jones

Dartmouth College, Hanover N H Sept 16 '38

Dear Sir,

It is with pleasure that I see your name announced in the papers as having arrived at Washington [as] Minister from the Republic of Texas.

My immediate object in writing to you at this time is to gain information in regard to the Estate of a Brother of mine who died while in the Texan Service in the autumn of 1836—Joshua Barstow[1] the Brother referred to was a resident of Nashville Tenn & at the time of the breaking out of the Texian war, was in the pursuit of an honorable & profitable business—Being an ardent Republican & at Enemy of oppression he no sooner heard of the difficulties in Texas than he resolved to go to their rescue. Leaving his business he attached himself immediately to a <u>volunteer</u> <u>company</u> of young men found in the city & started for Texas <u>at</u> <u>his</u> <u>own</u> <u>expense</u>. After a long & difficult passage in which they were well nigh being ship-wrecked he arrived in Texas in Jan. or Feb. 1836. & immediately joined the army. He was subsequently in the <u>battle</u> of <u>San.</u> <u>Jacinto</u> & after the capture of Santa Anna was placed as a guard over him, which station he filled till the time of his death.

He died in Sept '36 at Orozimbo of conjestive Fever & was buried with military honors at that place. His <u>trunk,</u> <u>clothes</u>, <u>papers</u> & indeed <u>all</u> his effects were left there—I believe in the hands of the Physician who attended him—I understand likewise that my Brother is entitled to Bounty Land—head right claim &c. Will you Sir inform me of the truth in the case as to <u>how</u> <u>much</u> he is entitled to—its <u>probable</u> <u>value</u> —the <u>means</u> to be used or the steps to be taken to secure it <u>according</u> <u>to</u> the <u>law</u> of the Republick & also the <u>probable</u> <u>expense</u> to be incurred in processing it. It is my design now to visit that country the ensuing winter on this business & should be very grateful for any information relative to it, in your power to give—

If you my Dr. Sir would take the trouble to notice this letter & would give me an answer <u>as</u> <u>soon</u> <u>as</u> <u>convenient</u> in regard to the topics mentioned you would confer a very great favor on me & the family—

With sincere regards for your welfare I am my Dr. Sir your friend & servant

E. Hale Barstow

✦✦✦

ALS. Tx, TLP. Ezekiel Hale Barstow (1815–1862) graduated from Dartmouth College in 1839. He taught school and from 1845 to 1851 was a Congregational minister in Walpole, Massachusetts.

1. Joshua Barstow (d. 1836) was a private at the Battle of San Jacinto. His heirs did not apply for the land bounty he earned as a veteran.

Edward R. Belcher to Anson Jones

Bolivar [Tennessee] Sept 18. 1838

Sir.

Mrs. Bomar[1] has handed me your kind favor the 29' of July, with a request that I should acknowledge the receipt of it. On mature reflection she is of opinion that it would be for her Interest to have one third of the Lands located for her and her children in Texas sold, provided a judicious disposal could be made of them. This determination is arrived at from a conviction that it would be more beneficial to her children. It is her desire to give them a good education, and the majority of them being girls, she will be necessarily compelled to spend much money on them. Her husband was not a thrifty man, and left her in destitute circumstances, and to do justice to her children it would be expedient to sell a portion of those Lands to forward their advancement at school,

She requests me therefore to authorize you, and through you your agent in Texas during your absence, to sell one third of said Lands which may be deemed marketable, when they shall have so passed the proper offices which may authorize Sales to be made.

Mrs. Bomar requests me to say that she is grateful for your kind attention to her interest, a total stranger, and which places her under obligations, not to be forgotten.[2]

The public papers will doubtless signify your return to Texas.

Nothing further as to troubles on the frontier.

I have the Honor to Remain Yr Ob St.

E. R. Belcher

✦✦✦

ALS. Tx, TLP. Edward R. Belcher (b. ca. 1805) was an attorney in Bolivar, Tennessee.

1. Mrs. Bomar is not otherwise identified.

2. Dr. William W. Bomar (1797–1837) enlisted in the Texas army at Bolivar, Tennessee, in February 1836 and served as a surgeon at San Jacinto. In 1837, he returned to Tennessee, where he died. His wife received 640 acres of land for his service. Apparently Mrs. Bomar kept the grant because her children settled in Prairie Lea, in Caldwell County.

Thomas Toby to Anson Jones

New Orleans 5 October 1838

Sir,

Enclosed I hand you my Commission as Consul of the Republic of Texas for this Port—

I must beg of you to procure from the Executive of the United States my Exequatur, and furnish by Express mail, and in so doing much oblige

Your obedt Sevt
Thomas Toby

✦✦✦

ALS. Tx, TLP.

Martin Van Buren to Anson Jones

Oct 9 1838

It gives me much pleasure, Sir, to receive you as the accredited representative of the Republic of Texas, and I reciprocate very cordially the assurances of good will which you have expressed in behalf of the government and people of Texas towards the government and people of the United States. The motives to the cultivation of the most liberal and friendly relations between the two countries are too numerous and the interests of both in their maintenance too obvious to allow them to be disregarded by the government of either. In your personal dispositions to promote so desirable a result, I have the fullest confidence, and you may confidently rely on our cordial coöperation in any proper measure that shall be calculated to advance it.

✦✦✦

Secretarial copy. Tx, TLP.

Aaron Vail to Anson Jones, With Enclosure

Department of State,
Washington, 11th October, 1838.

Sir:

I have had the honor to receive your note of yesterday,[1] stating that agreeably to a stipulation in the Convention for marking a portion of the boundary line between the United States and Texas, signed on the 25th of April, last, you are prepared to proceed on the part of Texas to the exchange of the ratifications of said Convention, whenever I might be ready to meet you for that purpose on the part of the United States, and asking to be informed of the time when the exchange may be effected.

I take great pleasure in stating to you that, tomorrow, Friday, at twelve o clock, I shall be ready to make the exchange, and for that purpose be happy to receive you at that hour at the Department of State.

Be pleased, Sir, to accept on this occasion, the assurance of my very distinguished consideration.

A. Vail
Acting Secretary of State

✦✦✦

ALS. Tx, TLP. Published in *DCRT*, 1: 348.

1. Anson Jones to Aaron Vail, October 10, 1838, *DCRT*, 1: 347–348.

Enclosure: Convention of April 25, 1838, between the Republic of Texas and the United States

CONVENTION

Between the United States of America and the Republic of Texas, for marking the boundary between them.
Concluded April 25, 1838; Ratifications Exchanged October 13, 1838.

Whereas the treaty of limits made and concluded on the twelfth day of January, in the year of our Lord one thousand eight hundred and twenty-eight, between the United States of America on the one part and the United Mexican States on the other, is binding upon the Republic of Texas, the same having been entered into at a time when Texas formed a part of said United Mexican States:

And whereas it is deemed proper and expedient in order to prevent future disputes and collisions between the United States and Texas in regard to the boundary between the two countries as designated by the said treaty, that a portion of the same should be run and marked without unnecessary delay:

The President of the United States has appointed John Forsyth, their plenipotentiary, and the President of the Republic of Texas has appointed Memucan Hunt its plenipotentiary:

And the said plenipotentiaries having exchanged their full powers, have agreed upon and concluded the following articles:

ART 1. Each of the contracting parties shall appoint a commissioner and surveyor, who shall meet before the termination of twelve months from the exchange of the ratifications of this convention, at New Orleans, and proceed to run and mark that portion of the said boundary which extends from the mouth of the Sabine, where that river enters the Gulf of Mexico, to the Red river. They shall make out plans and keep journals of their proceedings, and the result agreed upon by them shall be considered as part of this convention, and shall have the same force as if it were inserted therein. The two Governments will amicably agree respecting the necessary articles to be furnished to those persons, and also as to their respective escorts, should such be deemed necessary.

ART. 2. And it is agreed that until this line shall be marked out, as is provided for in the foregoing article, each of the contracting parties shall continue to exercise jurisdiction in all territory over which its jurisdiction has hitherto been exercised, and that the remaining portion of the said boundary line shall be run and marked at such time hereafter as may suit the convenience of both the contracting parties, until which time each of the said parties shall exercise without the interference of the other, within the territory of which the boundary shall not have been so marked and run, jurisdiction to the same extent to which it has been heretofore usually exercised.

ART. 3. The present convention shall be ratified, and the ratifications shall be exchanged at Washington, within the term of six months from the date hereof, or sooner if possible.

In witness whereof, we, the respective plenipotentiaries, have signed the same, and have hereunto affixed our respective seals. Done at Washington, this twenty-fifth day of April, in the year of our Lord one thousand eight hundred and thirty-eight, in the sixty-second year of the independence of the United States of America, and in the third of that of the Republic of Texas.

[L.S.] John Forsyth,
[L.S.] Memucan Hunt.

✦✦✦

Printed document. Tx, TLP. Published in *Treaties*, 4: 133–134.

On October 12, 1838, Anson Jones, in accordance with instructions earlier issued to Memucan Hunt on May 19, 1838, informed Acting Secretary of State Aaron Vail "respectfully but unconditionally" of "the formal and absolute withdrawal of the proposition for the annexation of Texas to the United States" (Jones to Vail, October 12, 1838, IAA, *12: 173–174).*

Aaron Vail to Anson Jones

Department of State,
Washington, 13th October, 1838.

The Undersigned, Acting Secretary of State of the United States, has the honor to acknowledge the receipt of the note addressed to him, yesterday, by Mr. Anson Jones, Minister Plenipotentiary of the Republic of Texas, announcing, under instructions from the Texian government, the formal and absolute withdrawal of its proposition for the annexation of Texas to the United States, and to state that Mr Jones' note had been laid before the President.[1]

The undersigned takes this opportunity to offer Mr Jones the assurance of his distinguished consideration.

A. Vail

✦✦✦

LS. Tx, TLP. Published in *IAA*, 12: 16.

1. Anson Jones to Aaron Vail, October 12, 1838, *IAA*, 12: 173–174.

Aaron Vail to Anson Jones

Department of State,
Washington, 19th October, 1838.

Sir:

Pursuant to the request in your note of this date, I have the honor to enclose the Exequatur of the President of the United States to Henry H. Williams, as Consul of the Republic of Texas for the port of Baltimore. The commission of Mr. Williams is likewise returned.

Permit me to offer you renewed assurances of my high consideration.

A Vail
Acting Secretary of State

✦✦✦

LS. Tx, TLP.

John Day Andrews to Anson Jones

Hanover C[our]t H[ou]s[e] [Virginia] 20th Octo 1838

My Dear Sir,

Your very kind letter by the last mail has been duly recd. for which I stand truly obliged; The information it affords me is truly valuable, but still leaves me much embarrassed as to what I should do.—In-as-much as it was my ~~wish~~ desire to carry out a considerable number of slav[e]s with me, and I feel unwilling to put so valuable an interest to hazard or to be engaged in any transaction that might wear the appearance of seeking to violate what I suppose to be a convention between the Governments of the U.S. and sundry Trans Atlantic powers.—I had hoped that there had been some positive stipulations between the Governments of Texas & that of the U.S. on this subject, till I recd. your letter—which advises that the only treaty extant ~~on~~ touching this subject, is the commercial treaty heretofore existing between the Governments of Mexico & that of the U.S. in which I can readily suppose that no such provision was incorporated.—May I not ask the favour of you to examine the laws of Congress on this subject and also enquire of the secretaries of the Navy, & war, as to my security venturing on what you propose of taking out with my family to Texas, my slaves.—Being at a remote situation from the points where I could make those enquiries for myself must plead my apology for thus troubling you again on this Subject.—The question is an important one I conceive to the rapid advancement of our new Republic and is worthy of your particular attention.—Indeed I am pursuaded you will render a most valuable service not only to the Government you have the Honor to represent but the information will be of vital interest to many individuals of interprise, whose wealth and industry would contribute much to give that strength to our infant Government that she at this moment so much needs.—

I feel satisfyed of the fact set fourth in your letter that many, very many slaves, are constantly from time to time being carried into Texas; but whether in a rather Smugled character or openly I am yet unadvised.—I rather Suspect under the former character. This I wish by all means to avail, as I hope to be extensively engaged in commerce between the two countries and would be utterly unwilling to do any thing that should be in any way subversive of what the Government of the U.S. & that of other Governments abroad might regard as conducive to the general good amongst nations. While I do feel well assured that the Government of Texas can not long consent to be subjected to restrictions that must have a more powerful tendency than almost any one circumstance in retarding her growth As I feel well convinced that the valuable lands of Texas cannot be fully developed without the introduction of slavery.—

I am quite anxious to get off in a few weeks, and shall carry all my slaves with me provided you can give me such assurance of safety in doing so, as a due regard to my own pecuniary interest as well as respect for my own integrity as a merchant and citizen, with that which the convention of nations in their wisdom might see cause to adopt on this important subject.—I feel truly sorry to trouble you again on this subject, but feel satisfied from the known urbanity of your feelings that you will take pleasure in doing what you can to advance the interests of immigrants & the growth of our common country. I shall aw[ait] your answer with great anxiety.—In t[he] mean time please accept the assurance of my most grateful acknowledgments for your past kindness. In great haste (as the mail waits)

I am Dear sir yours most truly
John D. Andrews

✦✦✦

ALS. Tx, TLP. Despite his concerns, John D. Andrews (1795–1882) and his family moved from Virginia to Houston, where he became a successful businessman and was elected mayor in 1841 and 1842.

Robert Strange to Anson Jones

Fayetteville N.C. Oct. 23rd. 1838.

A citizen of North Carolina residing near this place is desirous of obtaining some information which I take the liberty of asking from you in his behalf.

It appears that one William Sampson Tuton joined a company of volunteers from Mississippi under the command of one Captain Pratt and entered the Texan service.[1] Mr. Tuton served as a sergeant and we learn through Capt. Pratt is entitled from the Texan Government to fourteen hundred and seventy acres of land. Mr. William Tuton died in the year 1836 leaving heirs survivng his only next of kin, his mother then residing near this place, (but since dead), his brothers Oliver K Tuton still residing near this place and Charles Tuton who is residing in Mississippi—[2] I am instructed by Mr O. K. Tuton to ascertain what steps are necessary to possess himself of the land to which his brother was entitled and to whom he is one of the heirs.—A prompt reply giving explicit information upon the subject will much oblige

Yr Ob. sert.
R. Strange

✦✦✦

ALS. Tx, TLP. Robert Strange (1796–1854), a Jacksonian Democrat, served in the US Senate in the Twenty-Fourth through Twenty-Sixth Congresses, 1835–1840.

1. Thomas A. S. Pratt (d. 1847) led a company at San Jacinto. William S. Tuton was a member of his company, but has not been otherwise identified.

2. Oliver K. Tuton (1805–?), from Robeson County, North Carolina, settled in DeWitt County, Texas, in about 1840. The 1870 federal census lists him as a resident of Clinton. Charles A. Tuton (1808–1851) also settled in DeWitt County.

Alexander Henriques to Anson Jones

New York Octr. 26th. 1838.

My Dear Sir:

I have just had an interview with Mr. Catlett, and he advises me to address you and obtain your views on the subject; the only obstacle in the way of my enjoying the station is that immediately upon my entering upon the duties of my office, the New Secretary may arrive, which dilemma will be anything but agreeable to be placed in. Will you write me your opinion, & concerning the remuneration? by so doing you will greatly oblige

Your Friend & Servant
Alexr. Henriques

✦✦✦

ALS. Tx, TLP. It does not appear that Alexander Henriques (1817–1889) ever served as legation secretary, but apparently he did act for a time as private secretary to Sam Houston in Texas. Henriques, who was born in Jamaica, later became vice chairman of the New York Stock Exchange.

Edmund Carmick Watmough to Anson Jones

Washington 20th. Novr 1838

Sir

I have receive[d] the enclosed papers from Mr Harrison American Consul at Jamaica with a request that I would have it forwarded. I know no other way than by begging of you the favor to do so, which I hope you will not deem an undue liberty.

I am Sir with consideration & respect Your very Ob Svt

Edmd. C. Watmough

Answd. & forwd. packet to Dr. Irion
26th. Nov. 1838.

✦✦✦

ALS. Tx, TLP. Edmund C. Watmough (1796–1848), of Philadelphia, was US consul at Trinidad, Cuba, 1835–1837.

1. Robert Monroe Harrison (ca. 1778–1858), of Virginia, was US consul at Kingston, Jamaica, 1831–1858.

Daniel Gold to Anson Jones

Office H.R. U.S.
Nov. 27. 1838

Sir.

I am requested, by the Hon. E. Root[1] of Delhi N.Y., to submit the accompanying papers to your consideration, and examination, and solicit of you the favor <u>to point out to him the way in which the titles</u>

can be confirmed, and inform him whether any of the deeds can be made available, and if so, how that object can be accomplished.

Thomas Hastings, formerly a resident of a neighboring town to Genl. Root, established himself as a merchant at Nachadoches some eight or ten years ago.[2] He was a member of the Texan convention and Secy. of the same. He died of the colera at Cincinnatti, while on his way to visit his relatives in N.Y. state. The precise time of his death, I believe, is not known. I am advised that his death is mentioned in a letter recd by his friends, from Maj. Belknap[3] while Maj. B was with Genl. [Edmund P.] Gaines defending the Mexican frontier, and also in one from Genl. Harrison[4] dated 3d April '37.

Genl Root is the friend, and the agent in the premises, of the Mother and an only brother of Thomas Hastings, who reside near Delhi

I am Sir With high respect Your Obt. Servt.
Danl. Gold

✦✦✦

ALS. Tx, TLP. Daniel Gold (d. 1849), of New York, was assistant clerk of the US House of Representatives.

1. Erastus Root (1773–1846) represented New York as a Jacksonian in the Twenty-Second Congress, 1831–1833. The papers referred to are not with this letter.

2. Thomas Hastings (ca. 1805–ca. 1837), of Bovina, New York, arrived in Texas in the 1820s and established a general store in Nacogdoches. He took part in the Fredonian Rebellion in 1826, represented Nacogdoches in the Convention of 1832, and was secretary of the Convention of 1833.

3. William Goldsmith Belknap (1794–1851), a professional soldier. He later served in the Mexican War and as commandant at Fort Gibson, Indian Territory.

4. William Henry Harrison (1773–1841) was then living at his farm at North Bend, near Cincinnati.

In 1837, Vicente Filisola, military commander of the northern frontier, headquartered at Matamoras, sought to ally Indians with Mexico, promising them the restoration of their lost territories if they would join in a war against the Texans. In the summer of that year Indian leaders from several tribes met with

Mexican officials in Matamoras, where they discussed plans to retake Texas. On May 29, 1838, Pedro Julián Miracle, a former Mexican army officer, crossed into Texas from Matamoras with a force of about seventy Mexican soldiers and Indians. By July 2, they had reached the Trinity River, where they were met by Vicente Cordova (1798–1842), a large landowner and former Mexican official from Nacogdoches. Cordova had supported the Texan cause when its goal was to restore the Constitution of 1824, but he had opposed independence and joined in plans to restore Mexican rule after the revolution. Miracle and Cordova spent July and August meeting with Indians and encouraging them to join their cause. Miracle was killed by an unknown party on August 20, 1838, near the Cross Timbers on the Red River. Found in his possession were instructions from Filisola for recruiting the tribes and a diary recording his efforts. Secretary of State Irion sent a copy of the diary to Anson Jones, who forwarded it to US Secretary of State John Forsyth on December 31, 1838. The Miracle Expedition, among other issues, was part of Irion's instruction to Jones on November 29, 1838.

Robert Anderson Irion to Anson Jones, with Enclosure

Department of State,
City of Houston, Novr 29th. 1838.

Sir,

I have the honor to acknowledge the receipt of your 39th. and 40th. dispatches.[1]

The President is gratified to learn that ratifications of the Treaty of Limits between Texas and the United States have been exchanged; and is extremely desirous that the Commissioner and Surveyor, therein provided for, should be appointed on the part of that Government with as little delay as possible in order that this troublesome question, which has occasioned so much inconvenience to this Government, and dissatisfaction to the citizens of that border, may be set at rest.

Shelby Corzine having declined to accept the appointment of Commissioner on the part of this Government, the President, during the recess of Congress, appointed Charles S. Taylor in his place, on whose nomination the Senate has not yet acted.[2]

The Treaty of Limits, and the Conventions of indemnity to American citizens for injuries sustained in consequence of the acceptance of the Pocket and impressment of the Durango have both been promulgated in the usual form, by proclamations of the President.

The people generally manifest grea[t] anxiety on the subject of the boundary line, and desire that it s[hould] be marked out as soon as practicable.

The late indian disturbances in [Eastern] Texas have been aggravated [by the uncertainty of the true boundary and the absence of a military force at the most eligible points to restrain the U. States' indians] from crossing Red River into [Texas, which they now do at pleasure far above Fort Towson, without hindrance.]

In contravention of treaty stipulations the Cadoes numbering about 300 efficient and experienced warriors [sho]rtly after the sale of their lands to the Government of the United States in 1834, without asking the consent of the authorities of this country, removed to it, and associated themselves with the prairie indians; and have been ever since, with the exception of a few short intervals, committing depredations on our frontier settlements; and are at this time combined with them, and jointly waging an active marauding warfare against us.

By reference to the Journal of Julian Pedro Miracle, an [officer] in the service of Mexico, (a copy of which is herewith transmitted) it will be seen that an extensive indian and Mexican conspiracy against Texas, which was perhaps intended also to involve the southwestern frontier of the United States, existed under the direction of General Vincente Filisola, the Commander in Chief of the Mexican army.

Miracle traversed at the hottest season of the year upward of six hundred miles of our frontier among various indian tribes and was, even after the declaration of his purposes, treated kindly by all of these. He was killed about the 20th. of August last near the cross

Timber on Red River by a citizen of that country, and the original of the copy of the journal alluded to, written in spanish, was found upon his body.

The movements of this emissary of Mexico, when viewed in connection with the fact that in May and June last agents of sundry tribes of North American indians visited Matamoros and procured from the authorities there large quantities of ammunition, and returned about the time that Miracle passed through Texas on his way, in all probability, to the great Council of the india[ns] who have been removed west of the Mississippi, which was to take place in September last.

It is reasonable to suppose that the Mexicans, finding [that they] are unable to reconquer Texas, in order to gratify their [vindictive passions against us, would willingly see it desolated, and again fall into the hands of savages.]

Could Mexico by the efforts of her emissaries and sp[ies pro]duce simultaneously, an indian war on the frontier of Texas, and the southwestern frontier of the United States, such a res[ult] might be possible; and if the object could not be fully atta[in]ed the contest would, as they are aware, occasion the most calamitous events to Texas with no risk, and but little expense to Mexico.

The discontented indians of Arkansas are continually removing to Texas and giving those of their tribes who preceded them thither, which is gradually increasing their number, and consequently the danger to us in case of an open rupture with them.

It is most sincerely hoped that this circumstance will not be regarded with indifference by the Government of the United States, and that the greatest vigilance and precaution will be directed on its part to prevent, in future, such emigration to Texas. The fine hunting grounds afforded by the Colorado, Brazos, Trinity, Red rivers and their tributaries, present strong allurements to the bold, enterprizing and somewhat civilized indians of Arkansas, occupying, as they do, districts less favorable to the enjoyment of their pursuits and dispositions.

Those hunting grounds are now being surveyed out under the authorities of the Republic, which frequently occasions serious collisions between the surveyors and indians.

We learn by the latest official news from Eastern Texas that none of the North American tribes in that quarter except the Cadoes, are in open hostility against us; and seemed better satisfied than they were a few weeks since. There can be no doubt, however, that all those tribes entertain a secret [an]d undying hatred to the Texians, as well as Americans generally, which they will doubtless manifest by joining the enemy when future occurrences enable them to do so with the least prospect of success.

With regard to the Cadoes I am direct[ed] by the President to instruct you to make a representation of [these] matters to the Government of the United States and request the [adoption] of such measures as will [lead to their entire expulsion from Texas. Since they came to Texas their perfidious actions present a continuous catalogue of depredations on the most exposed and defen]seless settlements of the country.

The injuries which they have inflicted [so far] it is true are small, when compared with the consequences [whi]ch will necessarily follow should they be allowed to remain [a]mong the wild indians. The latter when the former went among them, carrying rifles, powder and lead in abundance, which had been obtained by the sale of their lands on Red River to the Government of the United States, were but little acquainted with the use of firearms. Since then by the facilities afforded them by the Cadoes they have become tolerable hunters, and are much more efficient in war; and will, ere long, should such a state of things continue, be equal to North American indians.

You will also furnish the Government of the United States with a copy of Miracle's Journal.

It clearly shows that Mexico does not hesitate to employ American indians to fight against Texas.

The circumstances and coincidences attending the visit of the Cherokees and Cadoes to Matamoros in June last, and the marching of Miracle to the villages of those bands in Texas and then leaving them and pursuing the direct rout[e] to the Cherokee country in Arkansas several hundred miles before he was killed, induce those in this country best acquainted with the indian character, and the peculiar relations which exist between them, the United States and Texas, to suppose that Miracle was sent to attend the great council in Missouri for the purpose of combining the Arkansas indians with those of Texas for the destruction of the latter.

This view of the subject is in accordance with the policy of Mexico, for she has long since regretted the institution of the colonization system, and would now greatly prefer a population of indians from the Sabine to the Rio Grande to her old [co]lonists, the Texians.

The withdrawal of the proposition for the annexa[tion] of Texas to the United States has given general satisfacti[on, and] will have a most favorable effect on our ne[gotiations in Europe. I have received despatches from General Henderson up to] the 5th of September, who was then in Paris negotiating [for] the acknowledgment of our independence by the Government of France. He had received no positive answer from Count Molé, Minister for foreign affairs, but expected to do so in [a] short time.

The difficulties existing between Mexico and France, I think, will have considerable influence on this question. Should the blockade be kept up, as it is likely to be, we may reasonably expect an unconditional acknowledgement.

If, on the other hand, the blockade should be raised and their disputes adjusted, nothing more than a commercial arrangement, similar to the one entered into between Texas and Great Britain, will be effected at present.

I rejoice to learn, as you doubtless have before this time, that the Navy Agent, Mr. Saml. M. Williams, has contracted for the building and equipping of Five vessels of War for the use of the Government.

This fleet will enable us to command the Gulf, shut up the enemies' vessels in their ports, and ruin their commerce, which will render an invasion of Texas by Mexico impossible; for they cannot march an army into this country, no matter how numerous, unless they can be provisioned by sea.

Harassments of this kind will soon force them to acknowledge our independence.

The acquisition of such a fleet will have a most happy tendency in securing the permanent and uninterrupted prosperity of the country, by inspiring confidence abroad, thereby increasing emigration to Texas, and promoting our negotiations in Europe.

They are to be built with all possible despatch, and, judging from the tenor of the latest news from Vera Cruz, France will keep the enemy occupied till our vess[els] will be afloat.

Exequaturs have been issued by [this Go]vernment to Young J. Porter, John A. Monges, and E. [A. Rhodes, since my last dispatch.][3]

[I have the honor to be, Sir, with great respect your Obt. Servant,]

R. A. [Ir]ion

[Postscript]

Mr. Catlett's resignation, as Secretary of Legation, has been accepted. The President regrets, however, that he would not remain longer in the office which he has filled with so much credit to himself and benefit to the country.

R. A. I.

✦✦✦

LS. Tx, TLP. Damaged, with missing text. Published in *DCRT,* 1: 350–354. Missing text inserted from *DCRT*.

1. Anson Jones to Robert A. Irion, September 26, 1838, No. 39, *DCRT,* 1: 344–346; Anson Jones to Robert A. Irion, October 13, 1838, No. 40, *DCRT,* 1: 346–349.

2. Charles Standfield Taylor (1808–1865), an emigrant from England, had signed the Texas Declaration of Independence. He owned a mercantile firm in Nacogdoches when President Houston nominated him as the boundary commissioner for Texas, but Mirabeau B. Lamar withdrew the nomination when he became president in December 1838.

3. Young J. Porter, of Mississippi, US consul at Brazoria, 1838–1842?; John A. Monges (1781–1840), of Delaware, US consul at Matagorda, 1838–1840; Elisha A. Rhodes (1791–1858), of New Orleans, US consul at Galveston, 1838–1842?

There are multiple versions of the Miracle Diary, which differ in many details, particulary in regard to names of persons and places. The secretarial copy published here is substantially the same as one published in Senate Executive Document 14, 32d Cong., 2d Sess., Serial 660, pp. 13–17 (and in IAA, *12: 176–180), which was sent by Anson Jones to Secretary of State Forsyth on December 31, 1838. Another version, translated by Dr. A. G. Wright, is published in Malcolm McLean, ed.,* Papers

Concerning Robertson's Colony in Texas, *18 vols. (Arlington: University of Texas at Arlington Press, 1974–1993), 16: 545–555. A third manuscript copy is described in Dale L. Morgan and George P. Hammond, eds.,* A Guide to the Manuscript Collections of the Bancroft Library, *2 vols. (Berkeley: University of California Press, for the Bancroft Library, 1963), 1: 286).*

Enclosure: Diary of Pedro Julian Miracle

Private Instructions for the Captains of the friendly Indians of Texas by his Excellency the General in Chief Vicente Filisola.—

As soon as you arrive you will invite them to a meeting and propose to them that they and their friends should take up arms in defence of the integrity of the Mexican Territory in Texas; this meeting being only composed of the principal chiefs who govern them. Afterwards you will invite eight or ten of each of the Tribes to smoke the Pipe, and in the name of the Supreme Government of Mexico distribute among them Powder, Lead, and Tobacco in the usual manner, this being done, you will keep an account of your operations and inform me officially of the same. You will make them understand that as soon as they have agreed in taking up arms, they will be reward[ed] according to their merits and that as soo[n as] they have taken possession of the places [that I ha]ve mentioned to you, you will advise me [by] an Extraordinary Courier, giving me a detailed account of the strength of the Mexican force and of the Indian Tribes, with the plan of attack, that I may be enabled to direct the forces that are to leave from this place to the assistance of those who are to operate in that quarter; make them understand that as soon as the campaign is over they will be able to proceed to Mexico to pay their respects to the Supreme Government, who will send a Commissioner to give each possession of the land they are entitled to.

++++

Companions and Friends

Never was the country in more need of your services than at the present time. To preserve the National Honor, I present myself in the field of battle, to share your fate. Such are the orders of the General in Chief who has desired me to notice particularly in my official returns the services that you may render so that the Nation may value your wor[t]h. You are not personally known to me, but I [can] assure you that often have I shed my [blood] in defence of the Country and in [conclusion] I may say that in the last struggle [in] Texas I was present on the field and expose[d] my life to the hazard or fate of war. I shall not be the first to present myself in the battle field neither shall I be the last.—

Provided. . . . .

✦✦✦✦

The President instructs me to take notice of your good behavior in the campaign and not only to recommend you in my official reports, but also to make a list of the widows and of the mothers who have been deprived of their children, in order that they may enjoy the amount of land to which they were entitled.

There will be a place of deposite fixed upon to keep Horses, Mules, Cattle, provisions, clothing &c. and when the campaign terminates all will be distributed among those who participate in it; those who may by some unexpected circumstance, be prevented from joining in the war will likewise be entitled to a share of the spoil.

As soon as the news of ou[r ope]rations are made known in Matamo[ros His] Excellency, the General in Chief, will [make] a forced march towards the point where our troops may be so that in the event of any sudden reverse, you will be aided, and a central position fixed upon for your reunion, to be head quarters during the remainder of the campaign.

Each division will have its own supplies of the munitions of war, which they will carry with them,—and the commanding officer will see that nothing is wanting in this respect.

✦✦✦✦

The other papers are 1st. a power of attorney to Pedro Julian Miracle, and a Letter of citizenship to the same individual from the Governor of the State of Tamaulipas, Vital Ferrandes.[1]

++++

Memorandum Book.

This book is written with a pencil and many of the words are completely obliterated, and the language is also very imperfect, making it difficult to give any thing like a connected or correct translation; the following is as near as I can come to the contents.

May [29th] Left Matamoras

[May 30 E]ncamped at the Fresnos where no no[velty] occurred

[May 31] Took a List of our force amounting to 72 citizens, 2 Indians, 34 Soldiers of La Bahia and 20 Cherokee and Caddo Indians, our horses were also accounted and ten of them were found to be unfit for service.

June 1st. Nothing particular occurred today.

[June] 2nd. We are waiting for Juan de la Garza, to commence our march; but still he does not appear. Don Rafael Cabasos presented himself with a passport from His Excellency the General in Chief, dated the 27th day of May; he is in search of his Goods, and is accompanied by his servants, in all to the number of ten.[2]

[June] 3rd Started from the Fresnos to the Anaquilas where we tarried for the night. John de la Garza joined us with Biscuit, Sugar, Coffee, and a supply of Cartridges; we are four days in expectation of a Drove of gentle Horses, but we cannot obtain them; started at midday, passing the Colorado Creek, encamping on the other side, at a place called the "Altos" where nothing of importance occurred.

[June] 5th Made our encampment this day at th[e "M]ulatos" where we remained to run wild Horses.

[June 6] th We were unable to catch any Horses. [A guar]d of twenty-four men were appointed to take charge of our Encampment, nothing of importance until

[June] 11th. When on the Hill of Purgatory (Purgatorio) a sentinel discovered several men on horseback, we advanced towards them, they were a party of Smugglers, they fired upon us, parties were dispatched in pursuit of them, they abandoned their Cargos of

Tobacco &c. and fifteen Horses, we encamped tonight on the Borrego.

June 12th Run wild Horses.

17th Encamped at the "Pastel" where were killed two Irishmen, one woman and her children.

18th Encamped on White Creek.

19th On today the Indians became dissatisfied, and asked Savariego[3] to let them go to fight at La Bahia, the request was not granted. Advanced as far as San Antonio River and put out spies who returned on the 20th bringing us news of 20 men (Americans), and 30 at the Copano, and that Villareal[4] was at La Bahia with Horses.

[June 20th] [T]he Indians crossed the River, I overtook [them shortly,] took leave of Savariego. Flores[5] join[ed me] intending to go as far as the Colorado Ri[ver] but the Indians and guides refused, saying the road was too public. We slept or encamped in a small Island of Trees.

21st Crossed the Guadalupe.

[J]une 24th. At one o'clock crossed the Colorado.—saw several Americans, but did them no injury at which the Indians were much enraged.

[June] 27th Crossed the Brazos.—between that River & the Navasoto in the Timber met the Kickapoos who received us kindly and accompanied us on our journey.

[June 31st] Cruz and Cordova[6] went in search of Buffalo and returned on sunday the 1st bringing abundance.

July 1st Kickapoos left us.

[July] 2d Encamped on Trinity.

[July] 4th Started for "Plazeta" Creek, soon after we discovered the farms of the Choctaw Indians we directed our course towards the Rancho of Buenavista.

[July] 5th Don Vicente Cordova presented himself and read this communication of His Excellency the General in Chief, Don Vicente Filisola.

[July 7th] We expect to meet the Indian Chi[efs or Ca]ptains.

[July] 8th About 3 o'clock on the afternoon Gu[imon,] Bolt[7] and their Interpreters made their appearance but on account of the rain nothing was done.

[Jul]y 9th At seven o'clock we started to a Rancho to hold a consultation with the Indians, we read the communication of His Excellency the General in Chief; the Interpreters being inefficient nothing was done, they left us without any understanding, but are to meet them in 10 days, when they will determine. They left an Indian to conduct me to Bolt's house which was done, and we reached that place drenched with rain. I am to take the first opportunity to speak to Bolts to show him my private instructions; but I can do nothing as yet, he has sent me to another of his houses where I could conceal myself, for he said that some Americans were coming with a communication from Houston, the contents of which I have not learned,—nothing can be done without trouble!—

[July 11t]h Belmon[8] went to invite the Tribes.

[July 12th] Remained concealed that no one might se[e me.]

[July 13th] [W]ent to another Farm (Rancho) about 8 mi[les] distant, where there were only two boys living.

[July] 14th Much rain and no business done.

[July] 15th I am in a great passion. We have nothing but milk to eat or drink, and small hopes of getting any thing else, because these cursed Indians are as lazy as the devil, and I am so much enraged that I wish the Devil would seize me Body and Soul.—about 4 oclock in the afternoon an Indian came. I told him that the Boys had gone out, that I was very hungry, not having had anything to eat. He took me to another Cherokee house where we obtained Buttermilk, cheese, corn Bread, &c. we then returned to the Farm.

[July] 18th. In the afternoon of these days several Indians made their appearance for the meeting.

[July] 19th. Bolt, Billmoor[9] and several other captains cam[e] in, but the non-arrival of the Kicapoos delayed our meeting.

[July] 20th. The meeting took place. War was agreed upon as soon as circumstances would permit, and as speedily as possible; the amount of our force to be taken immediately;—including Nacogdoch[es] we have 540 men. At 5 o'clock P.M. Capt S[aguan]o[10] began to raise objections to th[e making of any] movement until the arrival of the army [in the] country, when war could be carried on [wi]th energy; but finally it was resolved that our force should be in readiness at a moments warning. At 5 o'clock Bolt left us, and all went away including Cordova, and the people of Nacogdoches about 8 o'clock in the morning.

[July 2]1st I left the House to which Bolt sent me and where the meeting was held, and directed my steps to "Horels,"[11] arriving at Bolt's house he gave me a horse in exchange for a Lepan horse which I had, about 10 o'clock in the morning we united in the house of Guhuile[12] to commence our march.

[July] 22nd. Marched and slept at the house of a Cherokee.

[July] 23rd Crossed the Naches, and stopped at a Kicapoo village.

[July] 24th Left very early.

[July] 25th —About 12 o'clock arrived at the Chickasaw village, they gave us plenty of Beef, Honey &c. the chief of the Tribe went with us, we slept with the Caddos where we arrived about 8 o'clock.

[July] 27th We continued our journey without any thing of importance occurring.

[July] 28th. I am waiting to meet the Kichis, Wacoes, Ta[huacanos] and other tribes.

[July 28th Th]e Captain of the Caddoes presented h[imsel]f about 3 o'clock in the afternoon, saying that the "Coyate" did not send for either Goods or money for the lands he had sold to the United States, but that he had sent a Captain called Nehomeceno[13] to take his place; it was observed that he was a bad man and might betray his trust and be the cause of some of our pla[ns] being frustrated, therefore he must indispensa[bly] go himself, which he finally did.

[July] 31st. On this day we learned that the Indian Nehomeceno did not wish to go, preferring to remain with us and fight.

Aug 2nd. On this day Manuel started for the Cherokee village.

[August] 3rd. Unintelligible. something concerning a Caddo and meeting Seguanas[14] who were coming to b[e] informed as regards the contemplated campaign, or what was meant by the message requesting them to meet and smoke a pipe.

[August] 4th. A meeting of the Saguanos was held to enquire if the Caddos had got some horses stolen from them.

[August] 5th I spoke to them about the war wit[h th]e Colonists, they asked if the River Col[orado was] for them, and I answered, Yes, to indu[ce them] to join the campaign.

[August] 6th The Saguanos and myself started for the Kichi village for the purpose of seeing Casemero,[15] and to enable me to have a meeting with them and to invite them for the present campaign. We encamped about half a league from their village; in the morning early went in. I slept at the house of the chief Arajena[16] who treated me with much kindness. I visited all the chiefs and was received well by all of them.

7th. I proposed a meeting to march against Bexar but was unable to make them comprehend me for want of an Interpreter.

8th We are waiting an arrival from the Saguanos to know when they will return to their village. Seeing that they did not come I determined to go to the Caddo village the following day, and I made my arrangements accordingly.

Friday 9th - - - - - -

Saturday 10th - - - - -

Sunday 11th - - - - -

++++

Extract from the official commun[ication of] His Excellency the General in Ch[ief]

Your communications as well as th[ose] of the friendly Indians have been received, [con]veying your wishes for the integrity of the Mexican territory in Texas, and your determination to make a stand against the Pirates and adventurers of Texas.

The Supreme Government is well aware of the suffering you have been exposed to occas[i]oned by the Rebels who still keep possession of the Mexican territory against the will of ev[ery] good Citizen and friendly tribe of Indians.

The Supreme Government authorizes you to take command, for which purpose you will invite all the principal Tribes that are willing to carry on the war at all hazards and without loss of time.—As soon as the war commences, you will inform me by an Ex[tr]a[or]dinary Courier so that I may be enabled to send my troops to your aid, and to the most convenient and advantageous point as soon as possible.

All Horses, Mules and spoils of whatever description shall be divided equal[ly] among all.

The Supreme Gover[nment recommen]ds that the families should not be [killed or] injured, but conducted to and kept a[t the] villages, when the General in Chief will himself dispose of them on the termination of the campaign.

✦✦✦

Secretarial copy and translation. Tx, TLP. Damaged, with missing text. Missing text added from copy in Senate Executive Document 14, 32d Cong., 2d Sess., Serial 660, pp. 14–17. Pedro Julian Miracle (d. 1838), a Columbian by birth, was an officer in the Mexican army.

1. General Francisco Vital Fernández [vice Ferrandes] was governor of Tamaulipas several times during the 1830s, but not after September 15, 1835. He was again governor from 1841 to 1843 and 1846 to 1848.

2. Juan de la Garza and Don Rafael Cabasos, not otherwise identified. The general in chief at this time was Vicente Filisola.

3. Savariego, not otherwise identified.

4. Villareal, not otherwise identified.

5. Manuel Flores (d.1839) was an Indian trader among the Caddoes before he became part of the Miracle Expedition. In 1839, Flores returned to Texas with military supplies for the Indians. He was killed in a fight with Texas Rangers on the North San Gabriel River.

6. Cruz and Cordova, not otherwise identified.

7. Guimon, not otherwise identified; Bolt is Bowl (ca. 1765–1839), or Duwali, the principal chief of the Texas Cherokees. Bowl was born in North Carolina to a Scottish father and Cherokee mother. He led a group to the St. Francis River Valley in Missouri and to northwest Arkansas before finally settling in Texas, near Nacogdoches, about 1820. On February 23, 1836, Sam Houston and other representatives of Texas signed a treaty with the Cherokees and other tribes guaranteeing Indian lands, but the Texas Senate rejected the agreement in December 1837, leading Bowl to ally with the Mexicans.

8. Belmon, not otherwise identified.

9. Billmoor, not otherwise identified.

10. Saguano, not otherwise identified.

11. Horels, not otherwise identified.

12. Guhuile, not otherwise identified.

13. Nehomuceno, not otherwise identified.

14. This is perhaps a reference to the Shawnees.

15. Casemero, not otherwise identified.

16. Arajena, not otherwise identified.

John Forsyth to Anson Jones, with Enclosure

Department of State,
Washington, 3d December, 1838.

Sir:

I have had the honor to receive your note of the 26th instant[1] stating that various tribes of Indians who had emigrated from the United States are combining with others originally residing within the borders of Texas for the purpose of committing aggressions upon the inhabitants of that country, and that there is reason to believe that the combination extends to Indian Tribes now within the limits of the United States and requesting the interposition of this government in preventing the threatened hostilities on the part of the last mentioned tribes, the infliction of punishment for those already committed, the removal of the intruding savages beyond the limits of Texas, and the adoption of measures for their peaceful behaviour in future.

A copy of your note has, by direction of the President, been transmitted to the Secretary of War, who being charged with the superintendence of Indian affairs, will adopt such measures as may appear necessary for the fulfillment of the obligations of the United States under the treaty referred to in your note. With regard to questions arising from the past or future emigration of Indians from the United States into Texas, I cannot better acquaint you with the views entertained by this government on that subject than by referring you to the enclosed copy of a communication addressed by this department on the 22nd of October, 1835, to the diplomatic representative of Mexico near the United States.

I avail myself of this occasion to offer you renewed assurances of my great consideration.

John Forsyth

✦✦✦

LS. Tx, TLP. Published in *IAA*, 12: 17 (where it is dated December 2, 1838).

1. Anson Jones to John Forsyth, November [vice "instant"] 26, 1838, *IAA*, 12: 174–175.

Enclosure: John Forsyth to Joaquín Maria de Castillo y Lanzas

Department of State
Washington, 22nd October, 1835.

The undersigned, Secretary of State of the United States, has the honor to acknowledge the receipt of the note of Mr Castillo, Chargé de Affaires of the United Mexican States, dated the 14th instant,[1] relative to alleged encroachments of Creek Indians from the United States upon the Mexican territories. A copy of Mr. Castillo's note having been referred to the Secretary of War, who is charged with the superintendence of Indian Affairs, that officer has stated that no information has been received by the War Department showing that the Creek Indians from Alabama are removing into the Mexican possessions, that there has not been during this season, any emigration of Creek Indians from Alabama, and that the War Department has, on all proper occasions, by direction of the President, discountenanced the project of those Indians for removing into the Province of Texas. From this it would appear that the political chief of Nacogdoches[2] has been misinformed. But, should it be otherwise, it may be doubtful whether under the 33rd article of the Treaty,[3] the intervention of the United States could be claimed or afforded unless the Indians manifested some hostile intent. If Indians going from the United States or elsewhere should migrate to the Mexican territories with peaceable intentions, it will be for the Mexican government alone to decide upon their admission or exclusion.

Though the general terms used in the representation of the political chief of Nacogdoches would justify the President in expecting a more explicit statement showing at what times and places and under what circumstances the Indians are alleged to have entered the Mexican territories, he has preferred directing this explanation to be made without delay, in order that there may be no room for doubts as to his views on the subject.

The undersigned avails himself of the occasion to offer M. Castillo renewed assurances of his distinguished consideration.

John Forsyth

✦✦✦

Secretarial copy. Tx, TLP. Published in *IAA*, 8: 34–35. Joaquín M. Castillo y Lanzas (1801–1878) was chargé d'affaires to the United States, 1833–1837.

1. Joaquín M. de Castillo y Lanzas to Asbury Dickins, October 14, 1835, *IAA*, 8: 297–298.

2. Henry Rueg (b. 1798) was born in Switzerland and settled in Texas in 1821. He was the political chief of Nacogdoches from October 18, 1834, to January 10, 1836.

3. The Treaty of 1831, *Treaties*, 3: 599–640. Article 33 (pp. 622–623) obligates the nations to "maintain peace and harmony" among the Indians on their borders.

Oliver Hampton Smith to Anson Jones, With Enclosure

Washington City
19th. Decr 1838

Sir,

Will you be so kind as to furnish for the use of the writer of the Enclosed letter, the information requested. The writer is a gentleman of character.

Your Obt Sert
O.H. Smith

✦✦✦

ALS. Tx, TLP. Oliver Hampton Smith (1794–1859), a Whig from Indiana, was a member of the US House of Representatives in the Twentieth Congress, 1827–1828, and a US senator from Indiana in the Twenty-Fifth through Twenty-Seventh Congresses, 1837–1843.

Enclosure: Joshua Soule Jr. to [Oliver Hampton Smith]

Indianapolis Dec. 14, 1838

Dear Sir

Permit me to trespass a few moments upon your valuable time, upon a subject of much interest to myself and others.

My object in addressing you is to ascertain from the Texian Minister at Washington, what terms were in force in in the Republic of Texas, on the subject of Bounty land, and in what manner they are applicable to the following case.

In December 1835, my brother-in-law, John Lawson, emigrated to Texas, joined the Texian Army, and as far as facts have come to my knowledge, was killed in March following, at the storming of the Alamo, and was found by the side of the lamented Crocket.[1]

I have endeavored to ascertain whether or not he has any claims upon that government; but have thus far failed. Communications have been addressed to the Department of War of that Republic, but no answer has been received.

Will you, Sir, have the goodness to ascertain from the Texian Minister, what those claims, (if any) may be, and whether his Mother, who is a widow, is his sole heir, and also the steps necessary to secure those claims.

Your early attention to this matter will confer a great favour, the more especially, as if it be necessary for me to visit Texas, I wish to start soon.

Respectfully
Joshua Soule Jr.

✦✦✦

ALS. Tx, TLP. Joshua Soule Jr. was the son of Joseph Soule, who was a bishop of the Methodist Church. The younger Soule was a dentist.

1. John Lawson, not otherwise identified. His name does not appear on any list of Alamo defenders.

Anson Jones to Samuel May Williams and A. T. Burnley

Copy
Texian Legation
Washington
Decr. 21st 1838

Gentlemen

Agreeably to your request I have countersigned the two Bonds handed me by Mr. Henry H. Williams and returned the same to him.

I remain very Respectfully Your obt Svt
Anson Jones

Bond No. 1 dated 13th Nov. 1838 for	$280.000	Five Hundred &	
do » 2 » » » » for	$280.000	Sixty Thousand Dollars	
	$560.000		

✦✦✦

Secretarial copy. Tx, TLP.

Henry Howell Williams to Anson Jones, With Enclosure

Baltimore Decr 22d 1838

Dear Sir

This will be handed you by Mr P. G. Cadue with a letter from my Brother S. M. Williams for himself & A. T. Burnley which Letter I intended to have had the pleasure of delivering personally, but have been prevented from leaving home by business. I have engaged Mr Cadue to take the Bonds alluded to in my b[r]others letter to you, for you to countersign, I take much pleasure in Introducing Mr Cadue to your acquaintance.

I hope you will excuse me for sending to you on Sunday but I expect my Brother here tomorrow & after he delivers the bonds, I hope to have the pleasure of making you a visit with him.

With Great Respect I am your Most ob Servant
Henry H. Williams

✦✦✦

ALS. Tx, TLP. P. G. Cadue, not otherwise identified.

Enclosure: Samuel May Williams to Anson Jones

Philadelphia Decemr 6th 1838

Dear Sir

The loan law of the Republic of Texas requires that the bonds issued by the Commissioners be countersigned when issued in this country by the minister of Texas at Washington.[1]

My brother H H Williams of Baltimore will hand you two bonds signed by Mr Burnley & myself each for $280,000 Two Hundred & Eighty thousand dollars, which please countersign and return to him. These bonds are to remain in pledge for 12 months, to secure the payment of a contract made for a navy, unless the Government should prefer to adopt a proposition made and order issued other bonds, in conformity with the contract referred to.

I hope to have the pleasure of visiting you in a few days at Washington. In the mean time please accept assurances of my personal esteem and respect.

Very truly your Obt Servant
Samuel M. Williams
for himself & A. T. Burnley

✦✦✦

ALS. Tx, TLP.

1 "An Act to Authorize the President to Negotiate a Loan on the Bonds of the Government, not Exceeding Five Million Dollars," May 16, 1838 (Gammel, 1: 1484-1487).

The constitution of the republic prohibited Sam Houston from serving another consecutive term as president. In an effort to block Houston's bitter political opponent Mirabeau B. Lamar from gaining the presidency, the Houston party persuaded Attorney General Peter W. Grayson to become a candidate. Grayson, however, committed suicide on July 9, 1838. The Houston faction then backed Chief Justice James Collinsworth, but he fell, or jumped, from a steamboat in Galveston Bay later that month. Lamar won the election easily. The new adminis-

tration took office on December 10, 1838.

Barnard Elliott Bee Sr. to Anson Jones

Department of State
City of Houston
Decr. 26, 1838

Sirs,

In conformity with the Constitution, a new Administration of this Republic entered upon its duties on the 10th Decr instant. In accordance with the comity of nations, you will notify the Secretary of State, of the United States, of this change, and of the existing Government, which is as follows.—

Mirabeau B. Lamar, *President.*
David G. Burnet, *Vice President.*
Cabinet Officers.
Barnard E. Bee, *Sec'y of State.*
Sydney S. Johnson,[1] *Sec'y of War.*
Richard G Dunlap,[2] *Sec'y of the Treasury.*
Charles Wattrous,[3] *Attorney General.*

You will present from his Excellency the President, to the Government of the U. States, the assurances of his high consideration, and upon all points connected with your mission, you will communicate with this Department. A Secretary of Legation will promptly be sent to you.

I am with great respect Yr' Obt Serv't
Barnard E. B[ee]

✦✦✦

LS. Tx, TLP.

1. Bee means to refer to Albert Sidney Johnston.

2. Richard G. Dunlap (d. 1841) had been a member of the Tennessee legislature before removing to Texas in 1837. He served as Texan minister to the United States from March 13, 1839, to April 20, 1840.

3. John Charles Watrous [vice Wattrous] (1806–1874) practiced law in Tennessee, Alabama, and Mississippi before coming to Texas, where he engaged in land speculation. When Texas became a state Watrous was appointed a federal dis-

trict judge.

Charles E. Heath to Anson Jones

Dated at Washington D C
Jany 2nd 1839

Dr Jones

Will have the kindness when perfectly at leasure to enquire from his Government through the proper channel which he may think most proper, what had become of the Estate effects &c of the late Major Leander Smith killed at or near Nacogdoches about the year 1837 or 8 as the papers say by a Bowie Knife.[1] I wrote to W Barr P.M.G.[2] on the subject but reced no answer. I also held a correspondince with Gel Hunt on this Subject & he referred me to Mr Barr.

Yrs &c
Chas. E. Heath

✦✦✦

ALS. Tx, TLP. Charles E. Heath, not otherwise identified.

1. Leander Smith (d. 1836) arrived in Texas in January 1836 and took part in the Battle of San Jacinto. He died in Nacogdoches on September 18, 1836, while in the army.

2. The writer means Robert Barr (1802–1839), postmaster general of Texas.

William Bryan to Anson Jones

New Orleans Jany 6th 18[39]

Sir

I have the honour to enclose a commission granted me by the President of Texas, by & with the consent of Senate appointing me Consul of the Republic at and near New Orleans.[1] You will please use the necessary forms to obtain my Exequatur and forward the same to me at this place. It will give me much pleasure to open a correspondence with you when your official duties or private business may require attention in New Orleans. Assuring that it will give me much satisfaction to execute commands you may have in this place.

I have the honor to be Respectfully Yours &c

Wm. Bryan

PS On my arrival yesterday I forwarded to you xprs mail, Dispatches from the Government of Texas

✦✦✦

ALS. Tx, TLP.

1. *Secret Journals*, 119–120, 232.

Wilson Lumpkin to Anson Jones

Senate Chamber
Washington Jany. 7th. 1839.

Sir

Alfred Bynum was one of the massacreed in Col. Fannins Regiment in Texas—how long, or in what capacity he served I am not prepared to say. He has left a mother, brothers & sisters—one of whom is my near neighbor—and has requested me to ascertain how much land, the heirs of the deceased are entitled to, & what steps are necessary to secure the same.

Not being prepared to furnish the information sought, must plead my apology for the liberty I now take, of asking the favor of you, to have me furnished with the information sought by one of my worthy constituents.

With high consideration & Respect, I am yr. Obt. Servt.
Wilson Lumpkin

✦✦✦

ALS. Tx, TLP. Wilson Lumpkin (1783–1870), a Jacksonian Democrat from Georgia, served in the Fourteenth Congress (1815–1817), the Twenty-First through Twenty-Second Congresses (1827–1831), was governor of Georgia (1831–1835), and US senator in the Twenty-Fifth through Twenty-Sixth Congresses (1837–1841).

1. Private Alfred Bynum, of Georgia, was among those killed at the Goliad

Massacre on March 27, 1836.

Barnard Elliott Bee Sr. to Anson Jones

Houston
Jny 14—39—

Private
and in haste—
Dear Sir,

The Committees on Foreign Relations in both Houses are devising the best mode to instruct you upon the subject of the withdrawal of the application for Annexation—Congress you recollect refused their assent last Spring—and you through your instructions from Genl Houston have in effect accomplished the object—great delicacy will therefore be necessary. Mr Bryan[1] waits & I must conclude.

With great esteem Yours
Barnard Bee

✦✦✦

ALS. Tx, TLP.

1. Moses Austin Bryan (1817–1895) had just been appointed secretary of the legation in Washington to replace Fairfax Catlett, who quit the position in October 1838. Bryan was the son of Stephen F. Austin's sister, Emily. He had served at the Battle of San Jacinto and acted as interpreter between Houston and Santa Anna after the battle.

Barnard Elliott Bee Sr. to Anson Jones

Department of State
Houston Jan'y 14th 1839

Sir,

In introducing Mr Bryan as your Secretary of Legation you will recognize a young Gentlemen entirely known to you both as a soldier of the 21st and a Neighbour. You will introduce him to the Secretary of State as having the full Confidence of this Government.

I am respectfully Yours &c
Barnard Bee

✦✦✦

LS. Tx, TLP.

John Forsyth to Anson Jones

Department of State,
Washington, 14th January, 1839.

Sir:

Pursuant to the request in your note of this date, I transmit the Exequatur of the President of the United States to William Bryan, as Consul of the Republic of Texas for the Port of New Orleans. The Commission of Mr. Bryan is also returned.

I avail myself of this occasion to offer you renewed assurances of my great consideration.

John Forsyth

✦✦✦

LS. Tx, TLP.

Richard Mentor Johnson to Anson Jones

U.S. Senate 11 Jan. 1839

My Dear Sir,

Doctor John Bennet of Newport Ky., a Citizen of great merit & a physician of great skill & eminence wishes to go to Texas with a view to enter the army.

He wishes me to appeal to you for such assistance as you may be willing & able to give him before he leaves Ky by letters &c. your answers will be gratefully acknowledged by your ob. Sevt

Rh. M. Johnson

✦✦✦

ALS. Tx, TLP.

1. Dr. John Bennett [vice Bennet], not otherwise identified. However, he did publish an article in the *Western Journal of Medicine and Surgery* 2 (1840): 418–422, in

which he advocated prescribing oil of turpentine for a variety of ailments.

John Forsyth to Anson Jones

Department of State, Washington,
19th January, 1839.

Sir:

I have the honor to acknowledge the receipt of your note of this date, announcing by direction of your government, that a change had taken place in its administration, and that you had been instructed to present, through me, to the President of the United States, assurances of high consideration on the part of His Excellency the President of the Republic of Texas. I have laid your note before the President, who has directed me to state in reply that he cordially reciprocates the friendly sentiments expressed for him by His Excellency the President of the Republic of Texas.

I embrace this opportunity to renew to you the offerings of my high consideration.

John Forsyth

+++

LS. Tx, TLP.

Robert Strange to Anson Jones

Senate Chamber
Jany 21 1839

Dear Sir

A month or so I had the honor of troubling you upon the subject of the claim of the heirs and representatives of Mr. Tuton who died in the Texan service for land, and enquiring how his claim must be substantiated. You were polite enough to respond but I have had the misfortune to mislay your letter. Excuse the trouble I give in requesting a duplicate.

With high respect Yr ob. Serv.
R. Strange

+++

ALS. Tx, TLP.

Richard Biddle to [Anson Jones]

H. of R.
22 Jany 1839

Mr. Biddle takes the liberty of submitting to his Excny the accompanying papers which impose, he is aware, a very unwarrantable labor.[1] He will be quite content to receive an answer to that effect. The writer had coi[nc]idently heard of his Excellency's reputation for obliging such and is disposed to push very far his experiment upon it.

✦✦✦

ALS. Tx, TLP. Richard Biddle (1796–1847), of Pittsburgh, was an Anti-Mason in the Twenty-Fifth and Twenty-Sixth Congresses, 1837–1840.

1. The papers referred to are not part of the extant record.

Barnard Elliott Bee Sr. to Anson Jones

Department of State
Houston Jany 31st '39

Sir,

Your Draft in favour of [Thomas] McKinney of the sum for Two thousand Dollars was immediately accepted.

Yours respectfully
Barnard Bee

I have written you a short official letter, by this opportunity.

B Bee

✦✦✦

ALS. Tx, TLP.

Barnard Elliott Bee Sr. to Anson Jones

Department of State
Houston January 31st 1839

Sir,

I am happy to inform you that the withdra[wal] of the application for annexation, has been sanctioned by Congress, [so] that no farther action need be had upon it.

The President is determined to act with great energy towards the Indians, who have been powerfully excited by the Mexicans living at Nacogdoches, and he is particularly desirous that you should communicate with the United States' Government in order that efficient Steps may be taken to prevent any coalition with the different tribes of the United States. We have observed with great pleasure the remarks of Mr Poinsett in his late report and are satisfied that every thing wi[ll] be done.[1]

Mr La Branche has remonstrated to this Government at the crossing the line by Genl. Rusk, and disarming the Caddo in the absence of that officer although daily expected we have assured Mr. La Branche of the total want of authority from this Government, but attribute it to the necessity of the case.[2]

Caddoes have been found killed in the recent battles, and hen[ce] no doubt Genl. Rusks interference. He placed the arms in the hands of the United States Agent, until the border war [was] over, and agreed to furnish them with provisions, they alled[ging] they had obtained arms merely for support, and not with host[ile] intentions.

I write in much haste and merely to give you [the] current information

Respectfully Yours
Barnard E Bee

✦✦✦

LS. Tx, TLP. Published in *DCRT,* 1: 362.

1. In the Report of the Secretary of War, November 28, 1838, accompanying President Van Buren's Second Annual Message of December 3, 1838, Poinsett recommended strengthening troops on the western frontier and said that Indians within the United States had been "warned that they will not be permitted to take part in any contest between Mexico and Texas, or to pass into the territory of the latter with hostile intent." The report is published in the *National Intelligencer,* December 10, 1838.

2. In November 1838 Rusk led a force of Texas across the Red River in Louisiana in pursuit of Caddo Indians who had been raiding in Texas. At Shreveport, he took away their guns and ammunition and placed them in the custody of the US Indian agent at Shreveport. The incident is described in Senate Executive Document 14, 32d

Cong., 2d Sess., 1853, Serial 660, pp. 9, 18–27.

John Forsyth to Anson Jones

Department of State,
Washington, 8th February, 1839.

Sir:

Your note of yesterday's date announcing the appointment of Moses Austin Bryan as Secretary to the Legation of Texas in this City, has been received.

I avail myself of the occasion to renew to you the assurances of my great consideration.

John Forsyth

✦✦✦

ALS. Tx, TLP.

Stewart Newell to Anson Jones

Galveston February 28/ 39

Dear Sir

Excuse the liberty of my writing again to you relative to any matter that appears only to interest myself; but from the many requests made of me by our mutual friends, to change my location from Velasco to Sabine, and among those Friends are his Excellency President Houston and Dr. Irion, the former of which will also address you upon the subject, as he has told me, intended also to write the Department and the President to remove me from Velasco to Sabine where he thinks my Interests as well as those of the Government will be promoted by my removal, to the latter place.

It is quite unnecessary for me to say any thing relative to Velasco as to the various reasons for my wish to be transferred to this place or Sabine, and now the Sabine is vacant and presents no difficulty on the part of the Department, to granting my request, you being well acquainted with the bussiness, in a Comercial point of view, connected with Velasco, are apprised that it presents but few inducements to Natives of the Northern U.S. as to health, and more particularly to those possessed of only very moderate means as to Capital for a profitable Commerce, the Fees of Office of course very limited, therefore the result must be by retaining it, to loose Capital, became involved, and rendered unable to maintain the respectable position in Society which such an Appointment should command.

I have laboured hard at this place and watch'd over the Duties at Velasco unceasingly, until the Appointment of Col. Rhode,[1] at this place, and every attempt to remain at Velasco has been attended with Sickness and attendant loss of attention to official as well as private affairs.

You may from the detail entered into by me think my Letter rather out of place, but from your attention to my former Letter, and our friend, Dr. Irion assuring me that I need not have any hesitation to write you upon this subject, therefore I do so and wish this considered by you as a confidential Letter and private, but wish you to make enquiry for me to ascertain if I could succeed in my application and to ask your Influence to aid me. I shall address the Department, in a few days upon the Subject, accompanied by a Letter from his Excellency Prest. Houston, and with whom, I leave here Tomorrow, to visit Sabine. I do not wish however, to resign the Appointment at <u>Velasco</u>, unless the Appointment to Sabine can be obtain'd in that Case I would cheerfully do so and should your leisure permit will feel obliged by your early reply as to probable success and if the change will be effected to have it done at once.

Remain Respectfully Your Obt. Servant
Stewart Newell

✦✦✦

ALS. Tx, TLP.

1. Newell refers to Elisha A. Rhodes, appointed US consul at Galveston in 1838.

Greene Washington Caldwell to Barnard Elliott Bee Sr.

Ho. of Rep.
August 12. 1841

Dr Sir

I recd. a communication from one my constituents with a request to enclose it to you and of you the favor to answer its interrogations–

You will please therefore enclose to me you're a[nswer] when it may suit your conveninence—

I remain your obt.
G. W. Caldwell

✦✦✦

ALS. Tx, TLP. Greene Washington Caldwell (1806–1864), of North Carolina, was a Democrat in the Twenty-Seventh Congress, 1841–1843.

The finances of the republic were a matter of constant concern. In 1839 James Hamilton visited England and France in search of a $5 million loan for the republic. He met with enough encouragement that when he returned to Texas later that year, President Lamar appointed him a confidential agent with authority to contract loans in Europe as well as to negotiate a treaty of peace, amity, and boundaries with representatives of Mexico. Hamilton returned to Europe in 1840 seeking diplomatic recognition by European nations as well as funds. While he met with some success on the diplomatic side—signing trade agreements with the Netherlands, Belgium, and Britain—his *efforts to obtain funds proved unsuccessful.*

James McMaster to Barnard Elliott Bee Sr.

Washington City
Saturday [August] 14th 1841

I arrived this day from New Orleans—Eight days from that City —left your friends all well. Dr. Ritch[1] wishes to be remembered to you. recd letter from Col. Love[2] 30th July—all going on well in Texas I calld to see you—regret my disappointment Exceedingly—I am with many of your friends much interested in Texas Securities[.] [W]e hear & read such contradictory reports about the loan, that we hardly know what to think of it—I am & have been firm in the belief that– the loan is effected being assured that such was the case by Col. Love & Mr. Burnley & the many advan[ce] reports—has caused a depression— <…> the notes in N.O. were selling when I left at 14¢ & bonds 17¢ the dollar—can you give me any satisfactory intelligence on the subject of <…> has it been effected—or is it only <……> by writing to me on the subject and giving such information as is consistent—you will confer a favour that shall ever be remembered with gratitude & respect—I am verry anxious to hear as my investments have already embarrassed me much, & if no certainty of improvement in the price of them be certain I would sell at present prices—I sincerely hope you will appreciate my motive & pardon the li[berty] I have taken—& indulge me by a communication as early as conveni[ent].

Respectfully Yours
J McMaster

Address—"James McMaster"
Ballston Spa
Saratoga Co.
N.Y.

I would want to see you but am informed you will be absent a week or more

✦✦✦

ALS. Tx, TLP. James McMaster (1803–1873), from Ballston Spa, New York, had traveled as a trader in Mexico and started a banking house in New Orleans before establishing a sugar plantation on the Mississippi, below New Orleans.

1. Ritch, not otherwise identified.

2. Love, not otherwise identified.

E. D. Whitney and Co. to Barnard Elliott Bee Sr.

Philadelph[ia]
August [1841]

Dear Sir,

We thank you for your much esteemed favor of the 11th ultimo, which was <...> received.

In the "Pennsylvania Inquirer," published in [this] City, of the 11th inst. is a long article headed "Republic of Texas," in which the writer says "By the late advices from her Commissioners for obtaining loans, (Genl. Hamilton) we learn that negotiations respecting it, have for the present ceased[."]

As we have reason to believe there has been no such advice recd. from Genl. Hamilton, we have thought it well enough to direct your attention to the article in the Penna. Inquirer, (the paper you can no doubt see in Washington) that you may, if you think proper, contradict the Statement, Officially.

We have seen Mr. Jaudon[1] who <...> not long ago <...> who told us that he dined with Genl [Hami]lton in London on the 3d July, and Genl. H. <...> him then, that his negotiations were entirely [suc]cessful. Mr. Jaudon also said that he [had] seen Mr. Laffette[2] a few days previous, in Paris, who told him that the Subscriptions for the loan were filling up as well as could be expected. Mr. Biddle has no letter from Genl. H. by the late steamers. We should, therefore, think that the statement in the Inquirer of the 11th. inst, is erroneous, which you may be glad to contradict, and which is the reason of our writing you at this time.

Should you receive any information we should be glad if you wd. drop us a line.

And we remain, Dear Sir, Very truly yours,
E. D. Whitney & Co

✦✦✦

ALS. Tx, TLP. Document damaged, with words missing. E. D. Whitney (b. ca. 1807) was a Philadelphia merchant.

1. Samuel Jaudon (1796–1874), of Philadelphia, was the cashier of Nicholas Biddle's Bank of the United States.

2. Jacques Lafitte [vice Laffette] (1767–1844), head of the Paris banking house Lafitte and Company.

Sam Houston's reelection to the presidency in 1841 meant a change in the republic's Indian policy. Mirabeau B. Lamar hated Indians and believed that the best policy toward "the barbarous race" was to "wage vigorous war against them" in order to drive them out of the country ("Message to Congress," November 12, 1839, quoted in Yoakum, History of Texas from its First Settlement in 1685 to its Annexation to the United States in 1846, *2 vols. [New York: Redfield, 1855], 2: 280). Houston, in a message to Congress on December 20, 1841, proposed establishing trading posts to "conciliate the Indians, open a lucrative commerce with them and bring continued peace to our entire frontier." The prospect of reaching peace by means of war, he said, had proven "utterly fallacious" ("First Message to Congress, Second Administration," December 20, 1841, in Amelia W. Williams and Eugene C. Barker, eds., The* Writings of Sam Houston, 1813–1863, *vol. 2,* July 16, 1814–March 31, 1842 *[Austin: University of Texas Press, 1939], 402).*

In July 1842, Houston appointed commissioners to treat with the Indians on the part of Texas, and US Secretary of War John C. Spencer instructed Indian agent Pierce M. Butler to assist in facilitating an agreement. A meeting of representatives from several tribes was held at Tehuacana Creek, near present-day Waco, in March 1843, which resulted in a truce with an understanding that a "Grand Council" would be held at a later date. On September 29, 1843, the Texans and representatives of ten tribes concluded a treaty of peace and friendship at Bird's Fort on the Trinity River. Documents about these meetings are in Dorman H. Winfrey, ed., Texas Indian Papers, 1825–1843 *(Austin: Texas State Library, 1959).*

The Houston administration also changed the republic's representation in Washington. Displeased with Barnard Bee because of his frequent absences from his post, Houston removed him in December 1841 and appointed James Reily (1811–1864), Thomas J. Rusk's law partner, in his place. Reily, in turn, was replaced by Isaac Van Zandt in July 1842.

John Canfield Spencer to Isaac Van Zandt

Jany 18, 1843

Dear sir,

I Send you a copy of the draft of a Treaty, as I promised. It has been communicated to Pierce M. Butler Esq,[1] with intentions to proceed at once to the Waco village, either by the way of Fort Towson or Fort Jessup as he shall find most advisable and to be there by the10th of March at the [latest?].

In haste
Yours respectfully
J. C. Spencer

+++

ALS. Tx, TLP. John Canfield Spencer (1788–1855), of New York, secretary of war in the John Tyler administration. Isaac Van Zandt (1813–1847) came to Texas from Mississippi in 1838. He was a founder of the town of Marshall, where he practiced law. He died of yellow fever while campaigning for governor.

1. Pierce Mason Butler (1798–1847), of South Carolina, entered the army as a lieutenant in 1818 and was stationed at Fort Gibson, Indian Territory. He left the army in 1829, but took part in the Second Seminole War as a lieutenant colonel of the South Carolina militia. He was elected governor of South Carolina in 1836. From

1841 to 1846 he was US Indian commissioner at Fort Gibson. He was killed at the Battle of Churubusco during the War with Mexico.

William S. Derrick to Isaac Van Zandt

Department of State,
Washington, 18th Augt 1843.

The Undersigned, Acting Secretary of State of the United States, has the honor to acknowledge the receipt of the note addressed to this Department on the 16th instant,[1] by Mr. Van Zandt, Chargé d'affaires of Texas, upon the subject of a proposed joint treaty with certain Indian Tribes on the Southwestern frontier of the United States; and to inform him, in reply, that a copy of the note above mentioned has been transmitted to the Secretary of War,[2] whose answer, when received, will probably enable this Department to make a further communication to Mr. Van Zandt on the subject of his letter.

The Undersigned avails himself of this occasion to offer to Mr. Van Zandt the assurance of his high consideration.

W. S. Derrick.

✦✦✦

Secretarial copy. Tx, TLP. Published in *IAA*, 12: 50. William S. Derrick (1802–1852), of Pennsylvania, was chief clerk of the State Department.

1. Isaac Van Zandt to Abel P. Upshur, August 16, 1843, *IAA*, 12: 298–299.

2. James Madison Porter (1793–1862), of Pennsylvania, was acting secretary of war from March 8, 1843, to January 30, 1844, when his nomination was rejected by the Senate.

Daniel Parker to Abel Parker Upshur, with Enclosure

War Department
August 22d. 1843.

Sir.

In the absence of the Secretary of War I have the honor to transmit herewith, in answer to your letter of the 17th instant, a copy of a Report of the Commissioner of Indian Affairs.[1] You will see by the endorsement of the Secretary of War, that he confirms the views of the Commissioner and that instructions have been given relative to treating with the wild Indians referred to by the Chargé d'Affaires of Texas.

Very Respectfully Your Obed Servt.
D. Parker C[hief] C[lerk]

✦✦✦

Secretarial copy. Tx, TLP. In Senate Executive Document 14, 32d Cong., 2d Sess., Serial 660, p. 121. Daniel Parker (1782–1846) practiced law in Charlestown, Massachusetts, before his appointment as chief clerk of the War Department in 1810. He was appointed adjutant and inspector general in 1814 and was paymaster general, 1821–1822. He returned to the practice of law from 1822 to 1841, when he was again appointed chief clerk in the War Department. Abel P. Upshur (1790–1844), of Virginia, was appointed secretary of state following the resignation of Daniel Webster in July 1843. Upshur was killed in the explosion of the experimental gun "Peacemaker" on board the *Princeton* on February 28 of the following year.

1. Thomas Hartley Crawford (1786–1863), of Pennsylvania, served as a Jacksonian in the Twenty-First and Twenty-Second Congresses, 1829–1832. President Van Buren appointed him commissioner of Indian Affairs, a post he held from October 22, 1838, to October 30, 1845.

Enclosure: Commissioner of Indian Affairs to the Secretary of War

Extract

The Commissioner of Indian Affairs to the Secretary of War.

Department of War
Office of Indian Affairs
18th. August '43

Sir.

The note from the Department of State to you, under date of yesterday, has been referred to this office, and I have the honor to report thereon.

That the Communication of the Chargé d'Affaires of the Republic of Texas, made to the Secretary of State of the United States on the 16th inst. respecting a proposed joint treaty with certain Indian Tribes on and near the boundary between the two countries, has received the most respectful consideration. It is desirable, for the security of the inhabitants of the frontier of both Republics that we should treat with the Savages who roam about them and are alternately in either country, as promotive of individual safety, if it is not indispensable thereto. The effort that was made last Spring, although not productive of any compact, was not in any stage of its progress discouraging of future exertion. I confess that, upon the receipt of Govr. Butler's report, my impression was that any further attempt at present to bind these wild Indians by Treaty to the observance of friendly relations would be inexpedient—but the anxiety manifested by the Texan Government, through its Representative in the United states, that a renewed effort should put forth by both governments—that the weight and influence of the U. States with the Indians should be brought to bear in the collection of them to negotiate, as well as in the negotiations themselves—and the friendly relations and kindly feelings that exist between the adjoining Republics, have conspired to induce a willingness to gratify our neighbor in a step that may result usefully to us both—and can be effected at a very small expense. The object is pacification and amity—the greater age of the American Government, the larger population and ampler means will give effect to its suggestions—and these advantages, which time has given to us, we shall be happy to make operative to our neighbours benefit, while we are attending to our own interests.

I, therefore, think that it would be advisable to send a Commissioner (the respectable gentleman who represented the Department last Spring would in every respect be well qualified, and because of his former engagement better, perhaps, than any one else) to meet the Indian Chiefs and Texan Commissioners in November next at some suitable point, not far from the boundary, but within the Territory of Texas, say a short distance West of the Mouth of Cash Creek on Red River, or at other more eligible place. The collection of the Chiefs and other details will be matters of instruction from this office, under your direction, to the Commissioner.

✦✦✦

Secretarial copy. Tx, TLP. In Senate Executive Document 14, 32d Cong., 2d Sess., Serial 660, pp. 121–122.

James Logan to Isaac Van Zandt

Washington City D.C.
30th May. 1844.

Sir

In accordance with my verbal promise to you, in regard to the Indian relations affecting the Texas Government of Texas. I take the liberty of making the following suggestions.

I regard the remnant of the tribe of Cherokees, who have been driven from the inhabited part of Texas, and are now on the head of the false Wachita and between the Wachita and Red river as being in a position to excite more mischief than any other tribe. These are a people with whom concilliation might be made, if proper steps were taken. This could be better accomplished through some of the influential Cherokees west of Arkansas, than any other way. There is a Cherokee warrior of much distinction by the name of Dutch,[1] who now resides in the Cherokee Nation and was once a Chief among the western Cherokees, and I believe also among the Texas Cherokees; (at any rate he is of the same clan;) He is a full blooded Indian, but a man of strong mind, and much influence, and as a brave there is not his equal found amongst the Cherokees. His communications to the commanding officer at Fort Gibson show his great wish or anxiety to bring about reconciliation between those Cherokees and Texas. I would suggest that this man and James Starr[2] and Stand Watie,[3] who are men of much influence and character in the Cherokee nation, should be employed, by some arrangement between your Government and the United States, to go to the dissatisfied Texas Indians and make some arrangement for permanent peace. The great attachment of the persons named to the whites, their Superior address, and well known bravery would enable them to accomplish more for a pacific arrangment than could be accomplished by any other pacificators.

My long experience among the Indian Tribes, and my deep anxiety for the inhabitants of Texas, and my personal knowledge of that frontier, who I already regard Citizens of the United States, must be my apology for this communication which I trust you may find useful. I would further suggest that if it should be made the duty of one of the Agents, residing within the Southern Superintendency of the United States, to visit the wandering Tribes of Indians residing on the Red river and its tributaries, and use all proper influence to ensure peace, it would be a most powerful means of preserving pacific relations, who would be required to report annually, the condition of those wandering Tribes. The expense of these precautions would be nothing compared with the benefits, which would result from a proper selection of Agents. Should any danger be apprehended on the western frontier, it would be most likely to commence in the regions of Red river, an arrangment of this kind would supersede the necessity of a roving agent, such a one was appointed two years since to the northern Superintendency (A. J. Dripps)[4] and of much more importance to the frontier Citizens of Texas and this country.

I have the Honor to be with high consideration your obt. servt.

James Logan

✦✦✦

ALS. Tx, TLP. James Logan (1791–1859), of Arkansas, was US agent to the Creeks from 1838 to 1848.

1. Dutch (ca. 1790-1848), or Tahchee, was born in Alabama, but moved to Arkansas about 1817. He was thus a member of the "Old Settler" Cherokees, who moved west before the Indian Removal policies of the 1830s. He was widely respected for his bravery and fighting skill. He moved to the Canadian River area of Texas about 1828. He represented the Cherokees at the Treaty of Camp Holmes, Oklahoma, of August 24, 1835, at which the western tribes agreed to keep peace with the new arrivals who had been displaced by Indian Removal.

2. James Harper Starr (1809–1890), of Nacogdoches, had been president of the Board of Land Commissioners during the Houston administration and secretary of the Treasury in the Lamar administration, 1839–1840.

3. Stand Watie (1806–1871), or Degadoga, was born in Georgia. He was among the signers of the New Echota Treaty of 1836, in which the Cherokees gave up land east of the Mississippi for land in Oklahoma. He settled at Honey Creek in the Cherokee Nation.

4. Andrew Drips [vice Dripps] (1789?–1860) emigrated from Ireland. He became a fur trapper and Indian trader. He was US Indian agent for the Upper Missouri, 1842–1846.

In 1843 the annexation issue was revitalized. Andrew Jackson and Martin Van Buren had resisted admitting Texas to the union, but John Tyler, who became president upon the death of William Henry Harrison in 1841, was eager to make the republic part of the United States. On October 16, 1843, Tyler's Secretary of State Abel P. Upshur suggested to Texas chargé d'affaires Isaac Van Zandt that "no time ought to be lost" in presenting an annexation treaty to the Senate (Senate Document 341, 28th Cong., 1st Sess., p. 37). Texas dispatched J. Pinckney Henderson as a special agent to assist in negotiations. The diplomats completed a draft agreement on Febrary 27, 1844.

But fate decreed a different plan. The day after completing the negotiations, Upshur and Van Zandt joined a distinguished party, including President Tyler among other dignitaries, for a cruise on the new navy steam frigate Princeton. *The vessel navigated the Potomac, thrilling the guests with demonstrations of its rifled cannon, "Peacemaker." Late in the day, when the crew fired the gun for the last time, it exploded, killing eight, including Upshur.*

Upshur's death was a great blow. Van Zandt informed Anson Jones, on March 5, 1844, that "so far as the question of annexation is concerned," no one would be "so well suited to carry out the measure" as Upshur (DCRT, 2: 261–262). His prediction proved true. The Texas emissaries signed an annexation treaty with new Secretary of State John C. Calhoun on April 12, 1844. Tyler sent the agreement to the Senate for ratification in executive session, but on June 8, after Ohio Senator Benjamin Tappan leaked the treaty, the annexation agreement was defeated by a vote of thirty-five to sixteen.

That fall James K. Polk, who favored annexation, won the presidency. John Tyler, determined to bring Texas into the Union before his term expired in March, in his last annual message as president announced that Polk's victory expressed the wish of the people "that Texas shall be annexed to the Union promptly and immediately" (Messages and Papers, *4: 344–345*). *He recommended that Texas be admitted to the Union by joint resolution of Congress. After spirited debate the resolution for annexation passed the House and the Senate on February 28, 1845. Tyler signed the measure on March 1, 1845, and sent a messenger to Texas with the news. A few days later Mexican Minister Juan Almonte requested his passports and left the United States.*

The Texas Congress met on June 16, 1845, to consider the annexation offer from the United States as well as a last effort by Mexico to reach an accommodation. The offer from the United States was unanimously accepted, and President Anson Jones called for a convention to draft a state constitution. That document was approved by the people of Texas and submitted to the United States. On December 29, 1845, Texas became a state in the United States, with J. Pinckney Henderson as its first governor. The Lone Star Republic was at an end.

Ashbel Smith to Charles H. Raymond

Department of State,
Texas, Feby 11.1845

Sir,

I have the honor to acknowledge the receipt of your despatches bearing date the 4th. and 16th ultimo.[1]

His Excellency the President wishes you to remain at your post until the 11th March next, and in the mean time to use your most strenuous exertions in every proper manner to accomplish the annexation of Texas to the American Union—a measure earnestly desired by this government. The Hon. D. S. Kaufman[2] has been appointed Minister Chargé d'Affaires of this country to reside near the Government of Washington on the Potomac, and will proceed to his post early in the spring. It is the wish of His Excellency the President, therefore, that as soon as may be convenient after the 4th of March, you take leave of the American Government in the customary manner, and return to Texas, unless the interests of this country should render it expedient to delay for some short time your departure. I am also instructed by the President to express to you his [entire] satisfaction with your efforts to accomplish annexation, and generally with the manner in which you have executed the duties devolving on you as Acting Chargé d'Affaires of Texas.

I have signed an order for the Comptroller to pay to your agent Mr. J. H. Raymond[3] your salary for the 1st quarter of the present year.

An exchange of official documents is a courtesy frequently practised between different Governments. From the British Government we have received publications made by order of Parliament of great value. Should a proper occasion present itself, you can intimate verbally to the Secretary of State that this Government would willingly make a similar exchange of public documents with the United States. The collection of "American State Papers" published under direction of Congress would be highly useful to us.

I have the honor to be with sentiments of high consideration.

Very Respectfully Your Most Obedient Servant

Ashbel Smith.

✦✦✦

Secretarial copy. Tx, TLP. Published in *DCRT,* 2: 358–359. Charles H. Raymond (1816–?) was born in New York and came to Texas in 1839. He settled in Robertson's Colony and practiced law. He represented Robertson County in the Sixth Texas Congress, 1841–1842. Raymond was secretary of the Texas legation from July 26, 1842, and became chargé d'affaires from Van Zandt's resignation until January 11, 1845. He was the brother of James Hervey Raymond.

1. Charles H. Raymond to Ebenezer Allen, January 4, 1845, No. 137, and January 16, 1845, No. 139, *DCRT,* 2: 334–335, 341–342.

2. David Spangler Kaufman (1813–1851), originally from Pennsylvania, studied law with John A. Quitman in Mississippi and began a practice in Natchitoches, Louisiana. He moved to Nacogdoches to practice law in 1837. He represented Nacogdoches in the Third through Fifth Texas Congresses, 1838–1841, serving as speaker in the Fourth and Fifth Congresses. He was appointed chargé d'affaires to the United States in February 1845. After Texas became part of the Union he served in the US House of Representatives in the Twenty-Ninth through Thirty-First Congresses, 1845–1851.

3. James Hervey Raymond (1817–1897), the brother of Charles H. Raymond, arrived in Texas in 1840. He was clerk of the Texas House of Representatives and served as treasurer from 1841 until annexation and then state treasurer from 1846 to 1858.

✦✦✦

Index

The sender and/or recipient of a letter is first identified in an unnumbered note following the document. Subsequent references and other individuals appear in numbered notes.

First identifications of individuals are indicated with a boldface page and note number.

Portrait illustrations are indicated by a boldface italic page number.